Transforming a Life:

A MEMOIR

by Joan Nelson Pierotti

ISBN #: 978-0-9966566-3-4

Storyweaving Press
PO Box 739
Accokeek, MD 20607

Book and cover design:
Patrise Henkel
www.patrise.com

This memoir is dedicated to Sheila Hansen
whose keen ear for dialog, genuine interest in listening, and
unfailing encouragement kept me writing
until I finished this book.

To be nobody but yourself

in a world which is doing its best day and night

to make you like everybody else

means to fight the hardest battle

which any human being can fight

and never stop fighting.

e.e. cummings

PART ONE

CHAPTER 1

A Principled Girl

1951 – CHICAGO, ILLINOIS

At sixteen, I was what some people might have called a principled girl, as was my best friend Marge since ninth grade. But we were definitely not GCMs, Great Christian Martyrs, the name we created as freshman in high school for some of the more sanctimonious Bible students who attended North Park College and shared the same campus with academy level kids like Marge and me. The GCMs were the ones who never wore make-up, nor did they dance, drink, smoke, swear, or even go to movies because they considered all those activities to be sinful. And they had lots of judgments about people who did.

They also believed that if you hadn't had some kind of "born again" conversion type experience, a specific time and date you could pinpoint when you had accepted Jesus "as your personal savior," then you weren't really considered a Christian by them at all— a judgment that some other students felt was off-putting and insulting since some GCMs also felt that if you didn't use that exact phrasing to describe that experience, then you probably weren't a real Christian, anyway.

Of course, Marge and I didn't consider ourselves to be GCMs, but I do remember taking a blood oath together in high school, via a pinprick in our forearms, vowing never to smoke. Since we both had parents who had come out of Swedish backgrounds, our anti-smoking motto became "Good Swedes don't smoke the weeds!" Unfortunately, it was a pledge neither of us ultimately kept.

I can remember how surprised I was at the age of fourteen when my first boyfriend, a tall, handsome, and quite intelligent Catholic boy from my neighborhood told me in all seriousness as we walked holding hands one summer evening that it was a shame I wasn't going to heaven because I would have made a very good Catholic! At first I laughed, thinking he was only joking, and then was dismayed when I realized he was really serious!

The tendency to accept the doctrines of any church unquestioningly was probably not part of my DNA. Though my mother attended the Lutheran Church occasionally, the relationship my father and older sister had with organized religion was almost nonexistent. Both of my parents had been born and raised in Sweden in the very early 1900s when the vast majority of people in Sweden were still profoundly poor. There was no public education for children after they made their confirmation at about the age of 12 or 13, at which time they were required by law to work either as farm hands or housemaids, the only work available to them. If they chose to move to another part of Sweden or decided to emigrate to America, as both my parents eventually did, they had to receive special permission from either the sheriff or one of the local parish clergymen. It was an oppressive system created by and for wealthy landowners and rich farmers in collusion with the local sheriffs and the clergy, who wielded considerable power as part of the State Church of Sweden from whom they received much of their financing. My father believed that most ministers were self-righteous hypocrites, and he'd occasionally referred to them as *prästafan*,- loosely translated from Swedish as priest-devils.

I sometimes was characterized as the "religious one" by my family, primarily because I still attended church even after my confirmation, but I never viewed myself that way. That word "religious" carried with it a kind of doctrinaire tone to me, although I've always tried to use my understanding and appreciation of the teachings of Jesus as a behavioral guide, holding as loving an attitude toward others as I could. But I never thought of myself as a goody two-shoes kind of Christian.

My primary vice, if one could call it that, was occasional swearing (mostly *shits*, *hells*, and *damns* and an occasional *fuck* or two—but rarely using the Lord's name in vain, which I believed was definitely "over the line.") When sorely provoked, I sometimes used a phrase I'd learned from my brother-in-law Bob— "Shit, piss and damnation, hell, crap and corruption!" all uttered in quick succession. He claimed it was a favorite among his World War II Navy buddies, and I found it quite satisfying to say when I was really pissed off.

A penchant for cussing on occasion probably came about early, when I was about six or seven and had come home crying one day after a neighbor boy had beaten me up. After asking why I was crying, my father put a consoling arm around me and said forcefully, "Don't cry, kid! Swear!" which I did from that time on whenever I'd been hurt. I don't recall ever being punished for it either, at least not by my father or mother.

Two characters from my childhood reading who captivated and possibly influenced my behavior were Honeybunch and Penrod Schofield. Honeybunch was an adventurous seven-year-old girl from the children's *Honeybunch* books, and Penrod Schofield was the main character in Booth Tarkington's *Penrod* series about an extremely mischievous adolescent boy and his buddy Sam, both of whose antics I found quite hilarious. Perhaps that accounts for the seemingly contrary nature of my personality as I grew up— the pleasant and somewhat compliant woman who also still has a part of her which even now delights in being somewhat risk taking, sometimes outrageously truthful, curious, independent, and quite salty— all characteristics which helped me enormously through the incredibly difficult shoals of married life, later as a single parent of three, and then quite suc-cessfully as a high school teacher in the inner-city of Washington, DC. for almost 40 years.

CHAPTER 2

Friends Written Off

My first love when I was about fifteen was with a college student named Harris, a nineteen-year-old freshman at North Park College. His father owned a funeral home in Lynn, Massachusetts, and Harris came complete with a delightful Boston accent. At first I'd been afraid to bring him home to meet my family because his being nineteen made him an "old man" according to my father's opinion of any boy more than a year older than I. I loved Harris but would not have used that term in the 50's since teenagers were thought to be incapable of "real" love back then. Adults would have called it "only a schoolgirl crush." I found that kissing someone I really wasn't attracted to was actually unpleasant and I avoided it, but it felt very different with Harris. Years later it was distasteful to even consider having sex with a man I didn't really care for. Whatever these crushes were called, if they were experienced as real love, they could be profoundly heartbreaking to many young women like me when they ended.

Harris and I went together that whole late winter and spring of 1952. All went well until my friend Marge asked if I minded if they asked Harris to escort their sorority president, Dorothy, to her senior banquet and perhaps the prom following it. Dancing was forbidden both at the academy and North Park because it was considered sinful. Instead, there were supposedly

5

"secret" sororities (none of which I'd joined) at the academy started mostly for the purpose of holding dances off campus.

Dorothy, whose father was a bank president, was a rather plain girl who didn't have a boyfriend. Marge and a few other friends couldn't bear to have their sorority president go dateless to the senior banquet and figured that I was understanding enough not to mind if they "borrowed" Harris just for one evening to be Dorothy's date. Perhaps Marge figured that since Dorothy was not particularly pretty, it wasn't likely that Harris would find her so attractive as to endanger his relationship with me.

Reluctantly I agreed, not wanting to appear selfish or possessive, but I secretly wished Harris had just said "No, I don't want to go to that banquet with some stranger." But he didn't, and I was quite upset, therefore, when I learned that he and Dorothy had gone out together a couple times after the senior banquet. Harris and I patched things up between us, and a short time later school ended for the summer, and Harris return home to Massachusetts to help in his father's funeral home. We began writing regularly, and I looked forward to seeing him back at school in September.

That fall, however, Harris didn't return to North Park to continue college. Instead, his father insisted he go to mortuary school so he could begin to take a more active role in running the family funeral business. We had talked about someday getting married when I finished high school and college, and we continued writing during my junior year in high school. I didn't date anyone at all and lived primarily for his letters and very occasional long-distance calls, which were prohibitively expensive in the Fifties.

One of the highlights of my school day was coming home each day hoping to find Harris's familiar beige envelope on the dining room table that signaled a letter from him. If there wasn't one and more than a week or two went by without one, I'd go into a minor funk for a while each day and then begin waiting in anticipation for the next day's mail. That spring came the happy news from Harris that he and his parents were coming to Chicago for a mortician's convention at the Edgewater Beach Hotel, which was only a couple miles from where we lived in Chicago. I began counting the days until we'd be back together again.

The Parkers arrived in Chicago in their long, black, Cadillac limousine used primarily in the family funeral business, and I finally got to meet his mother and father the evening of the mortician's convention banquet at the hotel where they were staying. Though Harris's mother was somewhat distant toward me, his father really seemed to like me. I wore a black faille dress with a flared skirt lined with red taffeta which my mother and I had picked out especially for this occasion. It was the first black dress I'd ever owned and was sophisticated and appropriate, I thought, for a mortician's convention!!

After the banquet, Harris took me for a drive along Lake Shore Drive near the hotel in the family limousine. Having never even been in a Cadillac (let alone a black Cadillac limousine), I felt rather self-conscious, and so making a joke of it, I pretended I was Mrs. John D. Rockefeller. I climbed into the backseat of the limo and taking hold of the side strap, I declared as imperiously as I'd seen done in the movies "Drive on, Parker," which I pronounced "Pahk'uh" with my best rich lady accent. Harris laughed and said in his wonderful natural Boston accent, "Veddy good, Madam," pretended to tip his hat, and off we went. The only thing missing was one of those little black chauffeur's caps for him to wear.

But the Parker's stay in Chicago was very brief, only three or four days, and soon Harris was gone again. It was back to the letter writing and infrequent phone calls which I endured only because he always told me he loved me at the end of each letter followed by a long string of V's like *vvvvvvvv* which was sort of code between us for "I love you, and you turn me on, and here's lots of kisses."

We had necked quite a bit when we were together, and a couple times I actually felt him getting hard when he stood close to me as he kissed me goodnight. Since we'd never been overtly sexual, I never mentioned that I noticed it because I didn't want to embarrass him. To allow him to touch my breasts, let alone any place else "down there" was unthinkable, at least according to the accepted Midwest mores of North Park in the early '50s and especially for a principled girl.

Perhaps my lack of sexual readiness and experience, along with having been drilled in society's beliefs about what a good, decent girl did or didn't do, coupled with months of physical separation from Harris, contributed to the end of that relationship. Harris's letters unexpectedly stopped with no explanations. Almost a month went by without a word from him. I became more and more downhearted, coming home each day to see the empty place on the dining room table where my mother always left any letters from Harris for me. Though I wanted to call him, I was too embarrassed to be that forward.

And then finally one day to my relief and joy, there on the table was the familiar beige envelope I knew was from Harris. Excitedly I opened the letter and a news clipping and picture fell to the floor. I picked it up, and there staring up at me was a photo of Harris and a girl identified in the article as Delores Duncan. I recognized that name as the girl Harris had gone steady with but who had broken up with him when he was in high school. But my joy turned to disbelief and then to pain. It was an engagement announcement. There was only one line written on his stationery— "Dear Joan, I trust this clipping will explain everything. Love, Harris." That was all. That was it!

How could someone so callously deliver a heartbreaking message like that? If somehow I had reacted with the anger that his deceitfulness deserved, if I could have called him up and raged at him— told him what a low-life, lying shit he was, it might have helped. That's what he deserved at least. But I didn't. I just accepted that betrayal almost as if deciding he no longer cared for me without telling me was his right. I didn't attempt to call or write to him again. I sank into a depression that lasted for a number of weeks until I finally got past it. Though I still developed crushes on boys off and on in high school, I became far more selective about giving my heart away after that.

1953 Chicago, Illinois - Alice

During our senior year in high school, Marge and I decided to attend the same college after we graduated from North Park. Though we'd been best friends all through school and now had chosen to attend the same college, we agreed not to be roommates our first year in college so that we could get to know the other people in our freshman girls' dormitory, as well as others. Our last summer in high school, we worked together waitressing at Toffenetti's, an Italian restaurant in downtown Chicago, and at the end of that summer of 1953, my dad drove the two of us to start our first semester at Augustana College— or "Augie" as everyone called it— a small Lutheran college, music school, and Lutheran seminary in Rock Island, Illinois, 175 miles from our homes in Chicago to start our freshman year.

It was at Augustana in the early fall that Marge and I met Alice, another new housemate, who became a close friend and was also rooming in West Hall, one of the freshman girls' dorms. She was a short, talkative, dark-haired, gamine, Greek-American girl who, like both Marge and me, was also from Chicago. Unlike most of the girls at Augie, Alice smoked, was plucky, and slightly, though delightfully, irreverent. (She was also Greek Orthodox, and later taught me how to cuss in Greek.) Underneath, she was a sensitive, beautiful soul. She was loyal, open-hearted, and would have given you the shirt off her back even if you didn't need it. However, she didn't fit the stereotypical blue eye/ blond haired "look" of so many of those predominantly Scandinavian college students.

She wanted to become a registered nurse, which required a college degree and the rigors of nursing school, but she wasn't particularly strong academically and struggled with her studies. Before long, she was over her head in college course work due in part to her worries about her parents' shaky marriage and other family problems. She desperately wanted to fit in at Augie, to belong, and was eager about the prospect of pledging a sorority. She would have liked to pledge Chi Omega Gamma (the "COGs" as they

9

were called) along with Marge and me as her first choice, but would probably have pledged any sorority that invited her if the COGs didn't.

Prior to Freshman Pledge Week, all the sororities held their pledge teas in order to look over the new crop of freshman girls. All of us girls at West Hall had been invited to these teas, and we'd excitedly discussed which sororities we wanted to pledge. We speculated on which ones might invite us. Marge was rooming with Doris Lorimer, who was our house proctor and also the president of the COGs, so naturally Marge wanted to pledge COGs. I figured she was a shoo-in under the circumstances, and so I'd decided that if I joined any sorority, I'd join the COGs, too. I didn't know how I was going to pay for it since I didn't think my parents would finance anything as frivolous as a sorority

On the day the sorority invitations were sent out, we all went excitedly to our mailboxes, filled with a mixture of hopeful expectation and fear of rejection. My heart was pounding as I reached into my mailbox. What if there was nothing there? What if no one wanted me? It wasn't that my heart was so desperately set on joining a sorority. Having briefly joined one during my senior year in high school, I actually thought that in many respects they were pretty dumb.

I had real misgivings about the kind of unswerving loyalty they demanded from their members, the pledge nonsense, the requisite humiliation and sometimes outright physical and emotional abuse one might suffer as a new pledge. But nevertheless, like most of the other freshman girls, I wanted to be wanted, and my apprehensions turned to relief when I saw the small, square envelope in my mailbox that signaled a sorority invitation. It was from the COGs, and I ran happily out of the mailroom to find Marge. She had a big smile on her face when I came flying up the front steps of West Hall and into the room she shared with Doris right next to the front hallway door. The proctors' bedrooms were always strategically located so that they could easily monitor our comings and goings and see to it that we kept the strict curfew regulations (8:00 pm on week nights, 12:00 on Fridays and Saturdays with one 1:00 a.m. a month.) I could tell by the expression on Marge's face that she'd already gotten her COG invitation and that she already knew from Doris that I'd gotten one, too. "Doris made me promise not to tell you," she explained as we hugged one another and then headed down to the Drug, the local pharmacy and coffee shop on the campus of Augustana, for coffee to celebrate.

When I returned to West shortly before dinner, I remembered Alice and headed upstairs to her room. Her door was closed and a wave of misgiving came over me as I knocked tentatively on her door. There was no answer, but sensing that she was in there, I cautiously called to her as I opened her door. She was lying on her bed with her face to the wall. "Al," I asked softly, "Are you sleeping?" She turned toward me, and I could see that her eyes were red and her face swollen from crying. I knew immediately that she hadn't received any sorority invitations— not from the COGS, and probably not from any other group. I sat down next to her and reached out to hold her. The tears came afresh and she sobbed there in my arms.

Anger rose up in me. "Those damned, snooty bitches," I thought to myself. I wondered what it had been that prompted all those hotshot sorority girls to blackball her. Was it her smoking? Her grades? Her nationality? Or that she wasn't popular enough? Or was it just that they thought she was somehow different from the many light haired, blue-eyed girls of northern European or Scandinavian descent at Augustana? Not being privy to their secret deliberations as they poured over their list of incoming freshmen girls, I couldn't say for sure, but I could imagine them chipping away at the relative merits or demerits of each of us girls as they sat in judgment of us all. All I knew was that Alice, someone I'd come to care for dearly, just hadn't "measured up" to those sorority girls' so-called standards (whatever the hell they might have been!). And I knew right then, as I sat there hugging her that there was no way that I wanted to affiliate myself with and be a part of a social organization that could arbitrarily inflict that kind of thoughtless pain on another person. "They're not worth it, Alice," I said lamely, trying to make her feel better.

"It's O.K.," she said softly between sobs, "They have a right to have who they want in their clubs. I'll be O.K." But her words sounded hollow and without conviction. But it was not O.K., and there was no need to wrestle with the decision of whether or not to join the COGs or any other sorority. The decision had been made for me in that moment. I never again considered joining the COGs or any other sorority while in college. Instead I joined the Independent Women's Organization or Indee's as they were called— a social club comprised of girls who, whether out of personal principles, for financial reasons, or because they'd been deemed too homely, too socially inept, or were otherwise considered unacceptable, did not pledge a sorority.

There wasn't any prestige whatsoever to being an Indee, but it did afford students the opportunity to compete in the homecoming parade, in intra-mural scholastics and athletic competitions with sororities, and to have parties and dances. I guess it also gave me a sense of some moral authority to have followed my conscience in this matter.

1953 Rock Island, Illinois - Ken

I hadn't turned eighteen yet, still a new freshman, when I first met Ken at the Drug. On a separate campus adjoining the college was the Lutheran seminary affiliated with the college. Ken, who had just finished four years at Tufts College, was a first-year seminarian at Augie. He also was at least six or seven years older than I. Most of the college boys in our freshman class seemed so much younger and far less mature than Ken and the other "Sem" students were. This added a certain intrigue and appeal to him for me. After our first several meetings over coffee, we began seeing each other almost every day, and eventually we were going steady.

At 17, the closest thing to sexual experience for me had been hugs and long kisses. Girls who let boys touch them on their breasts and below were regarded by most of my friends as slutty—even by the boys who yearned most to do it! Allowing a man to touch you below the waist was unthinkable if a girl wasn't married to the man, and even if they were already married, we thought it was somewhat disgusting or even shameful. It was an area that most women during the 40s, 50s and 60s (and probably long before that) accepted without question and were influenced by, the feelings of shame about human sexuality in general and especially about our own bodies that many of us felt were unattractive and consequently unacceptable. It all came from the morality of organized religion and society, especially for women.

No boyfriend of mine had ever touched me "below the neck" (actually what we called anything below the collarbone), and though I believed it would be all right to have sex with one's husband after marriage, I definitely wasn't prepared to let anyone touch me "down there!" or to see my less than perfect naked body. Where I had gotten these notions, I don't know— certainly not out of any book on human sexuality because in the forties and fifties those kinds of books hadn't been written yet, at least as far as I knew. When I first heard about something called French kissing and that people actually stuck their tongues in other people's mouths, I could hardly believe it and wanted to gag at the thought of it. It never occurred to me that there was any connection between touching, deep kissing, and the enjoyment of intercourse— of really making love.

I'd actually been inculcated with the belief that most men wanted to marry girls who were virgins, and God help the girl who wasn't one! She was "used" merchandise I was told, and so I intended to save my virginity for my husband, whoever he turned out to be. I fully expected that unmarried men were doing the same thing for me. Big mistake!

Now, during my first year in college, I was surprised to receive several letters that my former boyfriend, Harris, had written to me from Tokyo where he was stationed in the Army's medical corps during the Korean War. He excused his deceptive behavior by lamely saying that it had been his mother who'd always been promoting the relationship with his old girl-friend, Delores. Finally, he'd given in, as he put it, and married her. At least that's the explanation he gave me. By then I had just started college myself and fortunately had gotten over Harris. I'd found a replacement for my first Massachusetts love, but now it was in the person of a second one— Ken of the Boston accent, only this one was from Fitchburg, Massachusetts. Though it never occurred to me at the time, I think that Ken's accent was an unconscious part of the attraction I had toward him perhaps because of the unfinished relationship I'd had with Harris, one that was never dealt with nor concluded satisfactorily.

The evening of my 18th birthday was an awakening for me. Ken had taken me out for dinner and had given me a beautiful, fragile gold chain with five tiny seed pearls strung on it. We were sitting in his decrepit Model A Ford under some trees near the freshman dormitory where I lived. It was a bitter December night, and we were snuggling and kissing out there in the cold because men weren't allowed in West Hall after 10:00 pm and there was nowhere else to go.

Poor Ken didn't even have gloves on, and his hands were so cold that I finally let him put them inside my phony mouton lamb coat. He began touching my sweatered breast, and for the first time I didn't gently switch positions or move my arm oh so tactfully in the way of his hand as I had done so many times before when any boy's hand wandered dangerously close to my chest. I'd always been most careful in this diversionary tactic so as not to offend, always assuming that they'd accidentally trespassed into forbidden territory. Even an unwanted kiss was smoothly sidestepped with a turn of the cheek to save the boy embarrassment. Once in high school a boy had attempted on our first date to stick his tongue into my mouth during a light kiss goodnight. It was met with clenched teeth, tight lips, and a decision never to date him again.

But this time with Ken, however, shivering in that arctic-like auto, I welcomed his touch and allowed him to slip his hand inside my sweater. The breath-steamed windows provided protection from unexpected eyes, and as my heart began to pound, I relaxed into his kisses and the touch of his tongue as he gave me my first voluntary French kiss. I could hardly believe that not only was I allowing this to happen, but I was enjoying it as well.

Now if this were your routine Harlequin Romance novel, this is where it would describe the juices running in the heroine's "private parts." But it's not, and I didn't know what was running where. I do know, however, that it was at this point that I first began to have some inkling that touching "below the neck" might be an integral and important part of making love. Though, God forbid, that was the furthest thing from my mind right then. Or so I thought.

That was my 18th birthday present— a small appetizer into the world of human sexuality— a world of which, heretofore, I had only been dimly conscious. Later, as I was climbing up the steps to the second floor of West Hall, I wondered if my two roommates, Marcia and Sarah would be able to tell immediately by some telltale twitch or flushed look on my face, that I'd been playing "below the neck" with Ken. Evidently, however, something akin to Hawthorne's Scarlet Letter was not emblazoned on my chest or forehead, for when I entered the room they acted as if I were perfectly normal. I felt different, though— somewhat tainted, perhaps. And I promised myself that I would never let Ken touch me like that again!

I was soon to learn, however, what any couple could have told me— that once you begin to hold hands, to kiss, to pet, you never go backward. You may hit a plateau, the relationship may end, but you never go backward regarding physical expression of love. And within a few weeks, Ken and I were into somewhat heavy petting, as we called it. And every night that we were together, I'd come back to the dorm, flushed with unfulfilled sexual excitement, promising myself that this was as far as it would go. I felt guilty and was convinced that I was the only girl in my freshman house engaging in such activity. I certainly never thought of sharing my sinful secrets with my roommates, who weren't even dating at the time, nor with my best friend, Marge, until we were juniors or seniors. And I remember that I would pray each time we'd been together and promised myself that things would go no further than they had.

But we never went backward. Eventually we reached the point where I would allow Ken to relieve his sexual frustrations by masturbating on my leg. The first time he ejaculated (and it got all over my skirt), I was awestruck at this thing spewing out its slippery liquid. I had never seen an adult penis up close— except on several occasions when I was in lower elementary school that men exposed themselves to me from their cars after beckoning to me with the pretext of asking directions or a question. At those times, frightened and disgusted, I averted my eyes as quickly as possible, pretended I hadn't seen anything, and got away as fast as possible. I never could understand what sick kicks those men got out of exposing themselves to a seven-year-old girl.

Those early experiences with strangers elicited in me a feeling akin to revulsion, but somehow much later when it was Ken, someone I cared for deeply, I didn't feel that way toward him or his "equipment." Since this particular penis belonged to him, I viewed it initially with disbelief and then eventually a kind of fascination

But I can't imagine why Sigmund Freud insisted that all women suffered from penis envy. He was definitely wrong! What we wanted more, I much later learned, was the almost automatic authority and respect that seemingly went with being a man but was withheld from women. (I guess Freud never asked for the opinions of many women about that theory of his!) What a nuisance when they became hard at the most inappropriate or inconvenient times, and couldn't be camouflaged under one's pants, saluting out there under one's clothing for all the world to see. Though I had to admit that they were most useful if you had to relieve yourself behind a bush. Certainly, far more efficient than squatting down in tall grass, getting your fanny scratched with twigs, losing your balance with your panties around your ankles, or peeing on them or yourself if you didn't take proper aim and pee fast.

Most of my sexual information I learned from Ken, six years older than I. I'd never heard of words like "clitoris," "labia," or "hymen" before, let alone knew that I possessed them. Nor had I known that there were only a few certain days when a woman could become pregnant. During the late spring of that first year in college, Ken and I went walking in the cemetery near campus, one of the very few places where a couple could be alone. It was a warm evening, just at dusk, and we sat down behind someone's tombstone. I was leaning against the headstone and Ken began kissing me. Before I knew it, we were in a passionate embrace and Ken was unbuttoning my jeans and attempting to slide them and my under pants down over my hips. He begged me to let him just touch my vagina. "I won't put it in," he promised, "I just want to rub it against you." That had to be one of the oldest lies men ever invented! Reluctantly I agreed. I say "reluctantly" with reservations. I loved Ken, and I, too, was excited, but though we were by now talking of getting married when he finished the seminary, I still had this belief that we should both be virgins when we married.

We'd spent the last nine months making love just to the point of actually having intercourse, and that created a very real tension between us. So, when I felt him begin to push against me in earnest and I felt like I really wanted to have sex with him, something in me could not allow myself to let him enter me. Part of it was fear of pregnancy, but even more, it was the sense that something was looking down on this whole scene with disapproval. I knew I was about to yield, but something inside me said, "No, this isn't right!" and I thrust my body back away from Ken to safety, hitting my head against the tombstone behind me. "I can't, Ken. Stop! I just can't!" I jumped up to my feet, pulling my blue jeans up around my waist, angry with him for breaking his word to me, angry with myself, and just generally angry with the whole, frustrating situation. We returned to my dorm in silence. I was shaken by that close call.

Several weeks later, during a conversation with Ken about a former girlfriend of his, Glenna, he told me that he'd had sex with her when he was college. I was crushed! When I got back to my room, I actually cried. For some reason, though he hadn't even known me then, I actually felt betrayed, nevertheless, and was let down for several days. I could hardly bear the thought

17

that he'd shared that kind of intimacy, of special love, with someone else before me. Here I'd been turning myself inside out to keep my virginity for him until we got married, and he'd not done the same for me. It was as though God had played a dirty trick on me. I hadn't heard of the term "double standard" between men and women, but I was already beginning to learn just what that meant.

The following fall, when I went with him to Massachusetts for his sister's wedding, we stopped in Leominster to have coffee with his good friend, Eric, who had married Glenna. I dreaded meeting her, and it was really difficult to be in her presence even for a short while, knowing that she and Ken had been intimate. Somehow it was inconceivable to me that two people who had been sexually intimate at one time, could not still have loving feelings for each other.

I went into an absolute panic when at just about the same time that I'd learned of Ken's relationship with Glenna, I was late with my period. I'd heard about girls getting pregnant without ever actually having had sex. The claim was that they'd gotten sperm cells off of a toilet seat or from off of their thigh.

We got little or no sex education in a health class I'd taken at Augie. A medical doctor had been invited to lecture on women's health issues in my sophomore year. I still laugh when I think of a question by one of my classmates when she asked the doctor if it was true that a woman could get pregnant off of a toilet seat. He paused for a moment before answering her, and finally, fighting to keep a straight face, he replied slowly and deliberately "Well…yyyes…" and then pausing a bit more said, "Yes…I guess so," and then added hurriedly, "but that's a hell of a place to bring a woman!" We all laughed, but I'm sure there were a large number of girls who didn't get the irony in his reply.

For a week after my period was due, I was terrified that by some fluky chance, one of Ken's little sperm cells had weaseled its way from the top of my thigh into my vagina and made me pregnant. I'd go to the bathroom every few hours or so to wipe myself, hoping there'd be some tiny tint of pink on the toilet paper signaling the onset of my period. I fervently began to pray for the acute cramps and mess that I'd usually experienced with somewhat disgusted resignation when I'd get my period. My mother had told me years before not to even bother to come home if I ever got pregnant and wasn't married. I believed her. And I wouldn't have.

If the Seminary Board had learned that Ken had gotten me pregnant, they'd have kicked him out of the Seminary. They had dismissed one seminarian a few years before just for being seen coming out of a motel with his fiancé. Abortion was illegal, and the thought of an illegal one brought up the terrifying specter of dirty back rooms, coat hangers, and girls who hemorrhaged to death. Besides I hadn't a clue as to how one even went about finding someone who did abortions.

There was only one thing left. I decided that if my period didn't come that I would withdraw the few hundred dollars I had in my college bank account, take a bus to New York to the Salvation Army's home for unwed mothers, have the baby and just disappear from everyone's life forever. I would leave no note even. I was sick with fear and angry because Ken and I hadn't really even had sex together. As far as I was concerned, my life was over!

God may have rested on the seventh day, but on my seventh day He or She seemed to have saved my life. I opened my eyes that Sunday morning, noted the dull achy feeling in my hips, leaped out of bed and fairly flew to the john. And there it was— my life handed back to me in the instant when I looked down between my legs as I sat on the john and saw a trickle of blood drop into the toilet bowl. "Thank you, God! Thank you, thank you, thank you!" I murmured to myself. I knew I wouldn't have to go to the Salvation Army's Home for Unwed Mothers after all!! I truly felt as though I'd been given a reprieve from a kind of death sentence.

My relationship with Ken, though close, loving, and frequently fun was more often stormy and argument-filled. He was very critical of others as well as me. He criticized the way I dressed, the amount of makeup that I wore (which was very little, I thought), and how I spent my money. When I bought something new to wear, he criticized me for wasting money we would need when we got married. So I didn't buy clothes, but then he criticized me for wearing the same clothes frequently. He was jealous of the grades I was getting. I tried to assuage his resentment by reminding him that he couldn't really compare my grades in college to his in the seminary because his work was so much harder than mine. Finally, I just avoided telling him when I did well on tests or on my grades. If asked, I would lie about the grades I had gotten, down grading my A's to B's and the B's to C's so he wouldn't get sullen.

Ken spent his second year in the seminary on an internship at a church in Massachusetts near his home in Fitchburg. During my sophomore year in college while he was gone, I had ample time for studying. I never dated. I lived for his letters and occasional phone calls just as I had done in high school when I waited for letters and calls from Harris. That summer, I worked in the office of a machine tool company near home, and before beginning my junior year, I traveled to Massachusetts at the end of Ken's internship there. He gave me an engagement ring, which when he tried to slip it on was a size too small. Our arguments began again even before the jeweler had time to size it properly.

We fought over piddling matters, usually something he would decree that I didn't agree with. He didn't brook my having different opinions from him. He needed to be in control of everything, and I was not reared to acquiesce easily. I didn't like his telling me what to do and how to think. On that dreadful ride back from Massachusetts, we barely spoke to each other. I don't remember what the fight was about, but by the time we arrived in Rock Island and I began my junior year, I feared that maybe our engagement had been a mistake.

By the twisted, delusional logic that only someone in love can have, I then came to the conclusion that our continual quarrels were a function of sexual tension between us because of our half-assed attempts at celibacy; we weren't having "real" sex, I reasoned, and a lot of frustration built up for both of us. It never occurred to me that Ken was simply the wrong person for me. I thought that if only we were married, all the fighting would disappear. I suggested we consider getting married at the end of that year while we were still in school, but that just wasn't financially possible. I believed my parents would have stopped supporting me in college if we had gotten married.

The arguments between Ken and me became so frequent and he made me so angry with his continual nagging about one thing or another being wrong with me, that I was often tempted to give him his ring back. But it had just been a matter of weeks since we'd become engaged. My friends and classmates, hearing of our engagement, were still coming up to congratulate us and to see my new diamond ring; I was too embarrassed to have to explain that I didn't have it anymore, so I continued to wear it.

And we continued to fight. And then we had something new to fight about— my relationship with my speech professor, Ted LeVander. I was a speech and English major, and at the beginning of my junior year, I was invited by LeVander to represent our college as the woman orator from Augustana that year at the numerous intercollegiate oratory competitions around the State of Illinois. Another student, Nam Yearl Chai from Korea was to compete in the men's oratory competition. Augustana had a formidable reputation in the Illinois State Oratorical Association largely due to the numbers of Augie men and women who took first place year after year due to LeVander's expert coaching in public speaking. I felt deeply honored to have been chosen by him that year to represent the school in the women's division, but I was scared that I wouldn't be able to live up to our school's reputation.

Mr. LeVander and I began spending many hours working together as he critiqued the oration I was writing and then meticulously began coaching me in my delivery. It was a fantastic learning experience for me not only in public speaking but also in composition. I learned more about writing from him than I'd learned in all the English classes I'd ever had before. Ted was a tall, gray haired, distinguished looking man in his late fifties, and Ken couldn't stand him. He was jealous of the time I spent being coached by LeVander, and of the fact that LeVander was fond of me and flirted a little with me from time to time but primarily in jest. At least I thought so until the one time he tried unsuccessfully to coax me into his hotel room. I was beginning to win first place at the various intercollegiate competitions when we traveled around the state to different colleges, and the more often I won, the surlier and resentful Ken became.

Consequently, it was both with elation and dread that I returned to school with LeVander after having won first place in the women's oratory division at the Illinois State Oratory Competition. LeVander was on top of the clouds with yet another first place winner in the state championship. Naturally I was really pleased with myself and elated as well. It was the first time I'd ever placed first in any kind of academic competition! I loved the attention and having my picture in the city paper, and getting compliments and congratulations that I received all over campus. But I dreaded the jealous reaction and insecurity I knew would come from Ken.

He didn't say too much when I saw him the next day except, "So I hear you won the Illinois State contest. Guess I should congratulate you," but the lack of enthusiasm and almost grudging tone in his voice told me what he was really feeling. I could tell by Ted's unspoken demeanor that he thought Ken was kind of an ass, but he knew that I loved Ken, and so reserved his negative comments about Ken only for when Ken and I we'd had another fight, and I'd be in tears barely able to function as LeVander and I were preparing for some new speaking contest.

Our relationship came to a head one winter evening shortly after the championship when Ken and I were returning to my dorm from a movie.

He began criticizing a couple we'd just seen going into the 9:00 movie with their eight or nine-year-old son just as we were leaving. "When we have kids, you can bet your life they won't ever be up at this time of night," he declared. I said I didn't think there was anything wrong with a kid staying up late once in a while. Well, we were off to the races again, this time arguing about how we would raise our hypothetical children.

We were still arguing when we pulled up in front of the dorm, but the topic by then had expanded from the original issue of the couple with their boy. He had begun to make insulting remarks about my judgment, the way I'd been raised by my family, and finally became so nasty and derisive that I lost my temper and slapped him. I'd never done that to anyone ever before. Without missing a beat, he slapped me back, but much harder. My head reeled momentarily from that blow. I was stunned and speechless, then I began to cry and in anger pulled off the engagement ring, rolled down the window, and threw it out into the snowy gutter, not caring whether or not he ever found it.

I opened the car door, stepped out, almost losing my balance on the ice and snow-covered walk, and hurried past the couples kissing and embracing in from of the dorm door just before the 10:00 curfew, tears of humiliation and anger streaming down my face. I cried myself to sleep that night, vowing I'd never see him again and then perversely worried that it might be all over between us.

I'd given Ken's ring back to him several times after similar arguments, but we'd always made up later after I'd had a good cry and we both had time to cool off. After a few days of anger and unhappy resolves not to see him again, I began to miss him. Each time I'd hear the phone ringing down the hall, I'd hold my breath hoping the loud speaker would announce that there was a call for me, and he'd be on the line apologizing. Eventually I tried phoning him at his seminary dormitory, but he didn't return my calls. My roommate Marcia tried to reassure me that we'd make up, and she'd go down with me to the Drug, drink coffee, and hang out there in hopes of running into him.

Several days later as I was sitting yoga-style on my bed trying to concentrate on studying, Marcia came into the room with a long look on her face, her blue eyes wide and serious behind her glasses. "I've got something to tell you, and I don't know if I should," she began tentatively, "but you'll find out anyway. I just saw Ken in the lobby. He was waiting for Peggy Pearson— you know— the freshman who lives in the room right below ours on the ground floor. Someone told me he's been dating her recently." The world seemed to drop out from under me in that moment. Somehow, I just couldn't believe Ken was really seeing someone else. I didn't want to know.

Those late-winter weeks were bleak enough and only added to my deep depression about Ken's going with this girl Peggy, who was a tall, willowy girl with long, dark hair. And a freshman at that!! I actually felt like some old hag he'd cast aside for a young colt. (I'd just turned twenty!) I made sure to avert my eyes as I passed through the lobby or when walking on campus, not wanting to chance catching a glimpse of them together. I couldn't understand how he could just up and start dating someone so soon after we'd broken up. Once I saw them walking down the street holding hands, and I became so nauseated that I had to run into the dorm bathroom sick to my stomach. I'd be sitting in my room trying to study in the afternoons or evenings and hear the loudspeaker calling her name on the floor below us. I knew it was either Ken calling her or coming to pick her up, and I'd dissolve into tears.

I, who usually had a good appetite even for cafeteria food, could not eat. I lost ten pounds in less than a month. Though I'm sure that Mr. LeVander was worried about the effect this depression would have on my public speaking performances, I imagine that he was also secretly delighted that Ken and I had finally broken up. He knew how angry Ken got each time I came back from a speech contest having won first place and of his jealousy of the time I had to spend working on my speech with LeVander. "You're too good for him, Joanie," he said one afternoon, trying to cheer me after the break-up, but it was no use. I just wanted to get back together with Ken, and for things to be like they were before, even if he did criticize me.

The final competition to determine the winners of the country-wide Intercollegiate Oratory Association's competition at Northwestern University was coming up in just five weeks, and I was a leading contender according to Dr. LeVander, a few of whose students had won top honors nationally. He knew I had a good chance of winning first place, but I was in such a state of upset and depression that he was afraid I wouldn't be in any emotional state to perform well. To make matters worse, I'd recently had let Marge cut my hair short, and when LeVander saw me with my hair whacked off, he was aghast. "My God, you look like a rat chewed it off!" was his only comment. I felt even more miserable as I forlornly surveyed my dismembered hair each day in the mirror, but other than to have the raggedy edges trimmed off at the hairdresser, there wasn't much else to be done.

We spent long hours rehearsing for the National Intercollegiate Oratorical Competition to be held at Northwestern University located in Evanston, just outside of Chicago. My hair had grown out some by then and didn't look quite so bad. Unfortunately, the week of the competition, I became sick with fever, sore throat and a heavy cold and was quite under the weather on the day of the finals. My parents both attended the competition, as did Ted and his wife Barbara, and they all did everything to buoy my spirits when I placed second rather than first place. I delivered the best speech I could but not good enough for a first place.

Despite only getting second place, I received much attention and congratulations when I returned to Augustana after the competition. We were always proud when our small liberal arts college of about 1200 students was able to compete successfully against the top schools over the years. Ted's students had often taken first place in the Nationals and I'd wanted to do as well. He had a stellar reputation for coaching in the area of public speaking and oratory among colleges in the US.

The subject of my oration, "The Golden Pitcher," dealt with the illusions and problems inherent in American public education in 1956. It is even more relevant today. I had no idea of how hard I would work to research the topic, write, and learn to deliver that 10-minute speech without notes when I first undertook the task. Nor did I have any idea of how much I would learn from the experience or how much it would shape and inform the whole direction of my career in teaching and learning some years later.

CHAPTER 3

The Swedish Eleventh Commandment

1956 – ROCK ISLAND, ILLINOIS

The annual Indee Women's Sadie Hawkins dance was approaching just weeks after Ken and I had broken our engagement. Swallowing my pride, I decided to ask Ken to go with me in the hopes that perhaps this would afford us the opportunity to get back together. When my friends learned of my intentions, they implored me to ask someone else instead. I think the real reason was that they thought Ken was a jerk because of his bossiness and the way he frequently put me down. So they began making suggestions about whom I could ask who would make Ken most jealous.

"Ask Dan Pierotti," Marge suggested. "Eva Mattson thinks he's a really neat guy, and he's Ken's boss at the Seminary dining room. I've heard they don't get along all that well."

"That's a great idea!" Marcia chimed in at Marge's suggestion. "I think he's really cute and Ken will be livid!" she added with a devilish grin.

"But I don't even know him," I wailed but began to waver a bit now from my original decision to ask Ken. "And how do you know he's even available. He may have a girl friend?"

"I'll ask Eva. I'm certain she'll know," Marge assured me.

Eva Mattson was the wife of the Seminary President and the mother of Marge's fiancé, Karl, a senior at the college who was a year ahead of us and would be entering the seminary himself the following fall. I had only met Dan Pierotti twice. Once when Ken and I ran into him coming down the steps leading from the seminary to the college campus nearby. I remember being puzzled about Dan's Italian last name, which stood out in sharp contrast from all the Olsons, Johnsons, Enquists, Nordquists, and other Scandinavian names predominant in that Swedish Lutheran milieu. I remember wondering how he had ever ended up a Lutheran since all the Italians I knew were Catholic. I'd also wondered where he was going to find an Italian girl to marry who was also a Lutheran. He interested me because of his snappy dark-brown eyes and wavy black hair which were in such sharp contrast to the scores of blue-eyed, blonde Scandinavians so common on campus.

The other time our paths had crossed was one evening at one of the local restaurants and student hangouts. I was sitting at a table with a group of my friends when five or six guys from the seminary sat down at a table across from us. Dan came up and asked if we had an extra chair. Since it was obvious that we didn't, I stood up and with a low bow facetiously said, "Oh here, take mine." Without batting an eye Dan said, "Thanks a lot," grabbed my chair, took it over to his table, and sat down without a backwards look as his seminary buddies roared with laughter. I was stunned momentarily and then we all burst out laughing at his unbridled chutzpah. I found another chair, thinking it served me right for being such a smart-ass to offer him mine. And I was somewhat intrigued by him. Through Eva Mattson's grapevine, I learned that Dan didn't have a steady girlfriend that she knew of, and so I screwed up my courage to call him and invite him to the Indee's Sadie Hawkins Day sock hop. To my delight, he accepted.

We double-dated with my roommate Marcia and one of Dan's fellow students from the seminary. One of the events of the dance was a treasure hunt requiring that we divide into teams of two or three couples and go out into the city of Rock Island and find the items on the list. At one point as we were driving in Dan's old Chevy hunting for items on the list, he pulled up in front of the seminary dormitory, jumped out of the car, and returned shortly dropping into my lap a doorknob he'd just removed from his dorm room door and a set of ball & jacks.

As the four of us sped off to our next stop trying to complete finding the items on our list. "Where did these come from? How did you know you could find these in the seminary dorm?" I asked him. "They're from my room," he replied smiling. "Didn't I ever tell you I was the ball & jacks champion in college?" I sat there in delighted incredulity wondering what kind of guy this Dan Pierotti was, who even at age 26 had enough kid in him to still play jacks. He certainly seemed different from any man I'd ever known before.

After the dance, Dan and I sat talking in his car until after 2:00 in the morning in the driveway of the seminary president's home where I was spending the night with my friend Marge. She was staying there with Karl's younger brother for the weekend while his parents were out of town. She and I had both signed up for baby-sitting overnights so we wouldn't have to be in by midnight.

We talked about Dan's family and life in Pennsylvania before he'd come to the seminary and of how an Italian who'd been baptized Roman Catholic could end up studying for the Lutheran ministry. Actually he was only half Italian, his mother being English/German and a Presbyterian. To save unending family disputes, his father and mother had agreed to raise their three sons in no particular religion, allowing them to choose when they were mature.

Dan's pious, Italian aunt, however, not able to bear her nephew's not being baptized properly, spirited him away to St. Calista's R.C. Church where she had the priest baptize him in secret, or so the story goes. Years later, Dan joined the Luther League for teenagers at the Lutheran church in his teens because that's where his girlfriend, Carol went, and it was a way of spending more time with her. He continued to attend the Lutheran church even after he and his girlfriend broke up. After getting a college degree in English literature, he decided to enter the Lutheran seminary to the dismay of his whole family.

We laughed a lot that night as we shared stories, cuddled against the chill March evening air, and kissed several times before I reluctantly said goodnight and went in. I hadn't even gone through the usual internal debate about whether to kiss on the first date that I normally went through fearing that a guy would get the impression that I was "fast and loose." It just seemed right, and I really wanted Dan to kiss me.

Marge was waiting up for me like a mother hen expressing both worry and dismay that I'd stayed out so late— especially on a first date— and was bursting with curiosity waiting to hear how my date with Dan had gone. I remember lying awake that night unable to sleep with excitement, reliving the evening, the fun I'd had with Dan, and the attraction I felt toward him. He was a very special person— bright, funny, relaxed, articulate but also very soft-spoken, unlike Ken whose manner of being and speaking always had an edge of nervousness to it.

I was also perplexed because I hadn't thought about Ken once the whole evening. I felt a little guilty because I had been so in love with him that I'd been eating my heart out over our breakup, and here in one evening all of that seemed in the past. All I wanted to think about was Dan and the de-lightful glow I was feeling inside.

Dan called me the next morning and every day thereafter. We were together for at least part of each day from March until June when we knew Dan would graduate from his four years of seminary, leave Rock Island, be ordained into the Lutheran ministry and move to his first parish. Because time was short, there was an urgency to be together as much as possible. This was difficult because in addition to his studies, Dan also worked managing the seminary commons and was responsible for overseeing all the food preparation. I, too, had my studies and was also involved training for the National Intercollegiate Oratory Competition with Mr. LeVander.

The more I came to know Dan the more entranced I became with him, and soon it was clear to me that I'd fallen in love with him, and, happily, he with me. He was full of surprises, some of them romantic and some just plain funny.

One beautiful April evening as we were walking hand-in-hand around Augustana's campus, he began telling me what he said was an old legend about a young couple who were separated by an evil sorcerer, who decreed that they would never be together until apples grew on cedar trees. He continued with this tale, and just about the time in the story when all seemed lost for this poor, cursed couple, we happened to pass a stand of cedar trees near the college library. Dan stopped, reached up into the tree and plucked several beautiful red apples from one of its branches and handed them to me as I stood there in open-mouthed wonderment. I laughed with utter delight and surprise as I realized that he'd staged the whole event— the tying of those apples onto the tree, the walk, the story and the perfect timing just for me.

Dan didn't have much money to spend on traditional dates, but he was always surprising me by doing the unexpected— things which revealed his real interests, unusual facets of his personality— an afternoon together at the Davenport Zoo feeding the monkeys— an evening reading Winnie the Pooh stories to me (his first gift to me was the *Oxford Dictionary of Nursery Rhymes*)— reciting poetry to me, not anything as predictable as Robert Browning, but rather A.A. Milne. I'd have to say that he really won my heart with his ability to quote from memory poem after poem of Milne's, especially this one:

Half way up the stairs is a stair where I sit

There isn't really any place quite like it

It's not at the bottom. It's not at the top.

So this is the stair where I always stop.

Half way up the stairs isn't up and it isn't down.

It isn't in the nursery. It isn't in the town.

And all sorts of funny things run round my head.

It isn't really anyplace, It's somewhere else instead.

Something about that poem charmed me— Dan charmed me!! I would ask him to repeat that poem over and over, and I would listen to his soft, gentle voice and wonder about what special human being could live inside a man who fancied that particular poem. Dan also wrote poetry, as well, and had one published in the *Christian Century* magazine. And he figure skated and won medals for skating.

I felt so very secure with Dan. I never had to wonder about things like whether he would call or not. He always did. Or how he felt about me. I knew he really cared for me. And being with him was so different from being with Kenneth, who was so full of criticisms of me, who felt the need to dominate and diminish me, and with whom there were always arguments and major upsets. Dan and I never argued, never seemed to disagree about anything. And, most important, we laughed a lot.

With the advent of Dan into my life, I'm sure Coach LeVander was relieved to see my spirits lift. Though Dan was unable to take the weekend off to attend the National Competition in Evanston, he did get a chance to see me give the speech when it was televised live a few weeks later on Rock Island's fledgling TV station. And he seemed genuinely pleased that I had won Second Place. He also genuinely seemed to enjoy my comedic sense, laughing appreciatively at my crazy jokes and humor. And he didn't push me to have sex with him because he seemed to respect my wanting to remain a virgin until I was married. I never asked him what his status was in that department— how much sexual experience he'd had— because I really didn't want to know— especially since I remembered how upset I'd been learning that I wasn't Ken's first partner.

Several weeks after returning from the Northwestern competition, I was shocked when I received an invitation to the Augustana chapter of Phi Beta Kappa, the oldest academic honor society in the US. I was sure they'd made a mistake because, though my grades were pretty good, I was not a straight A student nor did I ever view myself as one of those brainy intellectual types I associated with Phi Beta Kappa.

So convinced that there'd been a mistake that I said nothing to anyone but made an appointment to see Dr. Naeseth, my American literature professor and the faculty advisor for Phi Beta Kappa.

"I think a mistake has been made," I told her upon entering her office. "I received this invitation, but I seriously doubt I have the qualifications. I know I don't have straight A's. Is it because of the oratory competitions?"

No," she replied, "No connection at all." She picked up a notebook, thumbed through it, running her finger down one of the pages, then looked up smiling slightly and said, "And, Joan, no mistake's been made!" She assured me that based on my grades and the courses I'd taken, I did qualify.

I stood there surprised and puzzled, many things racing through my mind— my fears that my classmates would be incredulous when they learned that I'd been eligible for Phi Beta Kappa. I could just hear them saying disbelievingly, "Joan Nelson? Phi Beta Kappa? You've got to be kidding!"— Also, if I accepted the honor, I'd feel like a real fraud since I didn't feel like any kind of "American Scholar" which the organization purportedly honored. I decided that this academic society with its worldwide reputation was definitely not what it was cracked up to be. I then asked Dr. Naeseth tentatively, "Do any students ever turn down the invitation?"

She said, "Well, I personally don't know of anyone here who has, but I guess it's possible some people have some place."

I stood there in her office weighing all these things, but then thinking how proud my parents would be to know that all their hard-earned money educating me hadn't been wasted. I decided not to turn the honor down, but I still felt like someone who'd gotten something she didn't deserve when I left the advisor's office.

That evening I called my mother long distance to tell her that I'd been asked to join Phi Beta Kappa. There was a long pause, and then she said slowly, almost tentatively, "Oh, that's nice," and too quickly added, "What else is new?" Though I felt rather deflated, I figured that perhaps she really didn't get the full import of this news. But there was also the voice inside that said, "See, that's what you get for trying to impress people," the eleventh Swedish Commandment. My married sister Violet was at the house when I called. Later she told me that when my mother hung up the phone, she turned to Vi and said disgustedly, "Can you imagine that kid? Four years she goes to college and NOW she joins a sorority and then wastes all that money to call me long distance to tell me!"

When my sister pressed her to find out exactly what I'd said, she guessed what I'd told my mother. I realized later that, not having had an education beyond seventh or eighth grade, neither of my parents would have been familiar with the honors of academia. And the worst sin among some Swedes is to appear to be a braggart or to praise your children too much so that they turn out to be braggarts. So, I rather think that even if my mother had known what Phi Beta Kappa was, her reaction might still have been quite measured.

Not long thereafter, I was sitting at the Drug having coffee with Dan and some of his close seminary buddies. The topic turned to a fellow seminarian, Irv, a guy who they considered to be somewhat of a blowhard. They were joking about his always wearing his Phi Beta Kappa key hanging from his tie clasp as though that act were too self-aggrandizing and inappropriate. Dan teased me about what I was going to do with my Phi Beta Kappa key.

Embarrassed, I stammered truthfully, "I don't know."

He replied with a laugh, "Well, you can always hang it from the handle on your toilet tank." Everyone laughed so I guess I did, too. It never occurred to me to even admit I had one, let alone to wear it proudly.

About three weeks after Dan and I had begun dating, Ken called and wanted to see me. Whereas two months before, my heart would have leapt for joy at his call, now I felt very little but curiosity. We met for coffee and it seemed strange— almost strained being with Ken again. He told me that he wasn't dating Peggy anymore. That had ended, he assured me, and hadn't meant anything, anyway.

"Hey, O.K., you've proven your point now by dating Dan. You've had your fun. You win. Isn't it time to get back together again?" he said with an embarrassed half grin.

I realized then that he thought my relationship with Dan had been just a game to make him jealous— to get back at him for dating Peggy. And actually, initially that had been true. I hadn't realized that Dan would come to mean so much to me. Even now, though Dan and I had begun to talk somewhat obliquely about getting married, I doubted my own feelings, my own judgment. That I could have loved Ken for two and a half years, been engaged to marry him, and now in just six weeks all of that seemed over? It didn't make sense to me. Could what I had felt for Ken really have been love? Was what I felt about Dan really love? I didn't know for sure, but I told Ken that I cared for Dan and did not want to end that relationship.

The next day I was surprised when Ken came down to the dormitory and left a large cardboard box for me at the front desk. In it were all his pictures of me, all the cards and gifts I'd given or made for him— the socks with the beer mugs containing his initials with the white angora "foam" coming out of them on the cuffs. I'd labored for weeks knitting them for his birthday. (Actually they were the first thing I'd ever knitted.) He included the long, burgundy knitted necktie I'd made for him for Christmas— the shirts, the sweaters, the cufflinks— everything, the large and the insignificant. I felt so bad that he'd found it necessary to return everything that I'd ever given him. It was really kind of sad but funny, too, in a way. And then he called again a few days later to tell me that he also wanted back the silverware chest that his sisters had given me when we'd become engaged. I returned it to him after my next trip home, and I was glad he'd asked for it back because it was a kind of reminder of what a small person he could really be, and how fortunate I was that the relationship had ended. It confirmed for me the rightness of my relationship with Dan.

I decided to bring Dan home to Chicago one weekend in early May to meet my parents and my sister Vi and her family. My family was cordial enough to Dan, but later I sensed some reluctance about him especially from my mother. Given her experience with ministers in Sweden, I shouldn't have been surprised. And she hadn't been particularly enthusiastic about my marrying Ken, either—she'd thought he was too "twitchy" or nervous. I'd been quite upset with her attitude because she really couldn't give a good reason for not liking him. "Twitchiness" simply wasn't a good enough reason to me for not liking your daughter's fiancé especially when he came from a solid Swedish family. I had not told my mother about Ken's frequent criticisms of me nor about our many arguments.

I decided that if Dan wasn't acceptable to them, then I'd go out, find and bring home the seediest, gangster-looking fellow I could find, and introduce him as my boyfriend! That would fix them! Ultimately (and probably long before that) such an extreme measure wasn't necessary. Dan must have seemed more likable to them than Ken had been, even if he was going to be a minister, and they said nothing more in opposition to him.

The last weeks of school sped by, and soon it was time for final exams and for Dan to graduate from the Seminary and leave Rock Island. In mid-June, he was ordained in Morehead, Minnesota, and then left to begin his first assignment as the pastor at St. Luke's, a small Lutheran mission congregation in Erie, Pennsylvania. I wanted so much to attend Dan's ordination, such an important day in his life, and to meet his family, who would be there, but I'd promised a friend to be one of her bridesmaids at her wedding that same weekend. The bridesmaid's dresses had been ordered, and there was no graceful way to get out of the wedding especially since Dan and I weren't at this point officially engaged. If we had been, I'd have felt I had a more compelling excuse to renege on my bridesmaid commitment. We'd talked about becoming engaged before school was out, but we'd not been dating for very long, and it had been less than three months since Ken and I had broken up. Dan was such a wonderful and dear person that I wanted no one to regard him as just someone I took up with on the rebound.

After his ordination in June, Dan stopped in Chicago for a short visit with me and my family before going on to his first church in Erie, Pennsylvania. It was hard to say goodbye since it would be many months before I would see him again. I had gotten a job waiting tables at an upscale restaurant/hotel on the Chicago lakefront for the summer and spent my evenings at home writing letters to Dan and dreaming about the time that we would be together forever. Long distance telephone calls were still quite costly so we could not talk together every day or even every week. Dan's beginning salary as a pastor was under $3000 a year, not much even in those days, and often his long distance bills to call me approached $50 a month.

The summer seemed interminable. Other than my waitress job, my life centered around writing to Dan, waiting on tables, and waiting for his letters. They were filled with all his news of getting used to preaching every Sunday, getting to know his small, struggling congregation, dealing as a wet-behind-the-ears minister with a hard-headed board of trustees and deacons, and the difficulties of living alone and single in a new city. In Dan's letters, he shared how much he loved me, missed me, yearned to hold me, and spoke of his vision of the happiness of our life together after we were married.

As had happened before meeting Dan when I had thought about marrying Ken, thoughts of what life would be like for me as a minister's wife sometimes concerned me. I didn't see myself as typical minister's wife material. I had this stereotyped image of ministers' wives based on books and films, and the wife of one of my confirmation pastors whose children I babysat for occasionally as a teenager. They seemed to have no identity of their own except as shadow extensions of their husbands— quiet, unobtrusive, plain to the point of blandness, unfailingly supportive of their husbands and expressing no opinions except those that reflected the attitudes and opinions of the minister. Of course I assumed they were also very righteous, soft-spoken, and probably quite boring. Their primary church functions were to attend the ladies' aide society meetings, teach Sunday school, maybe sing in the choir, and play the piano for Sunday school or church. They were definitely to keep a low profile!

One woman I'd heard about was an exception, though I never knew her personally. She was from a prominent Lutheran family in the Midwest, was a smart, well-connected and very active woman in the Lutheran church, having written several books on spiritual matters. Among some men in the seminary, however, her pastor husband was to be pitied, the object of "Casper Milquetoast"-type jokes, and she was derisively viewed as the one who wore the pants in the family. She definitely did not know her place, but she evidently hadn't let that hold her back from speaking her mind. She was not someone I could ever imagine myself emulating.

I felt I was different from the stereotypical minister's wife in many ways, except perhaps that I could play the piano. As a college sophomore, I'd briefly taken organ lessons from Mr. McDermott, the organist at Augustana, but it had taken me eight weeks to get through just one hymn playing with both hands and feet. With over 500 hymns in the hymnal, I figured it would take me 50 years to get through the whole hymnal at the rate I was going, so I quit.

Though I took my spiritual life seriously, I didn't talk about it publicly. My faith had not come without thought, questioning traditional Christian doctrine and doing some soul searching as a teenager. Even well before my teens I didn't believe that God or Jesus would only "save" Christians. What kind of egocentric God would that have been? The Jesus I knew and believed in would never have been so egotistical as to close off the possibility of whatever heaven there was to someone who'd never heard of the man Jesus or his teachings.

I must have been viewed by my classmates in high school as a bit of a Sarah Bernhardt since the school yearbook described me as "dramatic," which puzzled me at the time. Today I would describe myself as an extrovert: someone comfortable with most people, articulate, emotionally expressive, forthright, and somewhat fearless for a girl. I was also questioning of authority, independent, and unconsciously funny— a girl who told jokes in various dialects and whose language, when angry or upset, could sometimes resemble that of a sailor. I had to be very careful not to let some of those words slip out at the wrong time or place. And sometimes they did, quite unexpectedly. Somehow those were not words to describe a typical minister's wife. I wondered if I would I fit in. I was bright but not really aware of that because most of my classmates in high school were also quite smart. I never made the grade average required by the National Honor Society in high school, however. And I had opinions— frequently strong ones about certain things.

Everyone in my family had opinions— political, religious, and social. Frequently my sister Violet and I would have heated discussions with our father at the dinner table about all manner of issues— Chicago politics, the police (my father thought they were all bribe-taking crooks), Communism, capitalism, his pro-Socialist views (actually his refusal to demonize Russia as most people did in the US. at that time), and his disdain for the corruption and greed of the US. government, which, he said, was run by the industrial /military complex. I didn't have a clue as to what that was, so I'd usually ended up saying something inane like, "Well, if you think life is so great in Russia, why don't you go live there!" Voices would be raised and often my father, to make a point, would pound on the table till the dishes rattled. When he saw that he could not prevail against our arguments by

39

dint of loudness, he'd sometimes just leave the table (but not before he'd finished eating) either in anger or disgust at our faulty reasoning or our gullibility at believing what we read in the newspapers. "After all, Dad, they wouldn't put it in the paper if it wasn't true!"

Sometimes he'd just summarize in frustration by telling us that we were both just "full of shit" (as he put it) and he'd turn his back on us and retire to the quiet of his bedroom to read. I laugh now at my ignorance regarding the realities of the Capitalist system in the US. And today, if he were alive, he'd come to me crowing about how right he'd been all along, pointing his long, hefty index finger and saying jokingly in his booming voice, "I told you, and I told you, and I told you!" just as he used to say when he had proof he'd been right all along about something or other. But given the political situation today, I think we'd still be arguing!

My mother rarely entered these dinnertime discussions, but more often than not she'd just get upset watching as things heated up, and then she'd lecture my sister and me about arguing with Dad and ruining a nice dinner. Except for my mother, the three of us really never took the vehemence of these discussions seriously.

Ours was not a family to shovel disagreements and other unpleasant feelings under the rug. Anger, whenever present, was handled verbally and sometimes loudly with slamming doors just for emphasis, but never with physical violence. My father had frequently been beaten by his father in Sweden, as had his four brothers and usually as a result of his father's drinking. Once after having accidentally broken a neighbor's window playing stickball, my grandfather in Sweden, now long dead, flailed him with an umbrella till it broke over my father's back. Dad, who was just 11 or 12, subsequently ran away from home to work in a match factory. I think my father must have vowed never to hit his children, for he never laid a hand on either my sister or me ever.

I have always appreciated that in my family, my sister and I were allowed to express our anger, upset, or disagreements. We were allowed to argue with our parents, and we knew that love and relationships were not in danger just because one or the other person expressed anger. It was safe to get angry, at least within our immediate family. My father would sometimes become really irritable or blow up in anger especially if he'd been drinking, but invariably he would come around later to apologize and frequently give me a small gift of money as a kind of peace offering.

Growing up as one of seven children in a painfully poor family of tenant farmers in Sweden, my father, like most native-born Swedes, had strong socialist sympathies. Both he and my mother emigrated to the US. in the early 1900s, and when they became naturalized citizens, they usually voted the Democratic ticket. But I believe my father also supported the Progressive party and voted for Henry Wallace when he ran for President against Harry Truman and Thomas Dewey in 1948. That fall when I was in 7th grade, we were assigned to give a speech supporting the candidate of our choice in that election; I was the only student in my class who spoke on behalf of Henry Wallace. My father had coached me the night before on Wallace's political platform— especially his support of the workingman and strong unions. I spoke with quite a bit of passion for a 7th grader— especially about Wallace's concern for the poor. I was the only one in class who gave any supporting facts (thanks to my dad) about Wallace and was quite satisfied that I'd given the best speech that day even though none of the class had ever heard of Henry Wallace.

In 1954, when I caught snatches of Senator Joe McCarthy on TV holding congressional hearings to ferret out members of the Communist party and their sympathizers, I began to become concerned about my father's pro-socialist leanings as evidenced by the presence of the Progressive party newspaper that came to our house regularly through the mails. By this time, the Progressive party had been painted by the press as a suspected Communist front organization, and I was afraid my dad would be hauled away, charged with being some kind of Communist.

My letters to Dan that summer of 1956 were filled primarily with words of love and longing for the time when I would be with him forever. There were also complaints of the Chicago heat, my boredom with the routine of my waitressing job, and anecdotes of occasional work mishaps such as the time I dropped a large, wet, whip cream-topped strawberry shortcake into the lap of some well-dressed man. (Actually he took it rather good-naturedly seeing how mortified I was by the occurrence. He settled with the manager for the price of having his suit cleaned and still left me a rather generous tip.)!

There was also the "Cornish hen caper" when I was getting accustomed to carrying large oval trays laden with food. I still remember holding the tray with those three Rock Cornish hen dinners balanced on one shoulder with one hand while negotiating the swinging doors between the kitchen and dining room with the other. I had never heard of a Rock Cornish hen, but after that summer, I shall never forget it when I see it offered on a menu now or in the poultry section at the supermarket. I still carry the vivid remembrance of the sight and sound of those three sumptuous hens as they slid off my tray and went s-p-l-a-t onto the restaurant dining room floor, the wild rice scattering all over the place. The crash was so loud after the swinging door hit my tray, that the whole dining room full of people looked up to see what in thunder had happened. Surprisingly, I didn't get reamed out by my manager for dropping those three hens. Instead, he quickly summoned the custodian to clean up the mess and never said another word. I also remember the look on the chef's face when I sheepishly returned to the kitchen to ask him for three more Cornish hens. He didn't say anything; he just looked at me steadily, and shaking his head wordlessly filled the second order, his eyes never leaving my face. I do believe I saw an ever so faint hint of a smile playing around his tightly closed mouth as he handed me the new hens nestled in their beds of wild rice. This time I managed to get them each to the customers' table all in one piece.

When the summer was finally over, I bid goodbye to my waitress job at the Edgewater Beach Hotel and before returning for my senior year of college, took a week off and flew to Erie to be with Dan. It would be the first time that I met Dan's family. When I got off the plane, I was unprepared and somewhat startled to see Dan standing in all his handsomeness waiting for me at the airport terminal wearing his black clerics complete with the white clerical collar, but looking so much like a Catholic priest. And we certainly drew stares from people when we hugged and kissed. Ordinarily when not working, he wore regular street clothes, but he'd been making hospital calls before coming to pick me up. It would take me a long time not to feel self-conscious by people's double takes when we were out in public and he had on his clerics. Erie, Pennsylvania, has a rather large population of Roman Catholics, and people were not accustomed to seeing a young, handsome priest in public alone except for the company of a young woman; this was especially so later when I was very obviously pregnant.

The day after I arrived in Erie, we set out to visit Dan's family— a 90-mile drive to Kane, Pa., a small town of about 5000 people in a beautiful wooded area of Pennsylvania next to the Allegheny National Forest. Here Dan had lived his whole life until he left for college and where his mother and father and his two brothers and their families still lived. I was quite anxious about meeting his family— wondering if they'd like me— wondering what they were like— if they were the stereotypical exuberant "Mama Mia" Italian family. But they weren't. Actually, though they were friendly enough toward me, on the whole they were rather subdued unlike Dan, who was more outgoing. Dan's father Louie was a soft-spoken, retired electrician and had owned a store that sold electrical appliances until the start of WW II when it became impossible to get household appliances, and he was forced to close the store. Though Louie was born in the US., his father was one of five brothers who had emigrated from Italy in the late 1800s.

Dan's mother Marion was of German /English extraction— a very intelligent woman who spent her free time reading, working crossword puzzles, occasionally playing bridge or canasta with friends from girlhood days, and playing cribbage and other games with her eight grandchildren when they visited.

She was also an excellent and effortless cook as were both of Dan's brothers' wives. Like most of the women of her generation in that small Pennsylvania town, she had never attended college, but she should have because she had a very sharp and inquiring mind. She did, however, attend a music conservatory in Warren, Pa., for two years and studied piano before marrying Dan's father, Louie. She gave it up, according to family lore, because Louie didn't want a piano in the house—a fact, if true, that boggles my mind. After Dan and I were married, one of the first things she would do when visiting us was to sit down at my piano and play. And considering that she'd not played for forty years, she played well. What a waste of talent, I thought.

I liked Dan's family, and they certainly were cordial to me. But I knew that I was different from Dawn and Ann, the girls Dan's brothers married as soon as WWII was over. They worked so their husbands could go to college on the G.I. Bill; both also became excellent cooks and homemakers. The focus of their lives always remained the care and feeding of their husbands, children, and eventually their grandchildren. Though I had always dreamed of marrying a wonderful man (one that loved me, of course) and having three children (whose names I'd chosen years before in high school), I never envisioned a life focused solely on being a wife, mother, cook, and housekeeper. I wanted someday to be a teacher, as well. Beyond that, however, I had done little thinking or planning except to know that I wanted first to be married to a wonderful man and have three children. Women's career choices were very limited in the 50s— to be a nurse, secretary, teacher, or airline stewardess (if you were slender, pretty, not over 5'6", nor over 34 years old). Of course a woman could also be a waitress, cashier, or cook, though these jobs weren't considered "careers."

There were just a few short days until I had to return to school to complete my senior year. Dan and I returned from Kane to Dan's "parsonage," a tiny furnished apartment which was the remodeled attic in some lady's private home. We slept together on his sofa bed for a night or two before I had to return to school, and we hugged, kissed, and did most other parts of making love (at least that I knew about), but we didn't complete the act of having intercourse. And we probably would have done that, too, except I was sure Dan's landlady had her ears glued to the walls of that young, single minister upstairs.

We spent our last day together with Dan showing me around the section of Erie known as Millcreek where his church was located. His congregation of about 65 members had been a non-denominational independent Sunday school for many decades before the mission board of the Lutheran church offered to make it a new congregation and fund it with a full-time pastor instead of the part-time ministers who'd served it briefly before. And so they sent Dan as his first assignment to make Lutherans out of those folks. The church itself, located in a rather run-down section on the outskirts of Erie, was a cinder block, basement structure with a small makeshift worship center, a kitchen, a couple of Sunday school rooms, an electric organ and metal folding chairs to sit on. The only thing that could have identified that one-story dwelling as a church was a small wooden cross and a sign reading "St. Luke's Lutheran Church, The Rev. Daniel L. Pierotti, B.A., B.D." I was told that when Dan's family had come for their first visit to his church, his six-year-old nephew Jimmy asked, "What does 'B.D.' next to Uncle Danny's name mean?" To which Dan's dad replied, "That stands for 'Bad Dago!'" and everyone laughed. Actually the two sets of letters indicated that Dan had received a Bachelor of Arts degree from college as well as a Bachelor of Divinity degree from the seminary. The "B.D." had been a family joke ever since.

After the week together with Dan, it was extremely hard to say goodbye, but he was coming to visit me in Chicago at Thanksgiving, and I had that to look forward to. That fall I finished my practice teaching requirement for a secondary education degree. I completed my practice teaching in speech and English at Rock Island High School with the words to "Rock Around the Clock" that they'd played incessantly at lunchtime over the school loudspeakers still ringing in my ears. Though I'd taken several theatre courses, but with a double major in speech and English and oratory competitions, I'd never had time to audition for plays. Now after completing the few courses I needed for graduation, I had the time to enjoy playing the female lead in the winter play. Dan could not afford to fly to Rock Island for the play since he planned to spend Thanksgiving with me in Chicago. I did, however, receive a dozen roses from him delivered on opening night of the play— my first red roses ever.

During the Thanksgiving holiday break, Dan flew to Chicago to be with me, and on Thanksgiving Day, he gave me a beautiful, diamond solitaire engagement ring. Of course I was thrilled, but held my breath, nevertheless, as he put it on my finger. I feared that like the ring Ken had given me, this one, too, would not fit; thankfully it did. I've always been self-conscious about my size. Though a healthy 5'7" (which today is quite normal for women) and always weighing slightly more than the charts said I should weigh, I was always the tallest girl in my class in elementary school. Happily, the boys caught up with me by 9th grade. My ring size was 7 1/2 or 8, and I was always embarrassed that the fingers of all of my boyfriends' hands had been shorter than mine. This was true regarding Dan, as well, who at just about 5'8 or 5'9 necessitated my always wearing flats when out with him to make me seem a bit shorter. When I now look at photos of me taken back then, I can't imagine what I was thinking when I worried so about my height and size.

I'm not sure whether Dan had followed the old custom of his asking my father for permission to marry me, but when my dad and I took Dan to the airport at the end of the Thanksgiving weekend, they shook hands as though they'd been friends forever. Smiling broadly, my father said, "Well, congratulations, Dan, and best wishes. You're not getting much but good luck, anyway." He laughed, looking over at me, winking, and we all laughed. He was probably joking, but somehow I still remember that comment years later, as I did the comment Dan had made about the exuberance of my clapping after a concert shortly after we'd begun to date. We had just attended a wonderful concert after which I had enthusiastically applauded hoping for an encore.

I commented about it again afterwards at the restaurant and Dan said, "Obviously, you liked it. Your clapping looked like you were slamming two big frying pans together." He said this laughingly, as my father had made his comment about me at the airport. What was there in some men that impelled them to denigrate the women they loved and pass it off as a joke? Those words made me shrivel inside, and I still remember how humiliated I felt. I wasn't cut out to be a fragile flower, as many other women seemed to be. I felt more like a strong Valkyrie, and it took many years before I could claim that Valkyrie image and begin to be proud of that fact. I have looked at pictures of myself back then and wondered what had been the matter with me that I had regarded myself as unappealing.

The following spring as graduation approached, Marge and I spent hours together excitedly planning our respective weddings, poring over brides' magazines, discussing wedding dresses and bridesmaids' dresses. Years before in high school, we'd sat next to each other in typing class writing notes, planning how many children we wanted and what their names were going to be.

And here we were, still best friends, worrying about the importance of the right colors for our bridesmaids' dresses, oblivious to the much more important decisions of our lives— our choice of partners. We were caught up in the excitement of marrying our "true loves." Marge had become engaged to Karl earlier that year, and because he had a year-long internship ahead of him in California before completing his last year in seminary, we decided to have our weddings a week apart just after graduation so we could serve as each other's maid of honor before we started whole new lives as the wives of ministers probably at opposite ends of the country. I doubt that neither she nor I could possibly have imagined how becoming ministers' wives would totally change our lives.

Mr. and Mrs. Almlof, Marge's parents, were both teachers whose incomes enabled them to have a much higher standard of living than my family had. My dad worked as a carpenter, my mother as a part time cleaning lady and then later as a school cook at North Park. Neither of my parents had gone beyond elementary school in Sweden.

It was my mother who first encouraged me to go to North Park Academy because of its reputation as a very good school academically. And she encouraged me to go to college because, as she sometimes said, "You never know when you'll have to earn your own living and your children's as well if you have them." How prescient she turned out to be!! She'd also got a full-time job in my high school's cafeteria to help finance my college tuition. Marge and I decided to attend the same college but agreed to have different roommates so we'd get to know other people at school.

We made several trips home to Chicago early that spring to pick out our wedding dresses and to plan our weddings. Marge's wedding invitations were elegant and hand-engraved from Marshall Fields. Mine were just machine printed at a local "el cheapo" printers in Chicago. The print-style of the invitations I chose had an elegant script to it so it looked engraved, but if you turned the invitation over, you could tell immediately from the absence of the engraver's plate indentation that it wasn't engraved. The wedding dress Marge and her mother selected was a lovely traditional, silk *peau* de *soie* beauty with a long flowing train. I knew that her gown would be exceedingly beautiful and it certainly was.

In high school, Marge had owned several cashmere sweaters, much-longed-for luxuries too costly for me to buy for myself and which my mother would never have bought for me because of their price. My sweaters, made of a newly invented man-made fiber they called orlon, a much cheaper cashmere-like fabric but could never have passed for real cashmere. The difference between the Almlof's and my family's incomes was considerable. That however, didn't affected my friendship with Marge. I don't recall ever feeling deprived, for there were compensations. Mrs. Almlof was always much stricter with Marge than my mother was with me, which is why Marge especially enjoyed staying overnight with me. We had more freedom and could get away with a little more at my house— like not getting into major trouble when we sometimes came home late from a double date.

During the hunt for a wedding dress with my mom, I tried on a number of unsatisfactory gowns at several different stores, and we were both exhausted from the search. Finally, as a last resort, we headed over to Marshall Field's where I had worked one summer and part time in the fall in the credit department while in high school. To me it was the quintessential and finest department store in the U.S. Its reputation for excellent quality and service was known world-wide. When I worked in the credit office there, I was shocked to learn that anyone could charge anything under ten dollars without being asked for a charge card— to me a considerable amount of money in 1953. My job was to track down phony addresses given by occasional customers and attempt to collect from deadbeats who took advantage of Field's generous credit policy. I hadn't even thought to suggest to my mother our going there for a wedding dress because of their prices. But in desperation my mother suggested our looking at what they had at Field's.

The bridal department was like a large, sumptuous, private boutique. The salespeople stayed exclusively with customers until they left satisfied or gave up looking. Marshall Field, the original owner, had a famous store motto "Give the lady what she wants." And Fields store always tried to do just that. I viewed my surroundings with awe, strongly doubting we would find a bridal gown at a price we could afford here. But our saleslady gave no indication that my mother and I were out of our financial league. Didn't she know, I wondered, as she began bringing out gowns for me to try on, that she was on a fool's errand?

I tried on the first two gowns, each time surreptitiously straining to see the obscure price tags designed for people who didn't need to worry about prices. Avoiding drawing attention to my price preoccupation, I admiringly stroked the beautiful fabric, looking in the mirror at the image of a girl I hardly recognized as me wearing the kind of dress every woman dreams of wearing at some time in her life. My mother made no comment about either of the dresses. After the saleslady's third trip back to the stock room, she came out carrying what looked, at first glance, like huge billows of fluffy, white spun sugar which she needed both arms to manage. As she held up the fabric with both her arms, she allowed the full length of the dress to gently unfold downward to the floor revealing a gown of layer upon layer of exquisite diaphanous material.

I stood there in my bra and a floor length hoop skirt as the saleslady raised the dress over my head, easing it down onto my body, and began buttoning the several dozen covered buttons that ran down the back from neck to waist. In pure white charmeuse, the dress had just a slight suggestion of a capped sleeve with the fabric shirred snuggly across the bodice all the way from my collar bones to my waist. Attached was an incredibly full, floor-length skirt of many discrete layers of fabric, which extended far out with the help of the hoop skirt under the dress. But what made it most unusual was the length of gathered fabric that extended from the back shoulders all the way down the back of the dress and extended as a train behind the gown. I sucked in my breath thinking "Ohhh my..." as I gazed open-mouthed at myself in the mirror, a huge smile of surprised delight breaking out on my face.

The gown had a distinct Grecian look, like something Aphrodite might have worn. It was magnificent. I felt magnificent. Starting to breathe normally again, I glanced over toward my mother, seated in a chair close by, for her reaction. For the first time during our search, she, too, wore a big smile. This was it!! This was the winner. And it would be the winner 25 years later when my oldest daughter eventually wore it at her wedding. The dress cost $118— in 1957. I'm certain no one in my family going back generations had ever worn anything that beautiful or that expensive. Oddly enough my mother made not the slightest demurral. That wonderful dress had sold itself. It was a done deal, as they say.

The last college social event that year was the Indee's spring dance. I'd been elected their president my senior year, and I felt obligated to attend their spring dance even though Dan was too far away to take me to it. So, I invited Basheer Nijim, a good friend and classmate who was an exchange student from Palestine, to be my date. I chose him because I knew that by taking Basheer, there'd probably be no gossip about my attending a dance without my fiancé. I also asked him because Basheer was a good enough friend to forgive my somewhat clumsy, inexperienced dancing. And he was tall enough that I might look a bit more like the fragile flower that girls were supposed to look like compared to their partners.

What I didn't expect was that not only was Basheer an excellent dancer but also an amazingly strong lead. At the dance, he took hold of me and as though I were light as a feather, quite physically led me around the dance floor with such confidence that my feet didn't have time to get the message from my brain about where they should be stepping. They just followed him effortlessly. I stopped thinking and started dancing as though I really knew what I was doing. Everything just worked. I stopped worrying about trampling on Basheer's feet and actually started having fun.

Never before and never since have I enjoyed dancing so much. He really made me look like Ginger Rogers, or so I thought. Eventually though, a new nagging in my mind began over what people would think if I danced with him until the evening was over. Would the good time I was obviously having get back to Dan? Around eleven, I reluctantly suggested to Basheer that I needed to get back to the dorm, and so we left. It was the first and last time in my life that I really danced with such abandon and lack of self-consciousness. I still regret that I cut the evening short at the dance because of my concern that as a woman already engaged, the appearance of having too good a time with someone other than my fiancé Dan might elicit gossip.

Three weeks later, my parents drove to Rock Island when I graduated cum laude as the first member of our family ever to complete college. My proud parents then drove me and four years' worth of accumulated college stuff back to Chicago just in time for my wedding to Dan five days later. Marge's parents also were there for her graduation. She was to be married to Karl the week after Dan and I were wed with both of us serving as each other's maid of honor.

After four years of college, papers, and tests, and for some years afterwards, I sometimes had nightmares of coming to a test that I hadn't prepared for, not even knowing that a test had been scheduled. Was it the fear of being unprepared for something crucial or just a carry-over fear from all those years as a student? As it turned out, there were lots of things in my life that I hadn't been prepared for, but the last thing I wanted was to start studying for a master's degree— and certainly not then.

CHAPTER 4

Wedding Day Whiplash

1957 – CHICAGO · MICHIGAN · NOVA SCOTIA

Dan and his parents, two brothers, and their wives arrived in Chicago on Friday, the day before the wedding just in time for the wedding rehearsal and dinner following it. It had been months since I'd been with Dan, and I could hardly wait to be alone with him. After the rehearsal and the dinner, we were finally alone in his yellow '47 Chevy coupe and eager to make love as we sat kissing and holding one another in front of my parent's house. But since we'd held off fully consummating our love all those months since we'd met, I told Dan that I wanted to wait just one more day.

The next morning, my wedding day, I woke up only to discover that I'd just started my period and had to begin taking Midol to quell the cramps, which were already starting. Damn! Damn! Damn! What a cruel joke to play on such a reluctant virgin. But I decided that I wasn't going to let this ruin my wedding day. I'd have a whole married life together with Dan to make love. God knows, I'd already waited 21 years! I'd just have to wait a few more days.

It was a perfect Saturday afternoon for a wedding, warm and sunny but not beastly hot as Chicago could sometimes get, even in early June. The many pink and white peony bushes lining the walkway to the church's side entrance were in full bloom as my father dropped me off at church, and I carried my glorious wedding gown in so that I could dress in one of the Sunday school rooms. My three bridesmaids, my closest friends, Marge and Carol from high school days, and my college roommate for four years, Marcia, were already gathered and beginning to get into their bridesmaid dresses.

The caterers were busy setting up for the light supper wedding reception in the parish hall after the ceremony. I could faintly hear the organist settling in to begin playing, and already guests were starting to gather in the church. My much-loved confirmation pastor, Olaf Jonasson, was going to marry us. He was to me the quintessential pastor, a man really deserving of the title "Pastor" (from the word meaning a "shepherd,"); a truly caring man whose life seemed emblematic of the kind of person one could turn to in a time of real trouble, a fine preacher who got to the heart of the Gospel, a man who sought to serve people rather than spend his career as a minister conducting a well-planned politicking program to achieve higher church offices or serve in impressive thriving congregations. He was definitely not a *prästafan*, to use my father's favorite pejorative Swedish term for ministers. Soon the photographer showed up to take wedding pictures, and Marge helped fasten a small crown of seed pearls onto my head and then placed the tulle fingertip veil over it. Wearing a small bridal crown with or without a veil was an old Swedish wedding custom. Marge would wear one with her wedding gown the following Saturday when she was married and I was her matron of honor. She handed me my bouquet and after a few more pictures were taken, she gave me a quick hug, and we all walked into narthex of the church where my dad was waiting for me.

Most of the guests had already arrived and were seated, as were my mother and Dan's mother and father when the ushers rolled down the long, white runner. Then began the strains of Trumpet Voluntary and the bridesmaids, led by my four-year-old niece Carol, our flower girl, started down the aisle. My dad, whom I usually saw wearing workmen's overalls with the familiar, flat yellow carpenter's pencil sticking out of his pocket, now looked tall, dignified, and handsome in his black tuxedo. I felt joyous and excited as I took hold of his arm and stood watching from the narthex doorway while my friends walked down the aisle and assumed their places up by the chancel. Dan with his two brothers had already entered from the side and turned smiling to face me. He looked very handsome and un-ministerial in his white tuxedo, and my heart was filled with such love for him. I felt like I was the luckiest girls in the world to be marrying this exceptional man. It never once occurred to me that he might be lucky to be getting me!

Why, I wondered, did people cry at weddings? It was certainly the last thing I felt like doing as I radiated my happiness. Then the organist modulated from Clarke's Trumpet Voluntary into the familiar Lohengrin Wedding March melody, and, as I had dreamed of doing so many times when hearing that music as a girl, I started down the aisle smiling broadly with my Dad by my side.

After the wedding reception was over, we changed clothes at church and drove to a motel in Michigan City overnight. The next morning Dan and I drove up to Portage Lake, Michigan, staying at Marge's parents' summer cottage for four days so that we could come back for Marge and Karl's wedding the following Friday. Despite my being on my period, we made love twice that week; however, dealing with the resultant soiled sheets, which we had to wash and hang out on the line each time, plus the curiosity of Mrs. Olson, the next door neighbor, who came "just to say hello," as she put it, a damper that was really put on our potential passion. I felt disappointed and a little embarrassed by the mess these first attempts at lovemaking caused.

It didn't get much better when we arrived back at my parents' house in Chicago for Marge's wedding. My period was over, but then there was the distraction of possible noise from my bedroom, which had only a single twin bed we had to share in my parents' small house. My mother thought it was foolishness for us to struggle together in that small bed when we had a perfectly good couch in the living room that one of us could have slept on. But we thought otherwise.

I'd always dreamed of a romantic honeymoon somewhere near the ocean where the waves pounded up on huge rocky outcroppings, and you could hear the sound of the sea at night when you lay in bed in the arms of the person you loved. I must have seen a place like that in the movies. Peggy's Cove, Nova Scotia, sounded just like such a place. Though it was a three- or four-day drive from Chicago, it wouldn't be so long on the way back to Erie, Pennsylvania, where Dan's church was located. We had two more weeks of his vacation, which we figured would get us there with time to spare.

We did not plan on car trouble, however, which started on a Sunday morning near Plattsburgh, New York. Not exactly a honeymoon heaven kind of place. But after a two-day layover in a Motel-6, we were off again for Peggy's Cove, poorer for the costs entailed with car repairs, but glad it could be fixed.

There were rocks and ocean in Bar Harbor, Maine, where we stayed that night in a large, old Victorian-style guest house with spacious rooms decorated with elegant (though a bit worn), turn of the century, ornamental bedroom furniture with twin beds. It was long on giving one a sense of how the rich had once lived, but unfortunately those twin beds made it short on romance. But I didn't say anything because I knew that Dan was quite tired from the hours of driving he'd been doing.

The next morning, we visited an historic cemetery dating back to the 1700s filled with tombstones indicating the remains and sometimes fascinating epitaphs of early settlers and families of fishermen and seafarers, many of whom had been lost at sea. Then before heading for Canada and Nova Scotia, we stopped to look at the ocean, my first experience seeing breathtaking views of rocks being battered by the incoming tides. I took pictures of Dan standing astride some of the rocks looking like he was the Colossus of Rhodes and pictures taken at that elegant guesthouse. Looking at honeymoon photos later would have led one to think that Dan had gone on that honeymoon by himself. There were no pictures either of me or us together, largely because Dan never mentioned his taking one, and because I was too embarrassed to have to ask him or anyone else to take my picture.

In retrospect, we should have stayed in Bar Harbor because we under-estimated the distance and time it would take to go to Nova Scotia. It was a long two-day drive to Halifax over roads some of which were only two lanes and not in great condition. To make matters worse, Dan's old Chevy started acting up again, cutting out so that eventually we had to jam a large cereal box between the gas pedal and the dashboard so that the motor wouldn't quit if we needed to stop for a bite to eat, use the restroom, or get gas. Canada in the '50s did not have many motels along the way to Nova Scotia, and those we could afford were of minimal quality. Their once white sheets were grey— never having been bleached. They were probably clean but they sure looked grungy.

Dan was looking forward to visiting Moncton and the Bay of Fundy in New Brunswick to watch the sometimes 40 ft. tides change. It seemed that we'd driven interminably. By the time we got to Moncton, I couldn't care less about the tidal phenomenon going on there. Time was running out, and as things stood now, if we ever made it to Peggy's Cove, we'd only have a couple days there before we had to turn around and head back to Erie, Pennsylvania— a very long drive for a very short-lived destination.

Arriving in Halifax, we found a charming restaurant where I ate my first prime rib of beef and Yorkshire pudding— a savory treat of batter baked in the juicy fat of the beef 'til it puffed up and was cut into slices. It was the best food we ate on our honeymoon, especially compared to the places we'd eaten along the way from Chicago. Dan's salary at his first church was just $3000 a year plus his housing, a small apartment nearby in the Millcreek section of Erie. By comparison, my father, who worked construction as a carpenter earned $5000 a year— far from a king's ransom but considerably more than a minister earned. Consequently, I kept a little notebook on our honeymoon trip detailing how much we were actually spending.

We had an hour and a half farther to drive from Halifax, and dusk was settling in. Peggy's Cove had been described in a travel book as a small, idyllic, fishing village and lighthouse situated on a rocky coastline. It had sounded perfect— quaint and romantic— and I was tingling with anticipation. We had reservations at a bed and breakfast close to the water in Peggy's Cove, but by the time we found the place, it was dark with a fine mist enveloping everything. I'd hoped we would have the chance to walk down to the ocean before bedtime, but that was pointless. There wasn't much we could have seen by then. Our room was so unexceptional that I don't remember a thing about it except that Dan was tired from all the driving, gave me a quick kiss goodnight but gave no indication that he felt like making love.

We awoke the next morning to find that Peggy's Cove and all of Nova Scotia locked into what seemed like a wall of fog so dense you couldn't see more than 15 feet in front of you. The sounds of squawking seagulls and the foghorn from the lighthouse were the only things to tell that you weren't in London. Years later I learned that Nova Scotia had more fog then anyplace else worldwide. They didn't mention that in the travel book.

Though the fog lifted somewhat as the day wore on, it lasted the whole time we were there. I never did get to see the rocks and churning ocean spray nor much of anything else of the picturesque landscape at Peggy's Cove, for that matter, due to the fog. On the morning of the third day, we started back toward Halifax and my whole new life as a minister's wife in Erie, Pennsylvania. That endless, tiring 1300-mile ride from Chicago to Peggy's Cove; the time and expense of our car breaking down; my unfulfilled romantic fantasies of the roar of ocean waves on rocks below as Dan and I made love together all to the passionate melody of Rachmaninoff's 2nd Piano Concerto or "Full Moon and Empty Arms" (as the popular song words went) playing in the background. I was so disappointed I could have cried. But I didn't, nor did I share my disappointment with Dan, who seemed his usual cheerful self.

1958 – Erie, Pennsylvania

I guess the biggest disappointment of all during those early months of our marriage was Dan's seeming lack of interest in me romantically and specifically regarding sex. There were no popular books on the subject then, at least none that I knew of. There seemed to be an unspoken understanding, however, that it was men who initiated sex, and women who waited but certainly didn't make overt overtures. The most I felt I could get away with, without fearing I'd be viewed as some kind of nymphomaniac (I don't think I even knew there was such a word for a woman who liked to have an unusual amount of sex at the time,) was snuggling up like a spoon behind Dan's body and putting my arms around his waist.

I believed that if he found me sexually attractive or wanted to make love, he would have communicated that to me physically or verbally. He had certainly seemed affectionate and interested in necking and petting early in those few months after we'd met at Augustana before he was ordained and moved to his first parish. Now shortly into our marriage, it was usually I who initiated a hug or kiss when we were home together, and I that took hold of his hand when we were out walking in public, though not when he had his clerical garb on. He did look like a priest, however—black suit with a clerical (turned around) collar, black hat, coat, shoes, etc. though he wore civvies when he was home or not out working, going to church meetings, making house and hospital calls on parishioners.

And it was usually I who was the first to say "I love you, Dan," to which he'd respond almost like a parrot, "I love you, too." That is, until the time I finally asked him why he didn't ever just spontaneously tell me he loved me. I don't recall his answer, but he did say, "I always feel like you're expecting me to say 'I love you' back to you." His words felt like a cold shock around my heart. I couldn't understand why if you really loved your partner, it wouldn't be the most natural thing to want to tell them that, unless you felt false in saying it. After he said that, I was much more cautious when I said those words to him. In a strange way, I felt muzzled.

The intervals between our lovemaking grew longer until it was over a week or ten days and then sometimes several weeks— this just shortly after returning from our honeymoon. I'd seen a doctor before we were married and been fitted with a diaphragm for contraception. I was told to practice inserting and removing it, putting the spermicide in the middle, folding it in half like a tortilla, and trying to insert it into my vagina correctly without its springing loose. It was not easy, I tell you. It was messy and tricky to do. But it was necessary if I was not to get pregnant. And so I would put it in night after night "just in case" Dan would indicate that he wanted to have sex. But then nothing would happen, Dan would turn over and go to sleep, and I would lie there awake stewing after going to all the trouble of inserting the damned diaphragm, all for nothing. And finally, I just stopped putting it in because I'd only end up mad at him and feeling like some kind of loser whose wonderful paragon of a perfect husband didn't want her.

Why didn't I just ask him what was wrong? Just flat out ask why he didn't seem to want to make love more often? But this was before the Sexual Revolution, which didn't start until the late '60s. Couples didn't talk about sex in the '50s. We didn't even discuss our sex lives with good friends back then. Furthermore, women were told that it wasn't their place to initiate lovemaking. There was no Cosmopolitan magazine and very few books about sex. I hadn't the slightest notion of how often the average couple made love— once a week? once a month? I didn't know what was "normal," but I was pretty sure that in the first year of marriage, it was more than once a month. Why didn't I just ask my husband that question, "Why do you not make love to me very often?" I didn't, I guess, because I just couldn't bear it if he were to have said, "Joan, I'm sorry, but you just don't turn me on!" or something to that effect.

And then sometimes, low and behold, he'd start making the kind of un-mistakable romantic-type moves that indicated that he wanted to have sex. And then I'd lie there, without the needed diaphragm in place to prevent getting pregnant so soon after we'd married, trying to remember where I was in my cycle, counting on my fingers to see if this was a time I might be ovulating. All this to determine if I should excuse myself, go to the john, and put that damned messy diaphragm in place. But then I'd think, "Nope, Joan, you'd better not…Remember to carpe diem! 'seize the day' as the Romans would have said…. Better stay put or he might change his mind by the time you come back." What a wonderful frame of mind to stir up passion! Maybe if I'd only had Rachmaninoff's concerto playing nearby…

Three months after our wedding, I missed my period and though I was surprised, I shouldn't have been. Three weeks later my doctor confirmed that I was indeed pregnant. I had mixed feelings— part of me was happy about the news and part of me wondered how Dan would feel. I wished that it had not been so soon after we were married. We'd certainly not planned to start a family this early. But he greeted the news with equanimity— not ecstatic like the husbands in the movies reacted, but not unhappy or seemingly disappointed either. I knew my mother would think it was way too soon or maybe react like I was an unwed mother. So I stalled until I was five months along to call her with the news. "Couldn't you have waited a little longer after you were married?" she said with what I thought was a somewhat accusatory tone in her voice that suggested that we were like a couple of rabbits madly screwing the night away every night. She should only have known the truth. But of course, I would never have discussed my marital dilemmas with her since on several occasions she'd expressed the rather negative view about sex in or out of marriage: that if a man left you alone sexually, you should feel lucky.

Though I interpreted that comment as my mother's poor attitude toward sex, years later I learned that view grew out of years of fear about getting pregnant. Her older sister had died from septicemia caused by an infection from a birth control device in her uterus, which evidently went untreated by a doctor until it was too late because as a young immigrant from Sweden, she'd feared possible arrest. Supposedly it was an illegal form of birth control. She left two small boys, my cousins, for her husband to raise during the

Depression when times were so hard.

A year or so after we had gotten married, Marge, Alice, our Greek girl-friend from West Hall, and I happened to be in Chicago at the same time. We got together for a long-awaited visit. By then, Alice was married, also, and we got into a brief discussion about sex. Both my friends complained about their husbands' demands for sex "every night and every night," as Marge said disgustedly, describing the arguments over frequency of sex with her husband that ensued if she didn't feel like making love. And there I sat with absolutely nothing to say in that discussion, and was silent in the face of the fact that Dan and I had made love only eight or ten times that year. I was too ashamed to admit to them that he didn't want to have sex with me any more frequently than that.

CHAPTER 5

Faith in Heaven vs Faith on Earth

1958 – ERIE, PENNSYLVANIA - ST. LUKE'S LUTHERAN CHURCH

D an was busy visiting potential new church members and acclimating the new organist to the peculiarities of the Lutheran liturgical music. He had recently hired an older retired lady, Nellie Carter, as the organist. She'd claimed she was an experienced music sight-reader, but Nellie was not your typical church organist by a long shot. Her primary experience had been at the Diamond Horse Shoe Bar in Erie in her younger days.

She would sit at the organ, her cane hanging from the edge of the Hammond electric console and her ample bottom hanging out a bit over the organ bench, and vigorously lead the singing of the hymn with her husky, whiskey voice. Dan had hired her primarily because she was available, could read music, and was able with limited success to switch key progressions in any key desired as she moved from one part of the liturgical service to another. She could do this, however, only by using the tune to "America the Beautiful." So, of course, if you listened closely and were fairly familiar with the music, which most members of St. Luke's weren't, you could make out the familiar strains of "America the Beautiful" as she modulated from the melody of the "Kyrie" to the "Gloria in Excelsis." And sometimes she had to move all over the scales searching until she finally found her way to a

63

harmonious entrance to the next hymn, but she was better than who was in second place— which was I.

Sometimes I regretted that I hadn't continued longer with Mr. McDermott, the organ teacher at Augustana. Despite my lack of skill on the organ, I was pressed into service occasionally when Nellie was sick. Unfortunately, Nellie had taken ill shortly before Easter Sunday, and I'd had to play the organ for the Easter Service just two months prior to Eric's birth. I was dressed in a pale violet-blue maternity dress I'd made for dress-up occasions and was very much pregnant as I sat on the organ bench listening to my husband's carefully developed Easter sermon. The choir, all nine of them, were seated up front in our small church just behind the pulpit. Mr. and Mrs. Babe were in their usual places front center of the group, she, complete with her black wig, which barely covered her head. It had the distinctly artificial look like it was part of a costume. I suspected that it had actually come from the local dollar store's post-Halloween sale.

Mr. Babe, our only bass, had lost his upper dentures some weeks before and there was no time for a replacement, so their absence was quite visible when the choir sang. Mrs. Sauerwine, though she had volunteered to be responsible for preparing the repast (as they called the post-service luncheon) to be served after church, managed to take her place with the choir. Fortunately, she was minus the large bread knife she was usually seen wielding at church dinners as she cut thick slices of bread from a huge loaf of white bread clutched close to her chest AS she sliced away in the church's tiny kitchen. Dan and I would hold our breaths during this "culinary performance" fearing that she might accidentally give herself an unintended mastectomy.

In the congregation sat 84-year-old Harry Egelin, who could be counted on at least once every Sunday to quite audibly clear his sinuses and throat and hawking up (usually during Dan's sermons) a large wad of phlegm and after carefully examining it, store it in a little glass olive-oil container especially for this purpose. Lucy and Martin Proudler, a couple now well into their 90s, who had started the congregation as an independent Sunday school many years before, were always present. All in all, it was a rather interesting collection of people, and quite different than what one would find in a typical Lutheran church, especially on Easter Sunday.

The Easter morning service in most Lutheran churches was much more formal and festive with visiting clergy, processionals, special music by several church choirs, brass instrumentalists, musicians, and soloists, who were often not members of the congregation but "ringers" to flesh out the musical offerings; overflowing banks of flowers— especially Easter lilies. Easter Sunday for Lutherans was always comparable to the High Holy Holidays in Judaism— actually more sacred for Christians than even Christmas.

That Easter Sunday at St. Luke's, however, was not at all what I'd been accustomed to in other Lutheran churches. The Easter liturgical service and music were different from the regular Sunday service, and it was obvious that most of the perhaps 90 people present including the kids from the Sunday school and a group of four neighbor children seated in the first row directly in front of the pulpit were totally unfamiliar with the music, as was I, the substitute organist.

Some of the children had undoubtedly gorged themselves on Easter candy. And almost as if it had been orchestrated, just after Mr. Egelin began his hawking/spitting routine, one of the children gagged loudly and threw up a huge mass of blue-tinted Easter vomit which went splat noisily on the concrete floor. There was a momentary pause in Dan's sermon as he beckoned for the ushers to help the little boy who'd thrown up to the bathroom and then bring in a mop to clean up. It was a sorry scene. Having just turned 22, I was too young to have developed the kind of dispassionate sensibilities to watch disasters with a loving, sense of humor. It all looked so hopeless to me, and my eyes began to fill with tears.

This whole, sad, and too intimate a scene was nothing like what I'd once imagined it would be like for this new minister's wife, especially on Easter Sunday. I didn't have a handkerchief or even a tissue handy up there seated at the elevated organ bench, and I turned my head away from the congregation toward the wall to hide the tears of shame and embarrassment that began rolling down my cheeks as I attempted to unobtrusively mop them with my palms and knuckles, and rescue the music as best I could. It was far from the many Easter services overflowing with Easter lilies, candles, and glorious music typical of others Easter services I'd attended most of the time earlier in my life.

June 23, 1958 – Erie, Pennsylvania

Two months later, our first child was born the evening of June 23, 1958, the day after Dan and I returned from a trip to Jamestown, NY, after attending the Lutheran Convocation and Ordination held at Chautauqua about 90 miles from Erie. It was a bit of a risk to travel that far from home because our baby had been expected two weeks earlier. But I got tired of patiently waiting for his or her arrival and decided that if my water broke while attending the ordination of a new crop of ministers, then so be it. There were hospitals in Jamestown for such an emergency, and since I'd had to miss Dan's ordination the year before because I'd been in a friend's wedding, I wanted to see what I'd missed.

When we finally arrived safely back to Erie from the ordination ceremony on a hot June evening, I consumed the better part of half a watermelon, went to bed, and awakened at six in the morning with what felt like twinges and abdominal cramps that I suspected might be labor pains. Shortly thereafter my water broke and Dan took me to Hamott Hospital. I'd been reading about natural childbirth, and though there'd been no childbirth breathing classes available in those days, I'd been practicing the controlled deep breathing at home. They had also recommended that babies be breast-fed, which was done by very few new mothers in the U.S. in 1958. Fathers were still strongly discouraged from being in the labor room with their wives and were forbidden from being present at the actual birth of their babies. I mentioned what I wanted to my doctor early in my pregnancy, especially asking not to be fully sedated during the delivery. I wanted to be able to watch the delivery as much as possible. The doctor told me that he doubted the hospital would allow Dan to be present during labor and the delivery. They didn't want fathers fainting during the delivery!

So basically, I was alone dealing with labor pains except for the nurses who came in periodically to check on my progress dilating during most of the 12 hours waiting for the baby's head to crest. My doctor was also not available until the last few minutes of the delivery. I was hungry from having nothing but watermelon during the last 24 hours and wondered if eating all that melon had sort of forced my baby into leaving the comforts of the womb, ready or not. I was fully awake, especially uncomfortable and toward the end in much pain during the contractions but trying as best I could to follow the breathing suggested by the book I'd read on natural childbirth.

In the last minutes before the baby's birth after the doctor arrived, I'd asked for something for the pain but was told it was too late then to give me something which would interfere with the pushing necessary to deliver my baby. At 7:25 I delivered a healthy 7-pound baby boy and watched with fascination as the nurses cleaned and weighed him, anxious to hold him in my arms and get a good look at him. We'd chosen the name Eric, a Scandinavian name to signify his Swedish heritage, Daniel for his middle name after his father, and Pierotti for his Italian/ English/ German ancestry.

Dan was there when I was brought back to my hospital room. By now I was famished having not eaten since the day before, but since the hospital kitchen was closed, all I was given was toast and juice for a meal. Dan had gotten only a quick look at baby Eric in his little isolette in the nursery before he headed home to finish preparations for his sermon the next morning. After drifting exhaustedly off to sleep, I was awakened well before the first light of dawn appeared by a nurse who carried Eric all wrapped up into my room, helped me to sit up in bed and placed my first child into my arms.

The nurse had been told that I intended to nurse my baby myself and placed him as close as possible to my breast to encourage him to become accustomed to the smell, sight, and sound of his mother even though, she told me, no actual milk would be forthcoming from me for a day or so. It was an extraordinary moment for me, thrilled to really get a long, searching look at this amazing little creature who'd come into my life, feeling his slight weight and warmth, and chuckling a bit at his little nose which was still smushed a bit to one side from the struggle of getting born. Then the nurse left and it was just the two of us there in the dark stillness of the very early morning. That was a very special and most precious time for me. Oddly enough, I felt like there were just the two of us here alone against the world, and somehow strangely that was comforting.

With the exception of our good Catholic neighbor, Pauline, who'd just had her seventh child some months earlier, lived across the vacant field, and was our closest neighbor, I knew of no one who'd nursed her babies nor had I ever even seen anyone doing it!! I'd had no intention of even trying because I'd heard stories that some nurses in maternity wards actually discouraged mothers from attempting to nurse by feeding newborns sugar water before bringing them into their mothers so they'd refused to suck. Some nurses felt that it was too time consuming in their busy schedules to teach new mothers how to get their babies to suck and also required an additional feeding in the middle of the night for the babies of nursing mothers. Also, so many mothers had a hard time getting sufficient milk into their breasts. Besides all that, I thought the sight of women nursing their babies looked kind of primitive. Women in modern countries just didn't nurse their babies when formula was so readily available, or so I thought.

When I had told my mother some weeks before my first baby was due that I didn't intend to nurse the baby because it seemed so inconvenient, she retorted incredulously, disbelief heavy in her voice, "Inconvenient? Inconvenient?" she repeated like she couldn't believe what I'd just said or like I'd just spit on the flag! She then followed with a lecture on the nutritional benefits to the baby that only I could give the baby and that I'd be depriving it by not nursing it. So, I just sort of blew her off by assuring her I'd give it a try, which I half-heartedly intended to do, confident that with my small AA-cup breasts, I'd never be successful at breast feeding and that would end that argument.

In high school, I'd been really embarrassed when my friends Marge and Carol and I were shopping together for bras. Playtex had a new bra on the market called "The Hidden Treasure" which made you'd look really stacked. I tried one on, was really pleased at how it filled me out and confidently showed it off to Marge and Carol in the dressing room. "Oh wow," said Marge as she took her finger and lightly pushed in on one of the cups. It gave way and made me look like that breast was totally concave. We all broke out in laughter. That ended "hidden treasure" as an answer to my small chest.

But to my surprise, breastfeeding actually was the answer to my small breast problems. When my milk came in a day or two after Eric was born, I was shocked by what I considered to be my now huge breasts, filled with plenty of milk. And feeding him that way was incredibly convenient except for one thing. Since very few women nursed their babies at all and certainly not in front of others, women couldn't even sit discreetly covered up nursing their babies in the presence of others. When we had guests, how frustrated I felt having to retire by myself to the bedroom to feed my baby and having to miss out on adult company and conversations. I sometimes felt like some kind of brood sow.

My mother flew from Chicago to help me after I returned home from the hospital with our new baby because Dan was usually too busy with church meetings, visiting the sick, counseling people, planning services and sermons to be of much help. Shortly after my mother went home several weeks later, Dan was scheduled to spend two or three weeks at a teenage Bible camp, and I had to stay at home with our new baby and our Weimaraner dog, Hilda. I felt somewhat abandoned. One of those weekends, I was invited to drive up with a couple from church who were bringing their teenaged daughter to camp for the following week, and I got to stay overnight with the baby in Dan's cabin, but I didn't get to see much of Dan because he was busy with the campers most of the time. I felt in the way. I'd gained weight during my pregnancy and was fifteen pounds heavier even after the delivery. My sport clothes didn't fit me, and all I had were dresses with convenient openings in the front so I could feed the baby. And, of course, I had to do that hiding out in our cabin.

The one evening I could be with Dan after he'd been gone from home for two weeks, he didn't return to our cabin until almost midnight, having had to make rounds checking on all the kids with Carolyn, one of the attractive college girls working with Dan as a counselor that summer. At just 28 years of age, Dan was a young pastor with dark, curly hair compared to some of the other much older ministers— and handsome, fun, and very popular with the kids and the counselors. There I was, just having had a baby. I was twenty-two years old but feeling forty, fat, and dumpy with frequently leaky breasts from nursing our new baby and wondering where Dan had been most of the evening when he returned to our cabin about midnight. Though I tried to lay to rest those faint feelings of suspicion about the true nature of Dan's relationship with those young girls working at the camp, and my own insecurities about myself and my relationship with Dan never totally escaped my consciousness.

Now the Easter season was well behind us, and six weeks after Eric's birth at the Sunday morning service we celebrated Eric's baptism. He looked like a little angel in the long, white, embroidered, baptismal dress that I'd found on sale at Trasks. I'd made sure that Hilda, just a year-old pup we'd adopted six months before, was secured in our house before I headed over with Eric in my arms across the vacant lot to our basement church. There I met up with Dan's brother Tom and his wife Ann, who were to be our son's Godparents, with their four children, and we took our places close to the front of the nave near the baptismal font. When it was time for the baptism, I handed Eric over to Ann and Tom. Dan stepped forward looking very handsome in his long vestments, a black cassock covered by the white surplice and green stoles, and beckoned us up to the baptismal font.

As we approached the font, I thought I heard some sort of commotion in the back of the church. Then I heard the sounds of the ushers behind us whispering loudly to someone followed by the noisy clicking of what sounded like dog toenails on the basement floor. I chuckled to myself realizing that they must be coaxing somebody's dog that had wandered into the sanctuary. The next moment, our 60 pound Weimaraner, Hilda, came running up the front aisle panting excitedly as if to say, "Hey, you forgot about me!" The ushers were trying to get hold of her, but she was too fast and too strong for them. In a moment, she appeared at Dan's side panting loudly and jumped up on him, her big paws against his white vestments as he hung on to his Bible with one hand and Hilda's front paws with his other. I leaned over to pet her to get her to calm down, and it was decided to just let her stay there and join the small group as Eric was baptized into the family of Christ.

The following week when Eric was six-weeks-old, we took him to our doctor, who had delivered him, for his six-week checkup. After a thorough going over of his little body, Dr. Hirsch seemed satisfied with the progress he had made and especially his weight gain, which was most important since he was being breast-fed. I breathed a sigh of relief as the doctor was finishing up his examination. He then stretched Eric's legs out on the examining table lining up his right leg with his left. The doctor kept manipulating his legs and hips. I wondered what he was doing when he finally grabbed a ruler and began to measure his leg extensions. Finally, the doctor turned to us and said, "I'm not sure of this, but it looks like your baby has congenital hip dysplasia."

Mystified and with mounting apprehension I asked him what that was, sucking in my breath with fear. He then explained that we'd have to take him to an orthopedist for x-rays for a definite diagnosis, but that essentially dysplasia in newborns was caused by the hip sockets not being formed properly so that one leg would be significantly shorter than the other. If not treated it would interfere with a baby's ability to walk— in essence, Eric would be crippled if the doctor's suspicions were accurate and he wasn't operated on and put into a full lower-body cast. My heart sank and tears came to my eyes. I felt like our beautiful baby boy had the sword of Damocles hanging over his head. I cried all the way home.

Two weeks later an orthopedist confirmed Hirsch's initial diagnosis, and surgery was scheduled for the following week. We were reassured that the surgery and body cast usually were effective in treating this abnormality and that following three to four months in a cast, Eric's legs and hips would develop normally as well as his ability to walk. Just twelve weeks old, it was difficult to see my baby enveloped in heavy plaster from his chest to his toes with just an opening so he could urinate and have bowel function, his legs akimbo and bent at the knees when he awakened from surgery. He could not move below the upper part of his chest nor kick his legs, and we carried him like that for the three and half months he was in that cast. But that doctor had been right, and it was worth all the sacrifice when he was finally able to develop and move with full normal capacities thereafter.

1940 – Chicago – Gene Headen

Dan was a good preacher— better than most ministers I'd heard at that point of my life. His insights into the Gospels and scriptures in his sermons were a considerable influence on my beliefs about what the focus of living and service should be for people who call themselves Christians. But we had our differences when it came to some elements of theology. The biggest was about the efficacy of prayer. I'd had an expectation that it would be different in my home from how it had been in my childhood home where we never said a prayer of any kind together as a family when I was growing up. There was never a simple grace at meals, not even on Thanksgiving. Ours had been a "graceless" table though I would sometimes catch my mother, her hands momentarily folded quickly and unobtrusively in her lap, pause slightly before she began to eat, and I sensed she was praying. There was, however, one time in all those years that a prayer of thanksgiving was said at our table, and it came from a most unexpected source.

In the early-nineteen forties, my dad had a friend at his construction job, Gene Headen, a black man who'd come up from South Carolina during WWII and worked construction with my dad, who had a high regard for Headen and spoke fairly often of him. He was the first black person I'd ever met, living, as we did, on the North side of Chicago, whereas Mr. Headen lived with his family on the South side; Chicago was still an almost totally segregated city.

Mr. Headen had come to help my dad lay a new sidewalk in front of our house. I stood by fascinated, watching as he mixed the concrete and then poured and eventually troweled the new walk into its perfect smoothness, looking up from time to time, smiling as he patiently answered my many questions about that whole project. I couldn't have been more than ten at the time, but I was so taken with the fact that he talked to me like I was a person, almost like an adult and not like some pesky kid that some adults would jolly along absent-mindedly. He took time to actually explain what he was doing. At some point, my dad came out and admonished me not to bother Mr. Headen while he worked. Headen, however. just waved my father away good naturedly and said, "Oh, she's not bothering me, Leonard." It was Leonard and Gene between them.

Eventually my mother called us in to have lunch at the kitchen table, which she had set with a small tablecloth that she always used if we had company. After we sat down informally, Mr. Headen paused a moment, smiled broadly and said, as natural as breathing, "Shall we thank the Lord for this blessed gift of food?" And without waiting for an answer or to see if we white folks prayed, folded his hands, bowed his head, and began to say a short, simple blessing. Stunned? You bet I was. Nobody had ever done anything like saying a prayer aloud at a table at our house. That was a learning experience for this little ten-year-old girl, who, as young as I was, already knew something of the prejudices that many white people had about people of color— an occasion that taught me a lot about prayer, and a huge insight into who this man was as a human being, and what I might possibly expect from others like him.

That occasion also taught me something about my father, who some weeks later when I asked him, "When's Gene coming back again?" paused momentarily, looked down at me soberly over his eye glasses, pointed his large index finger at me and said not unkindly, "Joanie, it's Mister Headen to you!" My attitudes about race came more from what I never heard at home— those ugly racial words that could hurt so deeply— and the easy way that Mr. Headen and my dad seemed to have with each other. That was possible, in large measure, because both my parents had come to this country as young adults from Sweden, having escaped the entrenched virus of racial prejudice, borne of segregation, bred early on in family attitudes or in the streets where it was so prevalent and still is in America among many whites. In Sweden and elsewhere in Europe it was rarely the issue that it is here.

When I married, I had a very limited notion of what life was like for ministers and their families other than that they rarely ever realized tangible financial prosperity, not at least in the Lutheran church and other mainline Christian churches. Ministers were not paid well; they usually had enough to squeak by financially, perhaps, but not enough to acquire anything resembling wealth, that's for sure. We were supplied with congregation-owned living quarters as part of our salary, but the down side of that was that there never was the opportunity to acquire any equity in a home that eventually we'd own ourselves. But clergy were assured that theirs was a calling with treasures in heaven and not a job to store up treasures on earth. But I believed that marrying the person you truly loved was far more important than marrying someone because of what he had or someday would have.

I believed that alcoholism was rarely a problem in a minister's home and certainly never expected infidelity! For me these were trade-offs for not having a lot of money. Alcohol might have been the primary bone of contention between my father and mother, but it wasn't an issue that caused serious problems in our home. However, those times when there was active discord between my parents, they occasionally involved my father's having gotten drunk or becoming surly and disagreeable to which my mother countered by giving him the silent treatment. If his behavior had been bad enough, days and very occasionally even several weeks could go by when she wouldn't speak to him as retribution. Dan took an occasional drink, but usually we didn't regularly have liquor in the house because I was concerned about raising doubts in the minds of parishioners about their pastor in the event that they should see liquor in our cabinet.

Since the total absence of prayer had been characteristic in my childhood home, one expectation that I had was that Dan and I would have some form of prayer together occasionally.

After we married, I brought up the desirability of our doing so but was shocked when he said, "I don't really believe in the benefit of prayer. I don't believe that God or Jesus is somewhere listening to and taking our prayer requests like some kind of waiter in a restaurant and then answering those prayers." I didn't believe that was the way prayer worked, either, but I believed that prayer didn't just go out there to a void.

"Well what is prayer then?" I asked.

"I think it's basically a psychological crutch people use when things go wrong," he answered.

"A psychological crutch?" I repeated incredulously, "That's all?"

His answer surprised me considerably. I wondered if he really meant that. I wondered if it was I who believed in something delusional. After all, Dan was the supposed expert on the nature of God, wasn't he? I had a lot to think about, but I never brought up the subject again. So I did whatever praying I did in my personal silence. It took many years but eventually, however, I found an answer to that question that satisfied me, and it was much deeper than the notion of God or Jesus as a waiter taking orders in a restaurant. I did not know who, where, when or how it worked, but it worked. No Jesus as a waiter was needed.

CHAPTER 6

Falling Off the Pedestal

Eight months after Eric was born, Dan accepted a call to be the pastor of St. Paul's Lutheran Church in Queens, New York City, and we moved from St. Luke's in Erie, to St. Paul's, Floral Park, Queens. We traded one basement church for another much larger, 400-member one, but it still had the feel of a somewhat dank, basement church. Eric was still in his body cast when we made the move, but shortly thereafter the cast was removed and with good results fortunately. He began to learn to walk normally by the time he was a year old. About that time, plans for constructing a new, "real" sanctuary on the top of the foundation of the "basement" church were set into motion with the attendant fund raising to pay for it. All of this began to take much of Dan's time.

A daughter, Elizabeth Ann, was born a year later at Long Island Jewish Hospital just down the street from our house. I had become interested in the benefits of natural childbirth methods that a well-known British obstetrician had promoted, and I had been practicing the recommended deep breathing and relaxation exercises for pain control when I'd become pregnant with Elizabeth.

I'd discussed natural childbirth with my own obstetrician and wanted to give birth as drug free as possible for the delivery. But when the labor contractions and pains began to come so quickly and everything was rushed at the hospital, I'd agreed to be given "just a little something for pain" as Doctor Gozan suggested. Instead, I'd was quickly knocked out with the drugs and awakened many hours later not even knowing what kind of baby, if any, I'd had.

Elizabeth came about 2:00 am. on July 16, 1960. I was crestfallen not to have been aware when she was born. I felt like I'd missed something really important. But eight hours later when the nurse finally came into my room with my new baby girl, my disappointment ended. She was perfect and beautiful. We were living in New York by then, and my obstetrician, Dr. Gozan, told me, by way of explanation for the heavy dose of drugs he'd given me, that most of his patients told him they didn't want to be awake for any part of the birthing processes—period. He ignored my earlier request entirely.

Two years later Ann-Mari was born on December 3, 1962. She, too, came very early and very fast, at about 2:50 am. There was such a huge rush just to get me into the delivery room before she was taking her first breaths that there was no time for thought about my getting anything for pain. At the time of Ann-Mari's birth, a beautiful new sanctuary and steeple for St. Paul's had just been completed. Dan, however, was so busy with decisions involving the last details for the completion and dedication of the church that his visits to me at the hospital were very brief. So brief, actually, that there'd not been time to either discuss or make a final decision about her name. On the third day of my hospital stay, a rather officious hospital administrator came into my room for the second time, clipboard and papers in hand, demanding the name we'd chosen for our baby's birth certificate. I told her with chagrin. "We still haven't decided."

"Well," she said, "this document is going in first thing tomorrow morning, and your daughter will just be listed as 'baby girl Pierotti' on the City records if you haven't a name by 5:00 pm. today." I was annoyed that there hadn't even been time to settle on a girl's name with Dan if our baby was a girl.

When Dan showed up at the day's end, I told him, "Sorry, Dan, but you've lost your vote on our daughter's name. Today was the deadline for giving the hospital her name. It's going to be Ann-Mari Nelson Pierotti and that's that." Five days later I was back home and singing with the church choir at the dedication of St. Paul's beautiful, new sanctuary.

At Ann-Mari's six-week pediatric check-up, I learned that she, too, might have the same hip deformity that Eric had been born with, and I was given the name of an orthopedist in our area of Long Island. I was in tears when the pediatrician made his diagnosis, for this time I knew full well what that meant, having dealt with it before. After examining her, the orthopedist confirmed the pediatrician's diagnosis. I was told that Ann-Mari's condition was more severe. She was to be entombed— as I referred to it—for six months in the same full lower type body cast as Eric had worn for only three. I dreaded the six months without being able to feel her lovely little body next to mine when I nursed her.

I took a whole roll of pictures of her in her birthday suit to have in order to remember what her dear, sweet body looked and felt like during those long months. I wondered, as I reflected on my earlier refusal to acknowledge that I was really pregnant until I was almost six months along, if her hip problem had been a kind of punishment for my reluctance about being pregnant again. Dan and I had sex so infrequently that it didn't seem possible that I could be pregnant. But thank God, she, too, came through it with good, sturdy little legs and was eventually able to walk just fine. But in the meantime, it was a huge chore lugging around a new baby in her heavy cumbersome plaster cast, especially with Elizabeth 2 ½ and Eric just 4 following behind.

My parents were senior citizens when we moved to St. Paul's, and they were still living in Chicago. The same was true of Dan's parents, so they came only once or twice a year to visit. Fortunately, when we first came to St. Paul's, a church member, Jeanette Mayer, who was also the kindergarten teacher at the elementary school, a part of St. Paul's, had offered to look after Eric whenever I needed a baby-sitter and she wasn't teaching. She and her husband, Emil, a N.Y. City police sergeant, were childless, and so it was that Jeanette, whom we nicknamed Aunt Jaye and Uncle Emil became our children's unofficial grandparents. It was win-win for both of us. I had much needed help with the children, and she got to exercise some of her life-long maternal longings via our children. Since children were not permitted at the hospital for visitations, Jaye would put Eric and Elizabeth in the stroller and bring them the two or three blocks to below my hospital window so the children could see me waving and holding their new baby sister, whom I held up for them to see.

Dan pitched in on Mondays, his day off, taking Eric on outings on the Staten Island ferry, and to watch the Verrazano Bridge being built between Brooklyn and Staten Island. Because I was nursing Ann-Mari, it was difficult to get a baby-sitter who could handle all three of the children except for a few short hours between feedings. We also had a couple of teenaged girls from our church, Julie Preston and Linda Bahr, who looked after the children when I needed to get out if Jaye wasn't available.

With two small children and a new baby, I felt very confined to home except for choir practice and the afternoon unit, a group of the older ladies at St. Paul's, who were part of our women's organization but met in the afternoon. Though they were many decades older than my 26 years, I actually enjoyed them almost more than the regular evening group. I felt like their expectations of me as the minister's wife were far more relaxed and accepting, and I could be much more myself when bringing the baby and Elizabeth along to the delight of those dear elderly ladies. I was also a part of a group of church women who made monthly visits to Creedmoor State Mental Hospital to visit a group of patients, mostly older women, who needed help being fed and longed for outsiders to bring them treats, play Bingo with them, and have a fresh face to greet them. That was pretty much my social life those days.

Dan was busy six days a week usually with meetings with the deacons, board of trustees, and building committee in the evenings, Luther League on Sunday nights, hospital calls, visiting the sick to bring them communion, sermon preparations and other community and clergy meetings—on and on it went. We could not afford anyone to come in and clean the house, and when I was vacuuming the carpets I would occasionally work up a head of resentment inside me. My anger would usually end up focused on Dan, but to me the anger was inexplicable because he hadn't really done anything but do the work that was part of his ministry. And I kept telling myself that his was important work. And then I would feel guilty about feeling angry. And since I did not want to be one of those minister's wives who was reviled for running the show at Lutheran Church Women meetings, I kept a rather low profile.

I avoided initiating church activities where I would be called upon to speak in public. Actually, I doubt that any of our members, let alone my husband, would have considered that I might have anything worth saying. Public speaking had been a skill that won me special recognition in college, and I knew I was very good at it, but I was afraid that people would either say that I didn't "know my place" or possibly worse, compare me too favorably with Dan and say that I spoke as well or better than he did. And if so, he might resent me for that, and maybe love me less. I was told by women's magazines, such as Ladies Home Journal, and by other women's magazines that a smart wife was wise to hide those places where she appeared to be in competition with her husband. Dan certainly never encouraged me to show my speaking talents in that respect. The only public speaking I recall ever being asked to do was to read aloud *The Littlest Angel* at a Christmas program.

I was on the program planning committee for St. Paul's Lutheran Church Women. It was early 1963, and while the war in Vietnam was just beginning to ignite what evolved into serious protests in our country, black college students in the South were being beaten senseless by police for attempting to use lunch counter facilities and refusing to leave drugstores and restaurants in protest against the segregation of blacks all over the South.

There were mob lynchings of African-Americans, shootings of civil rights activists, and the disappearance and murders of three young men from the North who'd come down to Mississippi to help with voter registration. Rampant discrimination and other inhumane treatment of black citizens by southern lawmakers, White Citizens Councils and the Ku Klux Klan were commonplace. Civil and voting rights protests, marches, and boycotts were beginning all through the South, especially after bombings and burnings of the homes of black people and black churches which culminated in the bombing of the 19th Street Baptist Church in which four young girls and two young boys were killed in Birmingham, Alabama.

All of this was going on while the LCW (St. Paul's Lutheran Church Women) was planning programs such as "What to Do if Your Son or Daughter Wants to Marry a Catholic." While our mothers worried about their daughters and sons marrying Catholics, the U.S. was intervening in a war that was taking place in Vietnam that would end up killing 58 thousand of our sons and daughters and many millions of Vietnamese! And down the street from St. Paul's was Glen Oaks, a large apartment complex that was segregated not by law but by custom, for all intents and purposes, as were all the churches in our area. And so, Dan, along with Rabbi Tietelbaum at Temple Sholom, and Father Mondell, the Catholic priest nearby, was beginning to speak out against segregation from the pulpit.

Remembering my dad's friend, Gene Headen, from many years before in Chicago made what was happening in the South quite personal to me. I totally supported Dan's efforts and was proud of him. I was told by one member of St. Paul's church council that Dan and I eventually were referred to as "those n——lovers" by a couple other members of the church council. As I stood ironing in our basement, I watched transfixed at the unbelievable sight of the fire hosing of black citizens and attacks by police dogs by the all-white police in southern cities on TV. Those events and other more personal ones in the mid-60s helped forge an almost seismic growth of consciousness in me that eventually changed the entire direction of my life. As for the ugly epithet aimed at my husband and me, it was a name that in truth made me feel proud rather than insulted, as it had been intended to convey.

Despite some interesting challenges and growing friendships, somehow my life felt flat. After graduating from college cum laude and Phi Beta Kappa, winning second place in the national collegiate oratory competition, and completing a double major in English and Speech and the course requirements for a degree in secondary education, I had married a man I adored and had truly placed on a pedestal, and had three lovely children. I should have been supremely happy, but I wasn't chomping at the bit to make use of my speaking abilities or dying to get a job teaching. I knew that would happen eventually when my children finally started school. As for Dan's lack of interest in me not only sexually but emotionally, as well, that was profoundly disappointing; we had sex maybe once a month and sometimes not even that often. But my body had never experienced regular sex or orgasm very often anyway, so those fires of unfulfilled sexuality just got damped down even further so that I didn't think consciously about it except occasionally.

What I did miss sorely was affection— pure unvarnished affection! I missed the hugs, kisses, pats on the fanny, cuddling in bed, touching and verbal indicators that I was loved. I always seemed to be the one telling Dan that I loved him or reaching out to touch or express and receive (hopefully) affection. When I would occasionally get angry with Dan for seemingly little provocation other than that he wasn't around to help me much, in was usually when I was alone and when I was vacuuming cleaning. It didn't occur to me that I was angry because I felt so unloved.

Those first months in our relationship he'd seemed to love me— said he did when we were courting those few months after we met at Augustana and in all his letters that year when he was serving in his first parish in Millcreek on the outskirts of Erie, Pennsylvania, before we married five days after my college graduation. I would remind myself of how lucky I was to have him and the children, be grateful that on his one day off a week, he'd sometimes take Elizabeth and Eric on trips around the city, and that he would help with the diapering and care of the children when they were babies if he was home. And we never fought like I had done with Ken before I met Dan. But I would still feel guilty for feeling as resentful as I did sometimes.

It was early May of 1963 when I had what I would today call a "meltdown." I'd been particularly stressed and feeling overwhelmed as I'd just taken out the second load of clothes and diapers from the washing machine on the garage level of our split-level parsonage and carried them down to the dryer in the basement when suddenly I started to cry. I felt consumed with sadness and anger and I didn't know why.

As I put the clothes into the dryer and turned it on, my crying got harder, and I was relieved that the roar of the dryer muffled those sounds from the children upstairs. In total despair, I slid down the wall opposite the dryer and sat on the basement floor sobbing uncontrollably. It was a combination of anger and sorrow, I think—the rage building up inside me until finally I began banging the back of my head against the concrete wall. I wasn't sure if I was angry with myself, with Dan, or with my life. And then, aware of what I was doing, I became frightened. This was what crazy people did, I thought. I had three small children who needed me. I couldn't afford to end up in Creedmoor State Hospital along with the inmates I visited with the LCW every month. I had to get hold of myself. I realized I needed to get help, and I didn't know where to turn.

My friends in Floral Park were either church members or other ministers' wives, and we wives and families were not supposed to have personal problems. Advice columns in the newspapers always recommended that people get help from their clergyman or a counselor, but I knew no psychiatrists, and I couldn't go to Dan for help. He was part of the problem (though I wasn't sure why). Since Dan was not one to show strong emotion, he would calmly tell me to get a grip on myself when I got upset, as would my mother when we talked long distance. She would also remind me, as she had in the past, of how lucky I was to have a nice home (the parsonage owned by the church), my husband and children, and to count my blessings. The only ministers I knew, other than Dan, were his colleagues. I couldn't go to them and talk about my problems, whatever they were about, especially those of a sexual nature having to do with Dan. It would make him look bad or maybe even me.

In desperation, I found the phone number for a friend from college, John Nystrom, who had recently graduated from seminary and was serving a parish in upper N.Y State. He told me about a Lutheran pastor, Dr. Paul Qualben, who had gone back to medical school after finishing the seminary to study psychiatry and was now a therapist in the Bay Ridge section of Brooklyn. At the time, I believed that most psychiatrists were either atheists or agnostics who thought people who believed in God, and specifically Christians, were some deluded breed of people. They couldn't possibly understand my problems as a Christian and a minister's wife.

I found Qualben's phone number in the Brooklyn telephone book, and a few weeks later, I told him of my depression and a bit about my relationship, or rather lack of it. He suggested that I come back again before we really started talking after I took a couple psychological tests he had, one of which I remember being the lengthy Minnesota Multi-Phasic Inventory.

At my next appointment with Dr. Qualben, he said smiling, "Well, Joan, the MMPI confirmed what I'd already surmised from meeting you— that you're not crazy nor neurotic— at least no more than the rest of us are!" I laughed with relief, and he went on, "But I am going to be away on vacation for six-weeks and don't want to start with you until I get back at the end of the summer. Give me a call in September, and we'll set up some appointments for you."

I was disappointed that we couldn't start in right away. A middle-aged man with an easy smile, Paul Qualben seemed very approachable and a person I could easily talk to. He gave me the name of another therapist in the event I needed someone to talk to before he got back from his trip.

I did develop a warm friendship, however, with Lyle Guttu, a new staff member working with the teenaged Luther Leaguers at St. Paul's. Earlier that year, St. Paul's had the opportunity to hire Lyle, who was Lutheran seminary student attending Union Theological Seminary in Manhattan. He'd been hired to take charge of St. Paul's Luther League, our youth organization. This was part of his required internship for seminary training toward ordination. His support at St. Paul's became one less burden for Dan's heavy schedule. A recent Harvard graduate who'd had a hockey scholarship to that prestigious school, he was as open and introspective a person as anyone I'd ever known, an articulate but down-to-earth Midwesterner from a small town in Minnesota. He worked at St. Paul's with the teenagers and spent weekends at our house.

Lyle became one of the bright spots of the week for me. He enjoyed sitting drinking coffee with me and sometimes Dan, too, when they were finished meeting with the teenagers on Friday or Saturday nights. We talked about all sorts of things: theology, psychology, theatre, music, and the church. Lyle was at that time seeing a therapist he called Hart, and often his conversations would somewhere have a sentence beginning "Hart says…" and I'd be treated to some new insight Lyle had gotten from this man he obviously respected. I never knew if Hart was his first or last name, but the sentence would inevitably bring us into a discussion of some insights about himself, life, love, ethics, and often the conversations would go on until one or two o'clock in the morning.

Lyle was more open and honest about his life, beliefs, and early family life than anyone I'd ever met. Not only was what he had to say usually very interesting, but his level of honestly about his life was totally refreshing. I loved talking with him, as did the kids he mentored and worked with at church. He would usually stay over on Saturday night and attend church at St. Paul's on

Sunday morning. Though I was glad, on the one hand, that Dan didn't seem to be troubled that Lyle and I would sit up talking and drinking coffee until all hours of the night in my kitchen, it bothered me somewhat that he didn't seem the least bit jealous. Had I been Dan, I wouldn't have put up with it.

Living on the Westside of Manhattan and having close friends working in the theatre in Greenwich Village, he would occasionally invite us to off-Broadway plays, entertainers, and musicals such as *The Fantasticks* and *In Circles*. I remember our going to see Bill Cosby at a club called The Village where Cosby was performing as a stand-up comedian along with Flip Wilson, whose famous character was the hilarious Geraldine. These two African American comics were just getting their start and were among very few blacks who at that time became enormously successful in "white" show business. These opportunities to get out in the real world were a rare and real treat for me— a chance to get out of Queens and into the City. But a trip into Manhattan was almost an hour each way by car, so if we were going to have an occasional dinner or see a play, we needed to plan on staying at least five or six hours, far too long to be away from Ann-Mari's breast feeding time, so those excursions had to wait until I was no longer nursing. When she could go on whole milk and getting out became easier for me, I felt more comfortable leaving the kids with Julie, one of our baby-sitters.

Though only about fifteen, Julie Preston seemed level-headed enough to look after the three children and give Ann-Mari her bottle. Our four-year-old Eric knew her also because she worked part time at the Carvel ice cream store, and he looked forward to trips there for chocolate ice cream cones with his dad on Dan's day off. Ann-Mari was still in her body cast so she stayed fairly contentedly in her little, canvas bouncy chair and could not crawl around getting into mischief.

Eric and Elizabeth liked Julie. She was a pretty brunette, somewhat shy, and not too strict with them. She had a boyfriend, Paul Kalitaro from the neighborhood, who occasionally came with her when she was babysitting. Julie probably let the kids get away with more than Aunt Jaye did. When Elizabeth was born after we moved to Queens, we asked Jaye and her husband, Emil, to be Godparents for her when she was baptized. By then they were really like grandparents to the children and actually delighted in being asked to babysit.

Julie was a sophomore or junior in high school, and was close friends with Cathy Hogan, whose mother and dad, Lorrie and Al, were close friends of ours from church. Julie's parents, Marion and Joe, were also church members. Joe, who worked for the N.Y. Times, came to our house before St. Paul's dedication to take a family picture of Dan and me with the children to be used for a Christmas card for the congregation, and Julie had come with him to lend a hand if necessary.

During choir rehearsal, just days before the dedication of our new sanctuary and less than a week after Ann-Mari was born, my breasts began leaking through my dress, and I hurried home to change my wet clothes. Julie was babysitting that evening for me, and I was surprised to find her sitting at our kitchen table, schoolbooks spread out, with Dan of all people. He was helping her write a term paper for school. Evidently he'd come home early to find her struggling with that project after the children were asleep and was helping her. As an English major, I would have been happy to tutor her, but I knew she had kind of a crush on Dan, as did so many of the teenaged girls and possibly some women in our church, as well. So she probably wasn't going to turn down an offer of help from him on her term paper.

There's something about ministers that many women and girls find irresistible. They put them on a pedestal, often imagining what a perfect partner they'd be. When I was a sophomore in high school, I remember a little crush I had on Ernie Johnson, a seminarian at North Park, who was in charge of our study hall. That's all it was though, a crush. And Julie had her own real boyfriend, Paul Kalitaro. What bothered me about Dan's helping her was that there were so few times when he and I ever had time to just do something alone together. I guess I felt cheated that we had so little time together.

Perhaps we should have worried about Paul, however. Some weeks later, Dan came home from church looking drawn and somber, not his usual chipper self. He stood at the front door taking off his clerical collar, then his black suit jacket and hung it in the closet as he always did when he first came home. He came into the kitchen, a deep worry frown between his eyes.

"What's the matter, Dan?" I asked, not expecting much of an answer. My husband invariably carried with him the aspect of one who almost always had things well in hand. I don't recall ever seeing him out of control angry, and as of this writing, I 'd never seen him cry. I once said to him, half in earnest, half in jest, "Ya' know, Dan, if you don't at least cry at my funeral, I will come back and haunt you for the rest of your life."

But that didn't seem to worry him either. Finally, he poured himself a cup of coffee, sat down at the kitchen table, and said with a deep sigh, "It's about Julie Preston. Marion and Joe Preston were in to see me today and told me that Julie almost three months pregnant."

"Oh, no!" I exclaimed unbelievingly. I didn't even bother to ask who the father was. It was obvious that it was Paul Kalitaro, who though he wasn't some kind of young tough, was definitely not the choirboy type. He also didn't have the greatest reputation at St. Paul's, though I'd never heard of his being arrested or in any sort of real trouble.

"What are they going to do?" I asked. This was 1963. Pregnant, working class, and middle class white teenagers rarely kept their babies. Abortion, still illegal in the U.S., was a risky business. There were very few legitimate doctors who ever performed them, and if they did, it was always sub *rosa* for they risked losing their licenses and possibly getting a jail term if they were caught. Of course, those people who were rich enough to afford a huge payoff to the doctors who had their contacts. For enough money, they could always find someone who had the medical training and was willing to take the risk of being jailed if the price was right. But ordinary working people might have to rely on a back-alley, untrained abortionist operating under filthy conditions and risking even a botched job and loss of the woman's life. Other options such as coat hangers, caustic preparations introduced into the girl's vagina, and worse than that were used by those girls desperate not to have to carry the baby to full-term.

"Well, that's what the Prestons were in to see me about."

"Does she want to marry Paul?" I asked, "…at least until after the baby comes…to give the baby a name?" I thought about the time I'd feared that I was pregnant in college when I was engaged to Ken. Even though we'd not ever actually had intercourse, when I missed my period by a week, I was afraid some wandering sperm had found its way up my skirt to my vagina from heavy petting.

"Marion said Julie doesn't want to marry Paul," Dan replied assuredly. They're going to come in tomorrow with Julie and talk it over with me. They mentioned the possibility of sending her down to Marion's sister's house in Virginia to stay until the baby comes and then possibly giving it up for adoption through Lutheran Social Services."

I was heartsick for Julie though not entirely surprised. There was something quite vulnerable about her. She was the kind of girl, trusting, gullible, who often gets caught in a situation like this. She had her whole life ahead of her and then this happened!! Keeping the baby was rarely done, especially in white families where maintaining the family reputation was all-important; or possibly the child is passed off as belonging to some other relative beside the birth mother and then raised by the girl's family. It was felt that no man would want to marry a girl who'd had a baby by some other man. It certainly would limit her marital options. More often the baby was given up for adoption, and the girl never saw her baby again, never knew for sure what had really become of her baby. All of those were tragic non-options, in my opinion, but there weren't any other options, other than the usual rushed marriage and an "early" baby whose age in months and the dates the marriage had taken place that some people later suspiciously counted on their fingers.

I did not talk with Dan about what had transpired at that meeting with Julie and her parents. He rarely discussed with me the more personal issues of our parishioners that had been confided to him in counseling. I did not see Julie again before she left to stay with her aunt in Virginia, just south of Washington, DC. I wrote to her from time to time while she was away, sent her a maternity dress of mine and purchased a new one to send to her because she was shorter and smaller generally than I. I also sent along a few novels I thought she'd enjoy reading. I received a thank you for the clothing and books, but I didn't hear from her again nor see her until after the following summer.

That summer of 1963, Dan and I vacationed in Vermont with our three children and also invited Aunt Jaye and Uncle Emil to join us. We'd been renting an unused farm for several weeks every summer. It was on a beautiful 300 acres of woods and fields with a breathtaking viewed of the Green Mountains and a large, brick farm house with no electricity except for gas lamps. The road ending at the farmhouse had been part of the old Boston Post Road a couple hundred years ago but was now just an unpaved narrow road. A pond for fishing and a natural slate swimming pool made it an inexpensive, wonderful, restful vacation place. We were there from late June to early July when Dan learned that Julie Preston had her baby, a girl, sometime during that first week in July. That's all we knew or at least all that I was told. Later Dan told me that Julie had given the baby up for adoption through a social service agency in Washington, DC., before she came back home to Floral Park.

The summer passed uneventfully and since the whole pace of church meetings had quieted down and we'd had a family vacation, I felt much better about my relationship at home with Dan and had not as yet made the call back to Dr. Qualben's office. When we returned home from Vermont, Julie began once more to babysit for us when Aunt Jaye was unable to do so. She was still a lovely young girl, now almost 17, but her experience away in Virginia had taken its toll on that carefree energy she'd had just a year before. She called me one evening in late September and asked if she could come over and talk to me. It had now been three months since she'd given up her baby. The children were already sleeping, and I was ironing the usual 30-inch high stack of freshly laundered clothes (this being pre-wash and wear days) when Julie arrived. I continued ironing after offering her a Coke, which she refused. I tried to make conversation about this and that, but I didn't not know what to say to her except that I sympathized with the extreme difficulty of what she been through these past months.

Finally, Julie got to the point of why she'd wanted to talk to me. She told me a bit about her baby girl, whom she'd named Katherine, and was now having second thoughts about whether she'd made the right decision to give her baby up for adoption. She knew that the baby had already been placed with a couple and that the adoption would become final in a few more months when it would be too late to change her mind. She wanted to know what I thought about her telling the adoption agency that she'd changed her mind, wanted her baby back, and wanted to raise it herself.

I was stunned by the enormity of her question. No one in my memory had ever asked me to help them make such a momentous decision about anything, let alone a decision that could have such a huge impact on people I didn't even know, nor they me: the couple who'd adopted Julie's baby, that baby girl, Julie, the father of the baby. And who knows, maybe even me, for all I knew, as the giver of advice. But I told her what I would have told my own two daughters at that point in my life. I don't know for certain that now, at this stage of my life, many years later, older and wiser, I would have given the same advice. But I told her that she, Julie, was a beautiful young girl with a whole life ahead of her. To undertake to raise that baby so early in her life might have meant that there would be many opportunities cut off from her because of her responsibilities, as one so young, to that baby.

I told her that her chances to choose the man she might want to have married might be greatly diminished because of the presence of the baby in her life. I knew she would love that baby to the very best of her ability, but that the couple who had adopted her might have the maturity, material advantages, opportunities to offer that little girl that Julie might not have. Here was this advice from someone as young as I was, by then, just 26. What did I know at that stage of my life? I supposedly had the content of a B.A. but very little else in the way of "life" learning. That learning, however, was about to begin very soon, except that for me, this young, relatively inexperienced mother of three? I did not know it! But I was learning, and the real postgraduate learnings of my life were just beginning. But do we ever know when such momentous things are about to happen unexpectedly at that early age in life when one's whole life is about to be turned upside down?

In late October, just before his 34th birthday, Dan shared with me that Joe, Marion, and their other two daughters were going down to Virginia, to visit Millie's sister with whom Julie had stayed prior to having her baby. Julie did not want to go with them. Dan asked if I would mind if she spent that next weekend with us. Knowing what a painful experience that might be for her after her recent long stay with her aunt and all the memories of her pregnancy and the wrenching experience of giving up her baby, of course I was happy to do anything I could to be of help after what she'd been through.

That following weekend, Lyle was at St. Paul's working with the Luther Leaguers. I had made homemade waffles for lunch, a favorite with Eric and Elizabeth. Ann-Mari, whom we called Beaver because of her fascination with the beaver pond in Vermont, was 10 months old, finally out of her body cast and daring to venture out on her newly straightened, healthy-hipped legs, holding on from one person's finger to another's, to the couch, to the chair, and little by little, learning to use those newly healed legs and hip sockets for walking. She, too, loved sucking on the syrup-sweetened waffle.

When the children were fed and out of the way, we adults sat talking as we finished our coffee. Lyle was sitting opposite me at the counter-style kitchen table that my father had built for us in the parsonage kitchen the last time he and my Mom had visited. Dan was sitting across from Julie. Lyle was discussing some aspect of the Luther League program and while he was talking, my eyes happened to glance over across the table to Julie. She sat there, stock still, her lovely brown eyes looking fixedly across the table in Dan's direction. It was a look I can only describe as absolute adoration.

Puzzled, I slowly and almost fearfully turned my head to see where my husband was looking. My heart sank as I saw that he, too, was gazing into her eyes. They were locked into this embrace of looking at one another momentarily—like those meaningful glances that you see in the movies between two potential lovers. Somehow I managed to finish my meal, my heart beating rapidly, wondering what to make of what I'd thought I'd just seen— a look of unmistakable longing certainly on the part of Julie. It felt like a cold hand was holding my heart. I had to get out of there, out of the house. Anywhere!

Lyle had some kind of medical appointment in Brooklyn that afternoon, and I asked him if I could ride along with him. Julie was willing to stay with the kids for a couple hours. My mind was racing, trying to talk myself out of what I thought I'd seen. As we drove, I shared with Lyle my experience of seeing the look that had seemed to pass between Dan and Julie. I also shared with him how puzzled I'd been when a church friend, Lorrie, told me some months before Ann-Mari had been born that when she had told her daughter, Cathy, and Julie the good news that I was pregnant, Julie had said, "That's the most disgusting thing I've ever heard!"

I was taken aback Julie's reaction had been, but I'd attributed it either to a crush she might have on Dan or the realization that her pastor was having sex with me, his wife. I didn't think much more about it until now when talking to Lyle.

"Oh, Joan, I know what you're thinking," Lyle responded, "and you're probably right about Julie. She probably does have a crush on Dan, but half the girls in the Luther League do! Like lots of the other girls, Julie's often hanging out around the church office. But she's especially needy now, after what she's been through. Don't worry," he continued reassuringly, "As a pastor, you don't take seriously the crushes that teenagers have on you. And anyway, Julie is still involved with Paul Kalitaro, who's always hanging around Julie. I saw them together just last night."

Fortunately, Lyle managed to allay some of the concerns I felt. I began to relax, but decided that I'd better have a talk with Dan about Julie's feelings for him to alert him not to unknowingly lead her on in any way. She was just too vulnerable. Sometimes men could be totally oblivious to those kinds of signs from a girl.

Saturday came and went. When Lyle and I got back to my house, Julie was gone. The Prestons had already returned from Virginia and had picked her up from the parsonage. When Dan came home from Luther League later that evening, he had just left Lyle off at the train to Manhattan where Lyle had a late date in the city. Dan was alone. The children were staying over-night at Jaye and Emil's, and I was doing laundry. For Dan it had been an-other busy Saturday with afternoon visitations, evening Luther League, and three Sunday church services to prepare for. Dan sat down wearily on Eric's bed where I was sorting the children's newly washed clothes.

"I know you're beat, but I need to talk to you about something, Dan," I began tentatively in preparation to warn him about my sense of Julie's feel-ings about him. "Are you aware of what a crush Julie Preston has on you?" I started out, expecting strong demurral from Dan as soon as I got into the subject. "I couldn't help but notice how she was looking at you during lunch today, almost seemingly transfixed. She's obviously got a huge crush on you!"

Dan stood up and walked into the hallway near the doorway of Eric's bed-room, taking off his black, clerical shirt and collar, as I continued putting away clothes. But instead of assuring me of my imaginings, he paused, looked at me steadily, and then answered me, matter-of-factly, "Yes, I know she does."

My mouth dropped open, and I stood there for many seconds totally surprised by his answer. Instead of protestations about my imagining all this, I'd received a confirmation. Our eyes met and I didn't know what to say next.

"Do you think that's wise, I…I mean to lead her on…" I stammered, "to lead her on into thinking that you…you share her feelings?"

He didn't say anything, just looked at me. At that moment, I had a choice—to forge on almost inexorably with my questions or to drop the whole subject, having given him the information I thought he needed to consider. At that moment, I knew precisely what it meant to open a can of worms regarding an issue or subject. I actually had a visual image of just that flash into my mind. I intuitively feared what was coming, but I couldn't protect myself by not asking, and I forced the words out of my mouth.

"Do you… I mean… do you share her feelings?" I asked, stumbling, hoping against hope that he'd say, 'No, of course not,' but he didn't. He answered quite simply and softly,

"Yes, I do." And then there was no turning back. I had to know. Stunned, I went on.

"Do you… care about her? Love her?" I asked very slowly, finding it hard to breathe.

"Yes," he replied, "I think so."

And still hoping that something could be retrieved of what had been our relationship, I then asked, "Have you kissed her?"

He simply, slowly answered quite simply, "Yes,"

I felt like all the air had rushed from my lungs. There was no escape now.

"Have you…have you made love with her?" Everything inside me was screaming mentally, "No! No! Say No! Please say no!'

"Yes," he answered again without hesitating. And thus began a new world for me, totally changed forever from what my world had been a minute ago. And then the impossible.

"And her baby?"

"Yes, it's mine," he said with finality.

"But… but she's been seeing Paul Kalitaro. How do you know it's not his?"

I forged on trying to rescue something—anything—from this awful… I knew not what.

"Because it's not!" he snapped back forcefully as though angry that I'd even suggested such a thing.

I was stunned— speechless— as I let the meaning of those last exchanges sink into my brain. I wanted to pursue an argument with him about how he could be so sure, but it was clear to me that he did not even want to consider that Julie had relations with both him and Paul during the same time period, and so I said nothing else. And besides, to me it really didn't matter whose baby it was— his or Paul's. Just knowing that it could possibly have been his was enough. In those moments, ironically, there seemed nothing else to say.

Dan seemed to show little remorse that I could see. He didn't mumble how sorry he was. He didn't attempt to explain how or when it had all happened, nor to comfort me. None of the things one reads in books or sees in the movies with the husband on his hands and knees begging for forgiveness. Numb and in a state of shock, something had died and I was unable to fully process mentally the import of what had just happened. And as things began to register in my brain, without even removing my clothes, I crawled into bed, drawing my legs up to my chest in a fetal position, fighting for air in gasps but saying nothing else, I began to sob. And I continued to cry, eventually more inconsolably than I had ever cried in my life before for what seemed like the whole night. I felt that my life was over.

Exhausted from crying, eventually I fell asleep, blessedly unaware at least for those few hours of unconsciousness of the reality that faced me when I opened my eyes the next morning— that the whole trajectory of the rest of my life had changed even though it might not be readily apparent until much later. And not only my life and eventually my children's lives, but also my own self-identity which was already in the process of changing, though at the time it never occurred to me that maybe I might actually be becoming the self I was meant to be, that person, perhaps, that I really was. I wasn't cognizant of that possibility then— that people could change quite radically as the years passed and become who they really were. I might have actually been frightened at the thought of so much change. And it would be many years before I learned from a very wise teacher, that more often than not we must experience total breakdowns, be they physical, emotional, or spiritual, before we can experience the significant breakthroughs in our lives needed for us to grow fully as human beings. At that point, however, my heart certainly seemed totally broken.

When I awoke the following morning, I felt what it must feel like when a loved one has just died and one must somehow face the possibility of what seems impossible— not wanting to even open one's eyes to that reality. Ironically, it was Sunday morning, and the house was totally quiet. Dan had already left for the first of his three Sunday services at church just as though nothing unusual had happened at his house. This then was the beginning of the pretense and lies— at least as far as I knew. Jeanette and Emil had kept the three children over night, so thankfully I didn't have them to care for with their happy, innocent, morning chatter and having to pretend that everything was normal. Hilda, our Weimaraner, was unusually subdued as she came to my bed for her customary morning doggy kisses, but she seemed to sense that something was wrong and didn't come bounding up on top of me in bed, as she usually did.

Shortly after nine, the front door bell rang. When I peeped through the opening in the front door, I saw that it was just Lyle probably showing up for his usual Sunday morning coffee, having just attended the 8:00 am. service. I looked like the wreck of the Hesperus when I opened the door, my eyes and face still swollen from crying, hair standing on end at sixes and sevens, still wearing yesterday's clothes but clutching a robe around me. A feeling of relief washed over me. Lyle was the one person I knew that I wouldn't have to pretend with, the only person I trusted enough who I felt knew Dan and me sufficiently well and had the understanding, compassion, and capacity not to judge Dan's actions or him as a totally worthless person.

"What's happened?" were his first words slowly and deliberately as he looked at me wide-eyed, searchingly. I broke into fresh tears but felt like a load of grief had momentarily lifted as I began to tell him what had transpired between Dan and me the night before— or at least as much of it as I could remember since I hadn't plied Dan with any further questions other than the bare facts of his relationship with Julie before I stumbled numbly into bed. I just couldn't bear to know any more details.

After I told Lyle about last night's conversation with Dan, he just shook his head slowly and disbelievingly, but he didn't recoil in shock. He just listened calmly and non-judgmentally. I was correct about him on all counts. There'd always seemed to be something very real about Lyle, and consequently an uncommon bond of speaking the truth existed between us. Just having someone like him to whom I could unburden this grim story was an enormous relief.

Thus, began the many months of secrecy, lies, and pretense. Except for Lyle, I told no one— not even my family. There were almost six months when not a day went by that I didn't cry. And the tears would come unbidden, unexpectedly, without warning and in inconvenient places— in the A&P pushing a grocery cart with my three children in tow; sitting in church on a Sunday morning blinking furiously to keep the tears from being too obvious; driving down Union Turnpike near our parsonage in Queens in the pouring rain, four-year-old Eric next to me, frightened because we were going too fast, and he didn't know why his mother would inexplicably break down crying. Had he done something wrong? The girls seemed luckier. Elizabeth was not yet three and Ann-Mari just an eight-month old baby, still in her body cast. They didn't ask about the tears, but my thinking that they did not notice them was undoubtedly a lie I was telling myself— my own self-deception.

Pretending everything was normal between Dan and me was especially hard given that most of our social interactions involved parishioners or other clergy and their wives almost exclusively. Because I loved him, I had no desire to leave him. All I cared about early on was that Dan not leave me and our children for that girl—for Dan's life work not to end in a sea of shame and disgrace, which it surely would have if this became public knowledge. He would have been forced to leave the ministry and would have had no way to support us. I prayed for us to be allowed to escape from St. Paul's without having this thing blow up in our faces into a huge scandal; for our families and friends, and our whole world to avoid learning this terrible secret.

I didn't know if Dan was continuing to see Julie, or if he was planning to leave us for her. All he would tell me was that he felt like he was living in a box. I assumed what he meant by that was his life with me. We talked very little about this situation though I thought about it constantly. We didn't argue about it, nor did I even mention the sealed letter I found in his suit jacket pocket with the initials JP hastily scribbled on the envelope in Dan's handwriting. Those were my initials, too, but I knew the contents were not intended for me but rather for her. I was heartsick to find this proof that their relationship was still going on and angry to note that along with having my husband, Julie also possessed my initials!! I was angry, but I dared not open the letter nor create a scene over it for fear that it would push him further away.

Only once after that do I recall actually screaming in anger at Dan. While he had been away at a synodical conference, I had used his keys to gain entrance to his office and desk at church and found packages of condoms locked in his desk drawer along with notes from Julie. I knew then that the affair was still going on. I confronted him in tears screaming almost hysterically about the condoms I had found in his desk when he returned from the conference. And that's when he struck me.

That was the only time Dan ever hit me physically or showed real anger. Whether in anger or because he thought I was hysterical, he ended up slapping me hard enough so that I got a black eye. What was embarrassing was attempting to hide the colored bruise which showed up the next day. Two days later Dan and I were scheduled to emcee a comedy routine and program between us for the Church Women's yearly Everybody's Birthday celebration. I tried not too successfully to camouflage the dark bruise around my eye with makeup. No one seemed to notice it, however, nor even kidded me about it. I guess they couldn't have imagined the bruise's source being something I'd received from their beloved pastor.

I lived almost constantly in fear. And hidden under that fear was anger at Dan and at Julie, too, that I dared not reveal even to myself— anger that might end up pushing him into running away into the sunset with this teen-aged girl he said he loved and had impregnated. I avoided the 9:00 worship service because I didn't want to run into Julie, who usually attended that service. Having given up her baby, I was afraid she might eventually tell her parents that Dan was the real father of her child, and they would of course reveal the truth to the whole congregation. Everyone would know the truth, and that would be the end of everything for us as a family. I never asked Dan any specific questions— where they had sex, how often they had it, how long they'd been doing it. I didn't want to know any details because the more I knew, the more real it would be in my imagination and the more it would hurt. It wasn't till many years later— actually many decades later— that I learned that this relationship had gone on for two years.

One Sunday morning during the 11:00 service, I heard a woman cry out from the back of the sanctuary followed by the scuffle of ushers coming to her aid. Immediately I thought it might be Julie back there having a break-down or something. Someone had fainted. Thankfully it wasn't Julie, but that was my mind continuously conjuring up terrible possible future scenarios.

I dreaded having to call my parents and my sister to tell them what a train wreck my seemingly "idyllic" marriage was, especially to the man I think they'd really had not wanted me to marry in the first place. If Dan should leave me, I dreaded having to return alone with my three small children to my parents' home in Chicago, having to rent one of those small apartments across the street from where my parents lived on Berwyn Avenue, and having to find a job of some kind— maybe as a teacher some place. I didn't want them or anybody else to know what my husband had done, or what a failure I felt like I was as the wife he rarely wanted to make love to and seemingly had little love for. I didn't even want to think about the future since everything seemed utterly bleak and totally uncertain.

I couldn't even bring myself to tell my dearest friend Marge, who was then living in New Haven while her husband Karl, himself now a Lutheran pastor, worked on his master's degree at Yale. I had no friends in Queens who weren't either members of our congregation or clergy friends of Dan and their wives. How could I go to any one of them for counseling? Ann Landers always recommended people go to their clergyman for advice, but what did you do when your minister was also your unfaithful husband who'd gotten your teenaged baby-sitter pregnant? In 1963 this situation was unheard of... at least to me. Christian ministers didn't do those sorts of things! I was young— just 26— and very naïve both about sex and the world. I wondered if *True Confessions* magazine would even believe a story as sordid as mine, let alone print it if I'd ever sent it to them.

The stress I was under was palpable, though I didn't recognize it for what it was at first. No one talked about "stress" and stress related illness— the fallout of physical problems stress caused back in 1963. Even though Dan had told me he didn't believe in prayer early in our marriage, I still did, though it was a shaky kind of faith. The God I believed in at that time seemed very far away— out there someplace, but certainly not someone or something inside me. And so I prayed— for my kids, for myself, for Dan and our marriage, and sometimes for Julie, too, though part of me wanted to think that somehow she'd seduced him so that I could mitigate in my mind the dreadful emotional and physical violation he'd done to her. It was not until years later that I came to realize that it had not been just the physical violation of a fifteen or sixteen-year-old girl, but a spiritual violation that Dan had perpetrated on her as her pastor. The rollercoaster of emotions I experienced continued, nevertheless, and eventually the heartache, depression, fear, and anger I'd swallowed rather than dare to express, began to find its own expression by manifesting physically in my body.

I began getting canker sores inside my mouth so severe that at one point I counted twenty on the soft tissue encircling the inside of my lips. They were so raw and angry that it hurt to eat or even talk. I began going to church late and leaving early so I wouldn't have to talk to people because it hurt even to just move my lips. And I frequently had backaches.

Then began some of the worst pain I've ever experienced: intense, hot, shooting pains in the three main nerves of my jaw that would intermittently attack inside my cheek, slowly working their way up from my lower jaw to my eye. The doctor diagnosed what was happening as trigeminal neuralgia, probably related to stress. That was the first time that I had ever heard of emotions causing physical symptoms. There were no drugs or a cure other than some largely ineffective analgesic relief from pain. Though no one talked about the mind/body connection in those days, I had a clear sense that the cells of my mouth were sending a signal that my mind was afraid to even acknowledge, let alone to express consciously— a kind of protest about being "muzzled", about having to lie, actually living a lie, not just physically but emotionally. I dare not even tell Dan how hurt and angry I felt for fear that might drive him further away.

As strange and perverse as it seems, part of me could not entirely blame Dan for falling in love with that pretty, young girl. After all, here I was, still over-weight, out of shape after having three children without even the compensatory appeal of big breasts while I'd still been nursing Ann-Mari. I believed that 26 was old for a woman. And I felt like I was 40, someone who even before our children were born Dan had not seemed to love nor felt enough desire toward to want to make love to. That I had graduated from college Phi Beta Kappa with honors, was bright, articulate, funny, well educated, and artistically talented— those things didn't count for much in a woman those days. They were not the things that most men wanted in a woman— not the things that were considered sexy, desirable, or that I thought made a man fall in love with a woman. I'd been betrayed by Dan and Julie, but my thinking those kinds of thoughts about myself was the ultimate betrayal— my betrayal of myself— especially over the issue of whether or not I was pretty enough, thin enough, or desirable enough for a man to love me? At that time, I felt like my life was over.

CHAPTER SEVEN

The Wrong Person on the Couch

1963 – FLORAL PARK, QUEENS, NY

On November 22, 1963, just three weeks after learning about Dan's affair with our babysitter and just a few days before Thanksgiving came the shocking news by phone from a friend at church of the assassination of John F. Kennedy. I stood in the kitchen by the wall phone staring numbly at the bright Early American motif on the wallpaper as I tried to get hold of Dan by phone with the news about the President, but he didn't answer at his office nor was he anywhere else to be found. And all I kept wondering was if he was with Julie. Most people old enough still remember where they were when they heard the news of Kennedy's death after it was announced on the TV. But the memory I have always had is standing by that wall phone wondering where Dan was or more specifically whom he was with.

Kennedy's death cast a pall over the entire country, especially contrasted as it did with the upcoming Thanksgiving Holiday. Almost immediately thereafter was the announcement of the murder of Kennedy's presumed assassin, Lee Harvey Oswald by Jack Ruby, leaving the country further awash in death and talk of conspiracies. We had planned to spend Thanksgiving with Dan's family in Pennsylvania. The children and I were to fly to Bradford

Airport ahead of Dan, who felt that he needed to hold services at St. Paul's on Thanksgiving Day. He then planned to drive to Pennsylvania after the service at church was over.

I was not comfortable with his insistence that I should fly to Pennsylvania alone with our baby and two small children without him several days before Thanksgiving. It occurred to me that if the children and I were out of Dan's way, he would be free to be with Julie without any scandal. Though it may sound melodramatic now, before handing over our luggage to baggage-claim, I actually double-checked inside the suitcases to make sure there wasn't a bomb or some other device planted in one of them by Dan.

The assassination of our President; the on-going violence against Civil Rights activists and Voting Rights battles; the attacks on freedom riders who'd gone down South to help with voter registration; along with the public opposition mounting against our participation in the Vietnam War— our country was becoming increasingly chaotic. This all was the background for the chaos and grief I was experiencing inside me as I had to maintain the pretense, at least while with Dan's family and others, that everything was normal at home between us.

With all the shocking drama nationwide, this was the focus of almost everyone in the country. Not surprisingly, when the children and I arrived safely in Pennsylvania, Kennedy's death and its attendant events were foremost in people's minds. Dan's family spent most of the time glued to the television coverage of Lyndon Johnson being sworn in as President while Jacqueline Kennedy stood mutely looking on, still wearing her, bloodstained suit on the plane back to Washington from Texas. There were reruns of Kennedy's assassination; the viewing of Kennedy's casket in the Capitol by hundreds of thousands of people; Kennedy's funeral cortege and then his burial at Arlington.

Two days later, Dan arrived late Thanksgiving eve just in time for dinner. Thankfully there wasn't much time for anything but small talk among any of us. Actually, there'd been no real substantive communication spoken between Dan and me about his future marital intention nor his relationship with Julie ever since I'd first learned of his affair with her. Affair! What a weak, meaningless word for the catastrophe that was my life! Strangely enough, it was as though we both, perhaps for our own reasons, were afraid to bring up the subject. I feared pressing him about his possible decision to leave me for Julie, but somehow it never occurred to me that possibly he feared that I would leave him.

To this day, years later, I still don't know what had really been going on in his mind, but like the 600-pound gorilla in the living room, we both avoided the subject of what was coming next for us as we did about most of the really important issues in our life together. Dan had always been conflict averse. Early in our marriage, I'd thought that our never fighting— as I'd often done with my former fiancé, Ken, years before— was a sign of how well suited Dan and I were for each other. That lack of real communication and honesty between us turned out to be a major flaw in our relationship, at least from my point of view.

We made it home safely after that grim Thanksgiving of 1963 at Dan's parents in Pennsylvania and carried on in public as one happy family as though nothing was amiss. There were still many unanswered questions about the future. I hadn't seen Julie nor heard anything about her from Dan. I hoped no news was good news, but in my heart, I had my doubts.

1962 – 1963 Late Fall and Winter Queens, NY

I had agreed to call Dr. Qualben, the psychiatrist whom I'd seen briefly in June, when he came back from vacation in September, but so much had happened since then that I was reluctant to tell even Dr. Qualben about Dan's relationship with our baby-sitter. Along with living under a continual cloud of depression, I was profoundly ashamed, oddly enough, as though it had been I who'd somehow been responsible for this nightmare. And so I'd been stalling calling Qualben, using our lack of money to pay him as my rationalization to myself for not doing so— anything to avoid telling the awful truth about Dan's fathering a child with our teenaged baby-sitter, a girl whom he had confirmed when she was fourteen. I could barely get those words from my lips.

I was on my way to the grocery store when an event occurred that finally awakened me to the absolute necessity of my getting some serious help. I was alone in our car backing out of our front driveway on the way to the A & P grocery store. As I was preparing to back into the street, a strong, over-powering feeling suddenly rushed over me. I just didn't want to live anymore. That was it!! No more! And before I could think clearly, I jammed the accelerator down to the floor as hard and fast as I could and purposely steered the car back across the driveway and onto our front lawn. The car lurched forward and headed straight toward the parsonage living room window. I was in the flowerbed, less than three feet from the stone wall under the front window when something—what? A guardian angel? Or maybe just sheer survival instinct propelled my foot hard onto the brake pedal, thrusting my upper body hard against the steering wheel. Somehow the car stopped less than a foot from the brick wall. I sat there, open-mouthed, stunned, and then shaken as I realized what I had almost done to myself. I had three beautiful children, and I had almost destroyed myself, leaving them orphaned and alone except for their father.

I called Dr. Qualben's office first thing the next morning. Luckily the doctor picked up the call himself. Probably sensing the urgency in my voice, he scheduled an appointment for me to meet with him early the next morning. And so began the emotionally hard work of attempting to put my life back together.

I had no idea of how therapists actually worked, nor what seeing a psychiatrist would be like. Their modus operandi wasn't even mentioned in either of the two rather boring psych courses I'd taken in college. Even the very word "psychiatrist" carried with it a somewhat ominous sound to me— like something most people would associate only with the word "crazy." Thus, I had a lot of misgivings as I drove for the first time on my own from Queens over to Dr. Qualben's office in the Bay Ridge section of Brooklyn. I personally knew no one who'd ever been to a psychiatrist, except possibly Lyle, our youth director.

I wondered if I would be asked to lie on a couch, my eyes closed, with Dr. Qualben hidden out of sight somewhere behind me like Hollywood movies portrayed those Freudian-style shrinks, usually ones with German accents. At least I knew already from having talked with him that he didn't have a German accent!! I wondered what kind of questions he'd ask. I wondered if he would dredge up dark secrets from my past that I harbored deep in my subconscious, painful or shameful things psychologists say all people keep hidden even from themselves for many years. But try as I could to conjure up what those secret things might be, I drew a blank. The best I could come up with, however, was an experience I'd had in high school, which didn't seem like a deep, dark secret.

The high school academy I attended was part of a larger campus consisting of a college, music school, seminary, and school of nursing. Once during my junior year, Duane, a music major and casual friend from the music school, had wanted to try hypnotizing me when several of us were in the student lounge. I thought it might be fun to see what that was like. He began by having me watch a pendulum he swung back and forth, back and forth, several inches in front of my eyes to get me to relax as he tried inducing a hypnotic trance in me, and so I did begin relaxing. At a certain point, however, I became quite upset and refused to go on with Duane's "experiment" as I forced my eyes open. For some reason, I just didn't feel safe with him, though he'd never given me any reason not to trust him. And so that ended our hypnosis experiment.

Then in my last year of high school, Marge and I attended a lecture/demonstration by a professional hypnotherapist sponsored by the college psychology class but open to everyone including us academy kids. It was toward the end of the program that evening that the hypnotist induced a mass hypnosis on the whole audience. When he brought the group back to waking consciousness, slowly telling us that when he counted to five, we would all return to full awareness, awake, and refreshed. I could hear him speaking clearly, but I could not bring myself to open my eyes. The audience was admonished not to force anyone near them to "wake up." There must have been a few others like me with their eyes still closed, and he came around to each one, and quietly speaking to them one by one, got them to open their eyes as he eventually did to me. When I didn't respond, he took me aside and spoke softly to me. I heard him tell the group that he suspected that someone inexperienced had attempted to hypnotize me possibly against my will. I didn't feel initially that Duane's efforts at hypnosis had been against my will, but clearly my refusal to go just so far with his attempts indicated to me some unconscious lack of trust I sensed with him.

The stereotypical expectations about psychiatrists and the therapeutic process that I'd read about in novels or seen in movies turned out to be quite different from Dr. Qualben's approach to therapy, however— no couch, no "hidden" psychiatrist with prying questions to uncover subconscious secrets, at least not in any of those early visits. After greeting me warmly outside his office, Dr. Qualben or Paul as he told me to call him, led me into his inner-office, sat down across from me, each of us in a comfortable armchair, and just waited for me to begin talking.

I had come initially to find out what was wrong with me, what I'd done wrong in my marriage, where I'd failed, what I'd done to make Dan not love me, and what, if anything, I could do to rescue our marriage and our family when things looked so hopeless. Qualben just listened, for the most part, except when he wanted some clarification about something I may have said. And so it went weekly for several months. Through many of those sessions, I poured out the ongoing story of Dan's and my relationship after we married, but also how wonderful things had been between us while he was courting me, a time when I truly felt loved, especially compared to my relationship with Ken whose treatment of me had often been acrimonious and filled with criticism of me though sexually he'd always seemed easily aroused if I'd been willing and not afraid of an unwanted pregnancy.

Qualben also asked about my relationships not only with my family but with other men as well, along with men who were strangers when I was much younger. I told him about the three different times when under the pretext of asking me for directions or wanting information, several unknown men in cars had exposed themselves masturbating to me when I was between seven and ten. And then after pausing a few moments, I continued almost off handedly, "And then there was the time when I was three or four— so young that I still couldn't read— I was at a playmate's house— when her father offered to read the funny papers to me on a Sunday afternoon. He put me on his lap and eventually one hand went down into my panties, and began touching me down there as he read to me. I slid off him and left as quickly as possible, but I didn't tell my mother for fear of being somehow blamed for what the man had done."

And then I went on, "When I was about ten or so and out walking my dog Princey, a teenage boy, whom I didn't know, stopped his bicycle, and began asking me about the dog. He coaxed the dog up into the large, newspaper delivery basket on his bike. When I got close to him to take my dog back from the basket, he grabbed me sexually. Angry at being touched and scared, I yelled at the guy, got hold of Princey and hurried away. That time I did tell my parents, who I believe may have reported the incident to the police. Pausing momentarily, I continued, "But these events were no big deal," I said to Qualben assuredly. "I mean, I wasn't raped or anything!" With such ease, I'd seemed to brush off these experiences— they'd be called "sexual assaults" these days— events that I later learned can have a profound effect on one's basic sense of safety and self-esteem at one's core. It wasn't until years later that I was prepared to more fully explore those events and their effect on me more deeply in therapy.

But if I'd expected that the purpose of therapy was to get advice from Qualben in answer to those questions I'd come with, I was mistaken, at least in the short run. His goal, I think, was first to get a sense of who I was and what had happened . Not just in my marriage with Dan, but in other relationships, to impel me, if even momentarily, to want to end my life— to help me unravel how I'd come to be so hard on myself that I'd thought I'd be better off dead if my husband no longer loved me. Where or from whom I'd learned those harsh and largely erroneous judgments was part of Qualben's goal, I think.

We also discussed my choosing to have relationships with two men, Ken and Dan, who were both preparing for the ministry. I'd always thought it was because they were so much older, more mature than the college boys I knew. Qualben proffered the possibility that subconsciously I'd thought that they might be safer than some of the men from my childhood and teens, ones who'd deceived or betrayed me, belittled my abilities or attempted to sexually assault me.

I remember how surprised I was somewhere in those early weeks of counseling when Dr. Qualben described me as an exceptional person. I still remember his exact words, and though I puzzled over them, I didn't ask him specifically what he meant. Though I thought people usually liked me, no one had ever described me like that before— as someone exceptional and certainly not in so many words. It sounded nice, but I thought perhaps he was saying that to make me feel better. Despite the awards I'd achieved in college, I'd really never thought of myself that way.

Being somewhat dismissive of praise was a common reaction I often had when someone complimented me. Though inwardly I might glow with pleasure, part of me was embarrassed because I thought the praise a bit inflated or undeserved. Such was my reaction when I'd been selected to be Phi Beta Kappa in college. Whether this embarrassment was characteristic of the Swedish culture I'd been raised in, a culture where people tended to be reluctant to either give praise or receive it, or if this was something primarily true just for women, I couldn't say. Perhaps it was also true of most women in the days before women became more liberated in the '70s. I think it may still be true today for many women— a deep sense of unworthiness instilled by the predominant white male society we've been raised in, regardless of our nationality or color.

In any case, I began to sense by some of Qualben's questions that perhaps he thought the wrong person was seeking therapy. It was not because of I was not worthy of Dan's love that our lives were in such a mess. It was not because of something I'd done or not done, been or not been. Qualben spoke of the recklessness, the self-destructiveness evident in Dan's actions, not only toward himself, his reputation, his ordination vows when entering the ministry, but also his betrayal of me, his children, and of Julie, a girl many years younger than he, a member of his congregation, whom he'd confirmed just a few years before and had seduced and impregnated. Eventually Qualben called Dan and asked to meet with him, but Dan refused. His excuse was that he had neither the time in his busy schedule nor the money for both of us to see Qualben, even though Paul had assured me early on that we need pay him only what we could comfortably manage.

Late one afternoon shortly before Christmas after I'd been holiday shopping at A&S Department Store, I stopped off at church on the way home to show Dan what I'd gotten for the kids for Christmas. Since we only had one car, I also thought I'd give him a ride home. Things seemed to have settled down a bit between us, and I had hopes that he was not having thoughts about leaving us.

I knocked on his church office door but initially heard nothing. I crossed the hall that led into the sanctuary to see if he was there only to be surprised to see Dan coming into church by way of another door, which led directly from his office to the chancel. He'd been in there even when I'd knocked but pretended not to be. I sensed intuitively that he'd been with Julie. I walked back into the hallway, my heart racing as I found his office key on the key ring I'd borrowed earlier to use the car and unlocked the office door. There sat Julie staring at me, wordless with surprise. I looked hard at her, shook my head ruefully, saying nothing, and then turned on my heel, left the church, and drove home shaking with anger and profound disappointment. I was both heartsick and angry that they were still seeing each other.

The children were still at Jaye's house, so when I got home, I called her to say that Dan would pick them up and left a note for him to do just that. Though it was almost dark, I was determined not to be there when he came home. I had no plan at that point other than to find a place to spend that night. I packed a small bag, left the car at home, and took public transportation into Manhattan. My usual appointment with Paul Qualben in Brooklyn was the next afternoon, and now, more than ever, I needed to meet with him.

I remembered that my sister-in-law had a friend in the city— a possible place I could stay overnight. Luckily I found her name and number in the Manhattan phone book when I got into the city and called her asking if I could spend the night with her. Even though I'd never met her, she welcomed me warmly without asking a lot of questions. With her help, I was able to find the right trains to Brooklyn the next morning to make it to my appointment with Paul.

Dan must have gotten in touch with Paul, for when I was finished seeing him, Dan was there waiting for me at Paul's office. Evidently when I never came home the night before, Dan called Qualben looking for me and learned that I had an appointment with him. In the morning, he drove to Brooklyn to pick me up and made an appointment for himself to see Paul the next week. Dan's willingness to finally meet with Paul was the first hopeful sign to me regarding the future of our marriage.

I still had not told even my parents nor my sister of the havoc occurring in my life. At some point during the late winter, in a phone call to my sister Violet in Chicago, I finally confided to her that I'd been seeing a psychiatrist because Dan and I were "having problems." That was as specific as I would get with her. I could not bring myself to tell her I'd been so distraught that I'd tried to run my car into the front of our house, so "marital problems" was the next best thing I could think of by way of explanation.

The next day my mother called from Chicago, greatly upset. "Your sister Violet just called me and told me that you're seeing a psychiatrist!! What have you done?" she asked imploringly, "that you need to see a psychiatrist?"

Hearing the anxiety and fear in her voice, I knew that I could no longer hide the truth from her. Knowing that her imaginings about me were far worse than the actual truth, I began to pour out the whole sad, sordid story to her.

Though shocking to her, it was also a relief to both of us that I hadn't done something— whatever that something might have been—arrested maybe for stealing from the offering plate? No, it was a relief to her that this was primarily Dan's doing and not some awful thing I'd done. My mother had grown up in considerable poverty. Many years later, when she was in her nineties and I'd been seeking information about her own early life vicissitudes, I was shocked when she told me that the hardest thing she'd ever gone through in her life was not some betrayal she'd experienced by my father or some other man. Her worst fear was that I would not emotionally survive this period of my life with Dan. Her response surprised me, yes, but how much my mother had worried about me during those early days of my marriage also touched me to my core.

CHAPTER 8

The View from Here

The Civil Rights Movement was in full momentum when Martin Luther King, Jr. and other clergy leaders of the Southern Christian Leadership Council (SCLC) held the March on Washington in August of 1963 with 250,000 people attending. The Civil Rights Act was signed by President Lyndon Johnson in July of 1964. This movement had been spearheaded almost exclusively by black Southern Baptist ministers; little if anything had been done for civil rights historically by white mainstream Christian churches in either the North or the South since Abolition or Reconstruction. White Christian churches continued to be among the most racially segregated places in the U.S., not necessarily by law so much as by societal practice.

In 1962, the Urban Training Center for Christian Mission (UTC), an ecumenical organization in Chicago to educate clergy not only to the extent of racism in the Christian church, but also to the problems of life among the urban poor and the training needed in urban community organizing to enable the clergy and their congregations to begin addressing these problems.

The program required that as part of their urban studies and experience, the participating clergy and their families must live for a year in a typical slum dwelling in Chicago that would rent to any family without regard to the race or ethnicity of the people. The housing, which was selected for the program's participants and their families, could rent for no more than $70 a month (roughly $300 in today's urban housing economy). It was minimally furnished by the UTC, which also paid the participants a basic stipend for food and living expenses.

Dan had just begun meeting with Dr. Qualben shortly before he learned of the UTC's Ministerial Training program. After talking it over with me, he made application for that training which required that we leave St. Paul's and move to a slum dwelling in Chicago. I would have moved to west Hell to keep my family together before everything exploded in my face, especially if that meant getting away from St. Paul's to avoid a congregation-wide ugly scandal if they learned the truth about Dan's relationship with Julie.

In the early summer Dan was accepted as part of the first UTC's group of ministers in this training, which would begin in late August 1964. It was only then that I finally began to have some assurance that Dan was not going to leave us. When he resigned from St. Paul's, he used the Urban Training Center as his reason for leaving.

Though it was not easy to say goodbye to the friends I'd made at St. Paul's, and especially to beloved Aunt Jaye and Uncle Emil, who had become like family to us. Like everyone else in our congregation, they knew nothing of Dan's affair with Julie nor the real reason we were leaving St. Paul's. I knew I would also miss Lyle, who been like a best friend and trusted confidant through those dreadful months of secrecy I'd endured. It also was not easy moving my children from the pleasant split-level parsonage in Queens to a tenement apartment in a slum neighborhood in Chicago, but at least I knew that we would finally be leaving St. Paul's at summer's end. I would miss our friends but leaving there would be a huge weight off my mind. That was enough for me. It was the answer to prayer that I'd asked God for many months before.

I also regretted having to end my relationship with Dr. Qualben when we left St. Paul's. In truth, he'd been not only a lifesaver for me but also instrumental in my beginning to look at myself with new eyes and with the incipient emergence of a considerably expanded self-identity though I still had a long way ahead of me.

I was especially sorry that Dan's therapy with Paul, though perhaps lasting only three or four weeks, had to be cut short. Dr. Qualben had encouraged him to find a therapist in Chicago to work with, but he did not do that.

We were still really not communicating in any meaningful way about our relationship nor his with Julie, and he still had not expressed any sorrow nor regret to me for his utter betrayal and infidelity. It was as though those things had never happened. I was, however, starting to read whatever I could get my hands on dealing with marriage and relationships, and my interest in psychology deepened.

I had begun this journey by asking, "What did I do wrong that my husband doesn't find me attractive enough to make love to me, and doesn't seem to love me?" and now I was asking the more fundamental questions of "Who am I besides somebody's wife or mother or daughter?" and "Who is this man I am married to?" Thus, began a lifelong quest, thereafter, for a deeper understanding of spirituality and human consciousness, my own and other people's, as well.

August 1964 – Chicago, Illinois

When Dan got word from the Urban Training Center that our new home would be a three and a half-room apartment at in Chicago, I let my family, who still lived there, know the address. All we knew was that our apartment was located on the raggedy edge of Old Town, on the near North side of Chicago, an area I was unfamiliar with except that it was near the Zoo and was scheduled for major redevelopment soon. What we didn't know was that whole section of the Near North side was slum scheduled to be torn down within a year or so.

My father and sister Violet drove from the Northside of Chicago where my parents lived and I had grown up, to see exactly where we'd be staying. Knowing we'd be living in a slum neighborhood, I had warned my parents not to expect too much. I guess I hadn't given them sufficient warning, however.

What they found was a shock to them— a string of rundown stores with apartments above them lining the 400 block of North Avenue. Located at that address was a decrepit TV repair shop with a large, rusted, metal, security gate across its front. Puzzled, my dad thought somebody had made a mistake. There seemed to be no such address… that is, until his eyes caught the barely legible number on a tall, ugly, ramshackle, black front door in desperate need of paint, with a kicked-in bottom panel located right next to but not part of the TV repair shop entrance. A mistake must have been made, my dad assured my sister. This could not possibly be the front door where his daughter and her family would soon be living. But it was, and that realization took him aback.

Tentatively my sister tried the handle of the door from the street, which surprisingly was open. It gave way into a dark, forbidding stairway that once had been painted but was now a barely detectable burgundy. There was no stairwell railing. A transom above the outside door was so dirty it barely let in any daylight. It was the only light source for the stairway, which led up to yet another questionable door on the second floor. This would turn out to be our three-room railway flat apartment. Another flight of stairs led to a third-floor apartment. When they later got a key for that second-floor door, they came back several hours later, my dad with his carpenter's tools in tow and this time with my mother.

The apartment had been abandoned long before; homeless people slept there when seeking shelter if they were drunk or cold. The place was an unspeakable wreck. Weeks later after we moved in, my sister told me that at one point that first day, my father put down the tools he was using, sat down on his sawhorse, and tears welled up in his eyes as he looked at my sister sadly. "I left Sweden for America when I was 17 to get away from this kind of squalor," he said, "so that my children would never have to live like I had once had to live. And this hellhole is where my college-educated daughter has wound up— is planning to live," he said with finality and disbelief. I could have assured him that we'd only have to live there for a year— that it wouldn't be forever. But somehow I doubt that would have been much comfort to him.

Even before Dan and I arrived in Chicago, my mother and father had been busy working hard to clean up the worst of the surface filth in the apartment. My father had torn out the vermin-infested pantry and built new shelves for food storage in the kitchen. The kitchen door led out to a roof over the TV repair shop. This was where our three children and Hilda, our dog, would eventually play after my father built a safety railing along the edge of the roof, and rails to hold onto when going down the steps to the back alley. Though there was still much to be done to make those rooms somewhat habitable, I was thankful that my family had done as much as they had to make that apartment bearable before we arrived days later. Had I seen that hideous front door without knowing that behind it lay my new "home," nothing could have persuaded me to enter it voluntarily.

There were three, long, narrow and very dirty windows looking down onto the traffic below from the high-ceilinged living room. Next to it was the doorway to a bedroom roughly 5 x 7, just big enough to hold a bunk bed for Eric and Liz. Eventually the view out those windows became an occasional entertainment for the kids as they gazed down into the street, fascinated as they watched the police routinely stopping cars each night and making drug busts.

Immediately adjacent to the living room without any wall of separation what probably was meant to be a bedroom and a bathroom with ancient fixtures and a claw-footed old tub. Then came the kitchen and what may have been a pantry, but now was being used to hold Ann-Mari's crib. Room followed room in a straight line with windows only at the beginning and end of what they once called a rail-road flat. The kitchen floor was covered by at least six layers of worn out linoleum, probably there from the turn of the century. Dan and my dad scraped up sheet after sheet of disgusting, rotted-out linoleum pieces after stuffing up all the rat holes with steel wool. Only then could they put down fresh linoleum flooring.

The condition of the walls with their multiple layers of old wall paper made peeling it off impossible. It just had to be camouflaged with paint. We used almost 12 gallons of paint on those four rooms. I remember my frustration and occasional fits of hilarity, as I would apply a roller full of paint, only to have the many old layers of wallpaper come rolling back down off the wall onto the roller. I can't count how many times I exclaimed, "Oh, shit!" or else just broke out laughing each time it happened. Sometimes we had to use a hammer and nails to nail the paper back up onto the walls.

We had left most of our furniture in storage in New York with the exception of our kitchen table, some chairs, a few end tables, our dishes and cookware, and our clothing and the kids' toys. The Training Center provided a few basic pieces of furniture— a hide-a-bed couch and an armchair upholstered in orange Naughty for the living room, a double bed and mattress, and two bunk-beds. I insisted we at least take along a few of our favorite pictures for the walls to remind us of home in New York.

Besides the hard-physical work that my parents had done for us both before and after we arrived, that which earned my eternal gratitude to them, they somehow had the wisdom to know what would make things easiest for the kids and me, too. They managed to treat my husband with a modicum of civility, which must have been difficult for them especially knowing, but never once mentioning, the sorry circumstances under which we'd left St. Paul's to come to this place. I don't know how they managed to do that, but they did.

Though I'd grown up in Chicago, my life had been spent primarily in two neighborhoods on the North Side, which was populated almost entirely by white people, the majority Jewish. I was part of a minority of Gentiles in the public schools I attended up to sixth or seventh grade. I knew no one who was Asian or Hispanic and saw very few black people, most of whom lived on the Southside. There were a small number of whites who lived in some sections of the Southside, my mother's Aunt Selma and her family being among them. They were the only white people that I knew personally who lived on the South Side.

My mother and I would take the elevated train— or the El as Chicagoans called it— which ran high above the street level, all the way down to the Southside to visit Aunt Selma when I was very young before the subway was built. I can remember sitting close to my mother as we looked out the L-train windows together at the back porches of families living there. The buildings were mostly rundown, wooden, four-story tenements, usually with people's laundry stretched out to dry, hanging on clothes lines from their windows on pulleys and reaching across from one building to the next. Sometimes we could actually look right into people's apartment windows or down into the streets below and see children playing there from the train windows.

I can still hear vividly the compassion and sadness in my mother's voice as she would look down at those tenement apartments, some of them peopled by low income African Americans, and some by middle-income blacks, who were restricted to limited choices of housing because of racial prejudice in Chicago, and she would say sadly, "Look at how those poor people have to live." Those words "have to live" made all the difference in the way I perceived them. There was not a trace of blame or condemnation in her words but rather a statement indicating that these living conditions were not of their choosing but of the policies of segregation in place in Chicago and every other city in the U.S.

The friendship and respect between my father and his construction buddy, Mr. Headen, the only black person I knew personally when I was young, had a profound influence on me, as well. There's an old Chinese proverb that says, "A child's life is like a piece of paper on which every passerby leaves a mark." That certainly was true for me regarding Mr. Headen. My parents had been invited to the Headen's 25th wedding anniversary. I still have a picture in an old family album of my parents standing next to Mr. Headen and his wife, he in a tuxedo-like suit and she wearing a long dress and a corsage at their 25th anniversary party taken at their home in the mid-1940s. How one's parents view the world and its people has everything to do with how we as children learn to view people. And now here I was back in Chicago with my own family, living at least for a year in one of the same tenement neighborhoods that I'd ridden over on the L Train with my mother on the way to Aunt Selma's on the Southside years before.

The curriculum at Urban Training Center consisted of training for clergyman in developing strategies and approaches to community organizing especially in urban areas. These pastors, who heretofore had been ministering almost exclusively to white, middle, and upper-middle class congregations, were to bring to their congregations an understanding of the necessity of community organizing as part of the Christian mandate to empower the urban poor and disenfranchised. Another of the goals of the UTC was to provide first hand exposure to some of the realities of poverty, segregation, and racism in this country to this group of mostly white, middle class pastors, who, like Dan, had been fairly oblivious to it or aware of it only as an abstraction.

One of the first, urban immersion experiences for him and the other participants was what UTC called "the plunge," which took place shortly after we arrived in Chicago. We'd been told about this aspect of the training before it began, and it seemed daunting to me and potentially quite dangerous especially for inexperienced ministers. Nothing in seminary training had prepared them for this, and I'd begun to worry early on about Dan's safety. Early on a Friday morning, all of the trainees were dumped out two at a time into disparate sections of the city totally unfamiliar to them, wearing their oldest clothes and carrying no identification other than a piece of paper containing just their name and the UTC phone number, plus a dollar in change. They were then left to their own devices until Monday evening to forage for food, subsistence money, shelter, or transportation, by any means they could, be it panhandling, searching for leftover change in phone booths, sleeping in flop houses, public buildings such as the train station, or even doorways, to be out on their own for the required days before finding their way back to the UTC. They were not to call home or the UTC unless it was an emergency. That was a nail-biting experience of worry for me.

It had to have been a real, skid row exercise in learning compassion for those who are homeless and friendless in the meanest streets of Chicago. I write of these aspects of the training not from any direct experience, unfortunately. I say "unfortunately" not because I'd have wanted an experience like that, but rather because I felt so disconnected from it all. Perhaps if I'd felt that Dan and I were more emotionally connected, I'd have felt differently. Never during that year were wives invited to hear any of the training center's guest speakers, such as some of the better-known clergyman and leaders in the Southern Christian Leadership Council (SCLC), or highly experienced community organizers such as well-known Chicago urban organizer, Saul Alinsky. Nor were we ever included in any of the Center's special training events. I never even learned precisely where the Urban Training Center was located because wives never had cause to visit there! This was 1964. Women's liberation and our inclusion in important societal decision-making had not, as yet, taken any significant foothold in most people's consciousness.

The experiences of those of us who were merely the partners of the UTC participants were far less dramatic than events like "the Plunge." We were the ones whose primary job was to keep the home fires burning. Besides staying home cooking, cleaning, and taking care of the children, I had some unexpected chores such as regularly cleaning or sweeping down the outside stairway in case it had been used the night before by some drunk or homeless person. Another chore of mine was picking up the garbage that invariably landed on the tar paper and cinder roof outside our kitchen door when little Vinnie Sullivan, the youngest child of the third-floor Irish family in the building next door, took out the family trash. He discovered that it was much easier for him to just heave the garbage over their railing and down onto the rooftop below which was also our back porch next door.

We wives also did the grocery shopping, which really meant picking through the unsold remainders from the suburban stores like the A & P and then sold presumably as first quality meat and produce when we shopped for meals at the A&P across the street. How did the A&P dare to sell inferior merchandise as well as the leftovers from the suburban stores, and at higher prices than in the suburbs? They dared to do it because they could get away with it, and they still do in some poorer places in the U.S. The politicians didn't care. There were no community organizations to speak for the poor who lived in that section of Chicago.

The laundromats out in the suburbs were much cleaner and to my surprise considerably cheaper facilities than the hole-in-the-wall laundry down the street from us on North Avenue. Unlike those who lived in our neighborhood and didn't have cars to drive out to the suburbs to grocery shop, I cheated by eventually ending up piling our three kids into the car and toting them out to Glenview, a northwest suburb where my sister and her family lived. I'd do the grocery shopping and our laundry, as well, in Glenview at the Laundromat out there.

Even shopping at the Neisner's Dime Store right across from us came as a shock to me with its higher prices and cheaper-quality merchandise most of which was frequently covered with dust. I still remember a framed picture of Jesus for sale in their gift department. When you held its somewhat soiled frame and tipped it slightly, the image changed from Jesus on the cross to Jesus seeming to fly off the cross to heaven— sort of like the images of naked ladies they sometimes had on matchbook covers. I was tempted to buy it as a souvenir of North Avenue, for my nephew Tommy, but it cost too much to buy as a kind of joke and might have been considered sacrilegious by some people.

Because of the dire circumstances that I felt we were in while we were still at St. Paul's, where at any minute I feared that Dan's relationship with Julie would become a huge scandal in the congregation, I never regretted our leaving St. Paul's, despite the conditions we were now living under. I was beginning to learn more about the realities and injustices of those living in poverty in the inner city than I had bargained for— more than I'd ever really wanted to know. I can remember the judgments I'd once held before leaving New York when the N.Y. Times carried tragic stories about the children, usually of poor mothers or grandmothers raising them by themselves, who'd died in tenement fires because they'd been left home alone unprotected. "How could they have allowed that to happen to those children?" I'd rant angrily to myself before my experience.

Then came the day on North Avenue when Eric, now five, became sick with the flu and had to stay home from school. I needed to pick up a prescription for him from the drugstore. He and Lizzie begged me to get them some game they'd asked for, which was on sale at Wieboldt's, the closest department store. Ann-Mari had just gone down for a nap, and I didn't think it would take more than 25 or 30 minutes to get both items. With our dog Hilda there in the apartment, I was sure they would be safe. But the trip took longer than I'd planned—almost an hour. When I got home, I discovered both Eric and Liz standing out in the unheated hallway in their flannel pajamas.

Ann-Mari was awake in the back of the apartment, and I could hear her in her crib crying. The children had accidentally locked the apartment door behind them when they mistakenly thought they'd heard me coming home downstairs. When they couldn't get back in and realized their mistake, they'd gone upstairs for help from the Hewitt's, but found nobody home. Now, unable to get back into the apartment, they were left standing there, outside our door, shivering in their PJs when I came up the steps from the street. I felt terrible for having left them and grateful that no one I knew had caught me at such parental carelessness. But I was reluctant to ever comment critically again on how the children of the poor could sometimes be left in harm's way. To add even more guilt to my state of mind, I realized that our apartment, heated by just two space heaters, could be especially dangerous. Many times in the years to come, I thought about how easily a fire could have broken out. I could imagine what the headlines would have said concerning a fire in my slum apartment on North Avenue and my supreme carelessness for leaving my children alone at home. "She was probably in some dive drinking!" I imagined people would comment as they read news about the fire. How easy it is to judge people without understanding the difficult circumstances they live under.

Three-year-old Elizabeth had her own adventure on the steps leading up to the Hewitt's flat on the third floor. A drunk had passed out in the stairwell and was lying there sleeping as she was making her way up the stairs to the third floor to play with Matthew Hewitt, so she just stepped over him to get up to the Hewitt's door. When no one was home, she turned around, stepped back over the fellow again and continued back down the stairs to our apartment. Sometime later, unaware that anyone had been in the stairway, we heard a ruckus of men's voices outside our door, and I looked out to see what was going on. It was the police, there to "escort" the "sleeping" man down the rest of the steps and out the front door.

It was only then that Lizzie piped up with total aplomb like this happened every day, "Oh, he was the man sleeping on our steps when I went up to Matthew's. I thought he was Santa Claus. Why did the police take him away?" I thought many parents would have freaked out by her response. I was at least glad she was able to take it in her stride.

Even our dog Hilda had her adventures. She found a rat out on the roof, caught it, and came proudly bringing it into the kitchen to show us. It looked pretty disgusting. Later when Dan was at the UTC for classes, he shared the rat tale with Archie Hargraves, one of the UTC leaders, who replied jokingly, "Aw, Pierotti, that ain't nothin'. You only need to worry when the rat comes in dragging your dog in its mouth!"

I, too, had what I referred to as my "Claws" Encounters of the Third Kind, though far less precarious. I was sitting on the john in our decrepit bathroom with its single, light bulb dangling from a long cord leading up to the nine-foot, paint-peeling ceiling and its ancient, badly stained, claw-footed bathtub (years before those tubs became "in" among the upward-mobile yuppies). I was staring glumly at the torn top layer of the nondescript linoleum under my feet, wondering if there was more under here than the six layers like we'd had to tear out of the kitchen to make it minimally habitable. Suddenly my heart jumped as something scurried along the wall within my vision field. At first I thought it was a rat, but I managed to quell my panic, stayed still and focused, as curiosity overcame fear. There, less than three feet from me sat a wee, gray-brown mouse intently staring up at me. I wondered if it, too, had its natural fear overtaken by curiosity at this giant monster that sat across from it on the toilet.

We sat staring intently at one another for several minutes. I noticed its tiny, almost translucent pink ears; its pink, quivering, little nose; its small, dexterous claws as it sat on its haunches washing its face, its bright eyes looking fixedly at me. I actually found myself fascinated by this creature and wondered how people could be so unreasonably afraid of something so small, really quite harmless, and almost beautiful in its own way. Now, mind you, I'm talking here about mice, not rats. It was my first experience being that close even to a mouse. Eventually losing fear and interest in me, the mouse ran off. And ever after that, I, too, lost fear in most unexpected mouse sightings.

I was fortunate to have my parents living in Chicago. My mother would occasionally babysit with the kids, which freed me to take several courses in portrait drawing, pastels, and calligraphy, which were offered at the YWCA downtown. My love of drawing and painting, and an adeptness I had with them had lain fallow since I'd graduated from college and gotten married. Being able to get back to my artwork helped brighten that dismal time in Chicago for me.

We spent almost a year attempting to make a decent home above that TV repair shop on North Avenue from the summer of 1964 to June of 1965. Shortly after we left, the city began a massive "gentrification" project. They tore down whole blocks of that area including our block and our apartment, to build expensive town houses and condos. That year was unlike anything I'd ever experienced anywhere either during the years I'd spent growing up in Chicago, or after I married Dan just after graduating from college. But however jolting and difficult the time spent in Chicago had been at times, there was never a day when we suffered the absence of any real life necessities. We had enough food, clothing, warmth, shelter, necessary transportation, and never any real kind of harassment from anyone in the neighborhood. As the keeper of our home, I was never really afraid for my family in that community and for some reason always felt an underlying level of safety aside from not knowing with certainty what the outcome of our marriage would end up being considering the nature of his relationship with Julie.

March 1965 – Chicago, Illinois

On a Sunday evening, early in March of 1965, we sat watching the nightly news in Chicago and the covering of what was scheduled to have been a peaceful march for voting rights in the South. It was also a protest of the shooting death of a young black voting rights activist, Jimmy Lee Jackson, two weeks before by one of the deputies of Selma, Alabama's sheriff, Jim Clark. The march from Selma to Montgomery, Alabama, was to be led by voting rights organizers with assistance from some of the Southern Christian Leadership Council (SCLC) staffers. We watched in disbelief and then shock, however, when Selma's sheriff, Jim Clark, riding on horseback and determined to stop the marchers before they crossed the city bridge, ordered them to disperse. Then, with local and national journalists watching, Clark ordered his force to charge the crowd. Several hundred state troopers, Selma Alabama police, deputy sheriffs, some of them also on horseback, and white Selma civilians, all of them armed with clubs, guns, cattle-prods, and whips charged into the crowd using their weapons along with tear gas and began bludgeoning the marchers, most of them African Americans.

Even from the distance of a TV screen almost a thousand miles away, I was shocked and sickened as I watched the rage and hatred on the faces of many of the white citizens of Selma, screaming filthy, racial epithets, and the violence displayed by these people on their own black towns-people and clergy, whose only crime had been attempting to peacefully protest the absence of voting rights and public accommodations for black people in Alabama.

Lynchings and attacks like this had been happening in other places in the South and elsewhere in the U.S. over basic civil rights for blacks and other minorities for many decades. There'd just not been television and other mass communications to make people aware of their prevalence. For me it became a life changing catalyst for the direction of my life beyond anything I could have imagined before we left St. Paul's. I simply could not fathom either logically or emotionally the kind of mindless fear or prejudice by some whites toward people of color whom they didn't even know. Most, if not all, of the white people I'd known at that point (with the possible exception of Lyle), had neither known personally nor ever even had any black people as friends. Their attitudes towards blacks were not necessarily as virulent, however, as were those of many whites growing up in the South who'd been brainwashed since birth to believe they were superior to people of color. But still they viewed blacks as something or someone other than themselves.

Some friends and family have said that the year in a Chicago slum took guts. Some described it as craziness on our part; some characterized our experience as just like that of the many poor people who lived there permanently. However, none of those was really true. There was an important difference between our being there and the experience of the other people who lived there permanently in that impoverished neighborhood. Dan and I were there by choice, unlike most of the other families on North Avenue, who had little hope of a different way of life.

From day one, we had known that this was a temporary situation and that within the year this experience would be over. Our knowing this made things infinitely easier for us. The experiences of that year alone forced open my eyes to the extreme inequities caused primarily by poverty, racism, lack of decent education, unemployment, and neglect towards people of color, not only in my hometown, Chicago, where I had lived much of my life, but also in most other places in the U.S.

1965 - Washington, DC.

In late April, Dan received an invitation to come to Washington, DC., to interview for the job of director of the Cooperative Lutheran Parish some weeks later. It was a newly formed organization made up of nine Lutheran churches in the District of Columbia. Its goal was to assist in the educating of members of these congregations to the deeper issues regarding poverty, racism, community change, and civil rights.

This would not be a job where he was working for one particular congregation in a position similar to a regular pastor. He would initiate and coordinate training in those Lutheran congregations in DC. When Dan learned that he'd been selected for the directorship, I was relieved to know for certain that he had no plan to leave me and our children for Julie, though we never spoke about that issue specifically. I had some certainty now that we would still be together as a family, and that our time on North Avenue, as important as it had been for both of us, would soon be over.

I'd been in Washington briefly only once before and thought it a beautiful city. I was excited at the prospect of living in the Nation's Capital. The Urban Training Center program ended for us in July, and after the movers came to pick up the few items of furniture we'd brought with us, we packed what was left and drove back to New York. Our dear friends Jaye and Emil from St. Paul's had agreed to keep our children while we drove on to Washington to find housing. DC.

Finding a home we could afford in Washington was more difficult than we'd imagined, especially one in a racially integrated community. Having little or no money after a year without a salary, we had borrowed $3000 from my parents towards a down payment. Finding a well-integrated public school in a community we could afford in the District was almost an impossibility since over 90% of the public-school children in DC. were African American (though that term hadn't come into use, yet. Back then it was either Black, Negro or colored, which by now was used only occasionally and mostly by older, black people, especially those from the South.) All of these appellations along with the N-word managed to insult someone or other in the African American community and left some well-meaning whites often befuddled by what word to use but yet not wanting to offend someone.

The District of Columbia itself was about 70% black in the 1960s. The few moderately integrated schools were mostly located in Northwest DC. where housing was priced well beyond anything we could afford and not available to us because we didn't live in any of the wards where they were located. While we looked for a house, we stayed with a clergy colleague of Dan's, Bruce Weaver, who was the pastor of a Reformation Lutheran Church on Capitol Hill. He and his wife Amelia lived in the Hillcrest section of Southeast DC., a lovely section of Washington on one of the highest hills in the city and just about three miles from Capitol Hill. We'd been told by one of Dan's other colleagues when we asked about housing in Southeast, "Don't even bother looking in Southeast for housing," he'd said dismissively. "There's nothing there!" What he really meant was that Southeast was predominantly black and the place where a large segment of lower income black people lived. Most of the people who lived in the Southeast section of D.C. were black. This was the result of one of the many unthinking, uncaring, racist decisions made by the U.S. Congress' Board of Commissioners for the District, who oversaw every aspect of the running of the District of Columbia for many decades.

This is still true to some extent. As of 2019, District residents still have no voting representation in Congress or the Senate, even though we pay among the highest Federal income tax and local DC. taxes as well. Hence, in protest over the lack of voting rights in DC., our local residents' car license tags still read "Taxation Without Representation!" The tax-paying citizens of the District of Columbia didn't gain the right to vote even in the Presidential elections until 1964. It wasn't until 1974 that we were permitted to elect our first mayor. We still have no voting representation in Congress!

Fortunately, Bruce and Emma Weaver knew more about Southeast than most white people do and had ignored the kind of advice we'd been given by Dan's other colleague who had initially warned us away from Southeast. Five years earlier, the Weavers had bought a lovely home as a parsonage in the Hillcrest section of Southeast just a few doors down from over twenty acres of National Park Service woods, and we began looking at houses for sale in that area. Thanks to the Weavers, we learned that a neighbor of theirs had an attractive split-level house, which was for sale at a price we could afford. We also checked out the Anne Beers Elementary School, just a short block away from the house we were looking at, and spoke with the Beers' principal, Ms. Maloney. When we expressed concerns about how well our kids would be received in an elementary school which was 90% African American, she said that the relatively small number of white children at her school didn't seem to have trouble fitting in, but she gave us the name and address of another white family, the Keeler's, who lived close by and whose four children attended Beers. Open and friendly people, they told us that in the three years they'd been in the neighborhood since George, who was an Air Force doctor, had been transferred to the Air Force base close by, their kids had no problems fitting in or being accepted as minority white children there.

And so, after all those years living in church-owned parsonages, we finally became homeowners for the first time. Kay Keeler and I became friends, and she introduced me to a women's discussion group at St. Mark's, an Episcopal church that our family began attending because we liked its worship service so much. Since Dan no longer had regular pastoral duties at any one particular church and was now preaching, teaching, and involved in many Lutheran churches in DC, he attended St. Mark's when he was not preaching somewhere else. I will never forget the Keelers. We were pretty broke our first Christmas in Washington. Kay, who had stopped in at our house just before Christmas, noticed the stack of un-mailed Christmas cards on the dining room table, and offered to mail them. I embarrassedly said, "Kay, we can't afford postage for them until the end of the month." "Nonsense!" she replied, picking up the stack of un-mailed Christmas cards as she departed. "Just consider it an early Christmas present from the Keeler Family!"

The community of Hillcrest, among the highest sections of the District, had been mostly middle and working class people and had been almost exclusively white until just a few years earlier because of the unofficial but pervasive practice among real estate interests of red lining neighborhoods in Southeast, a discriminatory practice based on race by which banks, insurance companies, realtors, etc. refused or limited loans, mortgages, and insurance policies to black buyers within specific geographic areas, especially in the suburbs and parts of the inner city. Now forbidden by federal law, it still takes place in some select areas sub rosa in order to control who can or can't live in select neighborhoods. Our immediate neighborhood was quite well integrated primarily with whites and African Americans, with most of the homeowners working for the federal or local D.C. governments. On our street lived three ministers, two teachers, a police officer, a dentist, and a pharmacist, while most of the others were employed at federal agencies such as the NSA (the National Security Agency), the U.S. Census Bureau, and NIH (the National Institutes of Health).

There were also a number of retired people. All but a small percentage of our neighbors were either high school graduates or college educated. I was fairly sure that Dan's salary as a clergyman made our family's income one of the lowest on the block— not that mattered much— but it was instrumental in my determination to find part-time substitute teaching work when our youngest child, Ann-Mari, turned three. Our family really felt the pinch financially with a mortgage and utility payments to make. We still found it necessary sometimes to return soda and milk bottles for the deposit near the end of the month when money got tight.

Since our neighborhood had only begun to be integrated three or four years earlier, mostly by younger black families with children, most of our children's playmates were from young black families. As expected with children, color never seemed to enter in as a factor in their friendships. They were already fast friends and familiar with one another's families long before we adult neighbors, a bit more cautious about color differences, met and got to know one another more than just superficially. By and large those seeming differences began to melt into genuine friendships as time went by.

Several months after we moved in, the Smiths, a black family with teen-aged twins moved in next door. Marea Smith had worked for the Department of Labor for many years, and her husband Ed was a supervisor at a large facility for children in the suburbs. The twins were about to start their final year at Ballou High School, one of the schools where I soon began substitute teaching. Jimmy intended to join the Air Force after graduating from high school and Jackie had recently been accepted at Bucknell University. She babysat occasionally with our kids before she left for college.

On the corner, next to the Smiths, were the Robinsons. Mr. Robinson was a pharmacist, who also owned several drugstores in D.C. He had been a chemistry teacher who served in WWII as a pilot in the all-black 99th fighter squadron and was one of the extraordinary Tuskegee Airmen whose heroism and success protecting U.S. bombers during the war ultimately led to President Truman's desegregating not only the War Department but other federal agencies, as well. To describe the Tuskegee pilots as "famed" depended on who was using it, for their success as pilots during WW II primarily as Air Force bomber escorts was rarely written about in the majority white owned newspapers, and its very existence barely acknowledged until decades later. I learned that in 1948 after the war had ended, Mr. Robinson, who'd been a chemistry teacher in South Carolina before he served as an escort pilot during WW II, had wanted to work as a commercial airline pilot after the war, but because of his race, the major U.S. airlines would not even accept an application from him as a commercial pilot when WW II was over.

A number of years later, my neighbor across the street, George Norfleet, interviewed and wrote a fine biography, A Pilot's Journey, about Curtis Robinson and his extraordinary family, which I helped edit before its publication. The Robinsons were one of the first African American families to successfully purchase a home situated two doors down from the house we eventually bought two or three years later after we moved to Washington. I use the term successfully because Hillcrest had been one of those areas in D.C. which had been red-lined and designated "for whites only" by the local real estate interests prior to 1962. The former owner of his house, who was white, had flown in the face of those real estate agents by selling his home to the Robinson family.

A general migration of whites fleeing from the cities to the suburbs had been taking place all over urban areas in the U.S. In Hillcrest, however, without our being aware of it, realtors had been busy "blockbusting" i.e. contacting white homeowners in the area, especially those of retirement age, informing them of the recent presence of black people in the community, what that would mean to their property values, and offering to buy their houses "while you can still get anything for your house," they warned. They then resold those houses selectively to African Americans at a considerable profit. That was the game real estate people and bankers played to make money and also keep America segregated.

I'd been distressed for many years over the virtually planned segregation of much of the U.S. and concluded that nothing would change in that regard until children could grow up knowing people of many different cultures and colors. Consequently, even before our move to D.C., our intention had been to raise our family in an integrated community, which was why we chose our neighborhood. But within two years after our moving to Southeast, there seemed to be fewer white families moving in, and I began to fear that we might end up being the only white family there. During the time we'd already been living there, we felt quite comfortable with all our neighbors, black and white, and the prospect of moving to the few more integrated neighborhoods in the District was just not financially possible for us. We decided that the only solution was to stay where we were and make a point to get to know all our newer neighbors, even if we did end up being the only white people on the block

Southeast Neighbors, our community association, had been started about the time that we moved in, and I began to attend their monthly meetings at the local library. One of their goals was to stop the real estate interests and banks from their illegal use of red lining tactics in the neighborhood. Another goal of Southeast Neighbors was also to create an integrated community where white and black people worked together to make our area better known to the press and general population in D.C. Because much of Southeast D.C. as a total area had been mostly black, all of Southeast had been treated for a couple decades like some neglected bastard child by the District of Columbia when it came to city services, schools, police, fire departments, parks and recreation facilities. The city politicians pretty much ignored Southeast D.C. except at election time. The "goodies" (recreational facilities, pools, parks, school services, etc.) were, for the most part, directed toward the moneyed and politically powerful parts of D.C. located in Northwest and parts of Southwest.

I began serving on several committees of Southeast Neighbors and eventually was elected to their board of directors. Southeast Neighbors and our proudly integrated board of directors received a special award for community service from the newly appointed mayor, Walter Washington, with our picture in the *Washington Post*. As a minister's wife, I had never served on the board of anything whether church-related or not. I never felt that I had any opportunities besides playing the piano for Sunday School to use my talents intellectually or otherwise in the church as an individual person in my own right rather than just as an adjunct to my husband, the minister. It felt good to have an identity of my own and be able to voice opinions in my own right.

Shortly after our youngest daughter, Ann-Mari, turned three and was now in pre-school, I began substitute teaching several times a week to augment our income. It didn't bring in much money— about $50 or $60 a day, but it certainly gave me a variety of experience from second graders to high school seniors both in the District and in adjacent county suburbs, which were predominantly white at that time. Eventually Ballou Senior High School, which had a predominately black student enrollment and was three or four miles away from our home in Hillcrest, began to call me regularly to substitute teach. This area at the time contained perhaps the highest concentration of public housing in the entire city. Of the school's population of close to 2000 students, more than 90% were African American with a high percentage of them from low income single-parent families struggling to make ends meet.

Though my areas of expertise and teacher certification were in secondary education and public speaking, I could be called mornings on the spur of the moment to teach almost any subject. Two of my earliest assignments at Ballou High School were month-long assignments in courses for which I was totally unprepared— Spanish and Mechanical Drawing! I'd keep one lesson ahead with the Spanish classes, who I learned had driven out their former benighted Spanish teacher. I was upfront with the kids about how little I knew of Spanish, and somehow I got through those weeks-long assignments mostly by keeping one step ahead of the students in their textbook until the principal was able to find a real Spanish teacher!!

As for my teaching mechanical drawing (about which I knew next to nothing), I used the skills I'd learned in the art and calligraphy courses I'd taken while with Dan and the children in Chicago, and had the class spend those weeks practicing the proper printing techniques for technical, architectural drawings. Somehow I was able to keep those classrooms, which were full of mostly 10th and 11th grade African American boys, engaged. The students were fun, even if at times quite noisy, and I guess they could tell that I liked them and was doing my best until a real mechanical drawing teacher could be found. As desperate as the administrators were for decent substitutes, I don't think they cared what I taught the kids. As long as I was able to keep students reasonably quiet and within the confines of the classroom!

My being white wasn't a problem, it seemed. I learned early on, though, that kids of all ages are phenomenal B.S. detectors. They know when you like and care about them, when you're straight with them, and when you're not. I came eventually to enjoy teaching the kids at Ballou. They and every adult who taught there learned early on that almost all schools located in

Southeast got what was considered the bottom of the barrel when it came to books, supplies, sufficiently trained personnel, athletic equipment, musical instruments— you name it, the school was invariably in short supply. Parents in predominantly middle-class schools would never have put up with the shortages that are commonplace for teachers and students in schools like those in Southeast D.

The real acid test with the students I substitute taught at Ballou came in the spring of 1968, our third year living in D.C. I'd been asked by one of the teachers to cover her junior and senior English classes over the ten-day Easter holidays while she and her husband were in Europe. I was to begin on Monday, April 8. On Thursday, April 4, however, an event took place countrywide that shook me to the core in any confidence I'd had as a teacher.

The entire country was shocked when we learned that The Rev. Martin Luther King, Jr., who was in Tennessee scheduled to address the striking sanitary workers in Memphis, had just been assassinated. That weekend and for many days after, rioting and looting broke out and fires raged in many areas aimed primarily at white-owned businesses most of which were in areas located in mostly black neighborhoods of Washington. Some of those areas were close to Ballou, but other parts of the city also were set afire, mostly in white-owned black neighborhoods. These outbreaks did not occur in our immediate Hillcrest neighborhood in Southeast, but just three short blocks away from us and in other parts of the Washington area, a military occupation in the form of armed National Guardsmen, sent there by President Lyndon Johnson, were standing guard on corners of busy streets to protect areas from fire and vandalism over much of the city.

It was all both frightening and yet somewhat exciting as my own children and I, and most other people all over town, were glued to our televisions until the fires in many parts of the city were extinguished, the extensive damage began to be assessed, and things began to settle down. Dan was out there somewhere in the city meeting with black and white clergy and also with the churches he was working with attempting to locate food, medical resources, shelter, and emergency clothing for people whose homes and businesses had been burned down. When we hadn't heard from him for many hours, the kids and I were concerned for his safety as the riots continued, but our fears for him proved groundless when we heard the sound of his car entering our garage when he arrived home.

Because the powers that be felt that if kids were in the classroom, they'd not be out in the streets getting arrested for looting or whatever other mayhem they might get into. This meant that I was expected to report to Ballou that Monday to cover Ms. Randolph's English classes. I was both sick-at-heart over the killing of Dr. King, and wondering how, as an unknown, white, substitute teacher in a mostly all-black high school in the heart of much of the rioting, I would be received by the predominantly black English classes I was teaching. I did not know what I was going to say to those students. I was ashamed and heartbroken as a white person at the utter racist stupidity of the white man who'd murdered King and angry, as well, at the loss of an extraordinary Civil Rights leader that King had been.

As for the mindless looting, it was somewhat understandable since some black people, especially those in the poorer neighborhoods, felt that white business owners frequently cheated them. Most of the black people I knew personally were totally disgusted with the loss of credibility the Civil Rights leadership suffered as a result of the looting and the consequent destruction of much needed businesses to people living in the black communities. Many of those businesses would not end up being rebuilt for decades after wards.

I prayed as I drove to Ballou that morning. I guess I was seeking some guidance as to what to do and what to say to those kids who'd once again lost a leader to violence— a man who, I believed, was a man of peace and extraordinary courage. What was I to say to those students when I entered that classroom? What was I to do? Certainly not business as usual. But I guess the look on my face said it all.

When I started to speak to the class, my eyes teared up and my voice broke. I don't remember all that happened that day, but I know I felt not in the least bit threatened. Words were not necessary. They knew how I felt. There was no ugly talk directed at me. Mostly we all talked, with the students sharing their own feelings and experiences in their neighborhoods as well as stopping to hang out by the windows of the classroom to watch the fires and other commotion in the distance. They were shocked— actually disbelieving— to learn that I, too, lived in Southeast rather than out in the suburbs where they assumed all white folks lived. Most of the remainder of those two weeks I spent with those classes went well and without incident. And then, once again, on June 6, 1968, just three months after Martin Luther King's death, it happened again. This time it was Senator Robert Kennedy, President John F. Kennedy's brother and a Civil Rights ally who was gunned down by a political assassin. Would it never end?

CHAPTER 9

Verna Dozier: Believing in Myself

1968 – WASHINGTON, DC

The faculty at Ballou High School, about 100 teachers, was fairly evenly divided between white and black teachers. The most senior teacher in Ballou's English Department was Verna Dozier, who was African American, quite erudite, and had the reputation of being the most demanding teacher in the department. Our school counselors would say that at the beginning of their senior year, students would come to them begging not to be given Ms. Dozier for English because she had the reputation of being the hardest of all the English teachers, and they were afraid they would not pass senior English if she were their teacher. Unfortunately, what they were not told by the other kids was that Ms. Dozier was also a very thorough and outstanding teacher. They would learn much from her.

I not only knew Verna from Ballou, but also from St. Mark's Episcopal Church where she was only one of three or four African Americans who were members there, and where my children and I, and occasionally Dan when he was free, attended church. Verna was an extraordinary person— highly intelligent, articulate, and perceptive. She was also somewhat of an Old Testament scholar, the senior warden at St. Mark's, a leading theologian and lay preacher in the Episcopal church, and author of several books. Had she not been born black and a woman, she no doubt would have become something like a U.S. Senator, Fortune 500 CEO or an Episcopal bishop.

When I was substituting at Ballou, we would occasionally eat lunch together in her classroom. She was years older than I and had a very wry and quick sense of humor. I remember once saying very earnestly to her, as I was expounding indignantly about the latest calamity in the fight for Civil Rights for all people of color: "You know, Verna, I really think black people are basically more moral than we whites are!" She broke out in peals of laughter, leaned over, put her hand on my arm, and still laughing said not unkindly, "Oh, my dear Joan, you are sooo naïve!"

I can still hear her voice. She was so right about my naiveté. What I really meant was that from my experience, black people operated more holistically than whites: thinking as much from their hearts as from their heads. Both of those functions were engaged together more often than just the "logical" parts of their brains. I wouldn't have used those words then because at that point I knew nothing whatsoever about either the brain or the mind. I don't think even neuroscientists in general knew or understood much about brain function and things like the split-brain theory (right and left hemispheres) or other aspects of human consciousness theory at that time.

In early 1970, Verna called to tell me that one of Ballou's candidates for the Urban Teacher Corps, which just had been instituted at Ballou and several other District junior and senior high schools, had unexpectedly dropped out of the program just before it was to start. The eight recent college graduates, who'd been selected to be interns in this two-year program to train teachers specifically for teaching in the inner city, would have the opportunity to earn a master's degree in teaching through one of the universities in D.C. Would I be interested in taking this person's place?

Teaching at the high school level in the District of Columbia required a master's degree. Though I had completed college with a double major in speech, English, and secondary education and hoped to teach someday, I really hadn't seriously considered ever going back to graduate school for an advanced degree. I always enjoyed learning and had graduated Phi Beta Kappa with honors, but I'd always dreaded studying for tests and writing the endless required papers. I still occasionally have dreams— nightmares, actually— about having to take some test I'd forgotten to study for.

Though joining the Urban Teacher Corps was a totally unplanned undertaking for me, thanks to the financial assistance available as part of the program, it would be an excellent opportunity to earn a master's degree I ordinarily could never have afforded. It would be a lot of work: lesson planning, on-the-job teaching, regular observations by the supervising teachers and other interns, plus two years of additional graduate courses for two summers and during the school years to meet the university's master's requirements, as well. Most importantly, I still had three young children to raise, though Ann-Mari was now about to start first grade, Elizabeth, 3rd grade, and Eric to begin 5th grade. How could I handle all the additional time and work?

I had to give Verna an answer the next day or two. When Dan got home from work that evening, I talked it over with him. He was his usual, busy clergyman-self, but he said he was willing to take over some of my household meal planning duties so that we could take advantage of this opportunity. I would then be able to handle the workload at home. The next morning, I felt like I was jumping off a bridge as I took in a deep breath and called Verna back to say, "Count me in!"

When I showed up for the introduction to the Urban Teacher Corps Program, I was not prepared when I met the other people on my English Department team. I was definitely the oldest at thirty-five. They all seemed so very young— recent college graduates, fresh out of college and all of them white in our English group. I was thankful I'd already had the teaching experience that I'd had as a substitute and in college. Though I had taken the

32 hours of secondary course credits in college including practice teaching, as any new teacher will tell you, that hardly begins to ready teachers for what they will encounter when they begin teaching for the first time. Unfortunately, too many teachers say that their college course work in secondary education was a total waste of time for the most part.

The time I spent in the Urban Teacher Corps, however, was extraordinary. Our English teams had the opportunity to try some very creative approaches to learning, especially with the large percentage of African American students, many of whom came from poor homes supported primarily by single parents or grandparents. Ballou is located in one of the most impoverished and crime-ridden areas of Washington. The Teacher Corps encouraged non-traditional approaches to learning, some as simple and effective as seating arrangements where students were allowed to choose their own chair/desks and sat sometimes in circles and other times in large semi-circles to encourage more open, class discussion and connection to others. Chairs were often arranged in small circles where students worked cooperatively on assignments and discussions. It was much harder for some students to hide out and not participate in those small groups.

Since many of our students had never read a whole book of any kind in its entirety by 10th grade, high interest literature was often selected on various reading levels, often by black writers about the experiences of black people in this country. They learned about the Harlem Renaissance, that period in the 20s and 30s when African American poets, artists, writers and musicians flourished— people largely ignored by white literary critics in those days and by some even today. We didn't aim for teaching the classics necessarily, the standard fare commonly used in most schools across the nation. Our goal was to get students wanting to read— learning that reading could be enjoyable, sometimes actually exciting, and could lead to discussions relating to their own lives and problems. And more importantly, having their reading levels increased.

Half of the day, we interns taught three courses and worked on lesson plans the rest of the time under the supervision of excellent, experienced teachers like Verna Dozier, the lead teacher. Frequently working in couples, we attempted to co-plan and team-teach creative lessons and high-interest learning activities when teaching literature, grammar, and writing. It was a teacher's heaven to have that kind of time to prepare creative lessons and unfortunately nothing like the real world!

Interns were encouraged to pay attention to their own tendency to do all the talking, the traditional lecture style, in their classes. Several times our UTC supervisors came into our classes, not just for routine observations of our teaching but armed with grids drawn on paper, each representing the teacher and each of the students. They sat unobtrusively plotting out who (teacher or student) was doing the talking at any given time to show to the teacher later how often they were doing most of the talking and how much attention they'd paid to encouraging the students to participate. It could be embarrassing for us to see how much non-stop talking we did as teachers.

One of the most useful "teaching" skills I learned was how to avoid if possible confronting troublesome students in the presence of their peers, but rather stepping outside of the class with them or addressing the problem at class end. It worked wonders to keep the confrontation from escalating out of hand to something really ugly. And a good personal sense of humor helped tremendously, too— always remembering these were adolescents I was dealing with!

Usually exhausted when I got home to my own family, I still had lesson plans and paper grading to do for the three sophomore English classes I was responsible for the next day. It was a huge help that Dan usually was there with dinner ready. But then he'd often be gone again in the evenings with meetings and more meetings.

I had to skip the two weeks of lovely summer vacation we usually spent at the farm we frequently rented in Vermont. Dan went up there with the kids those two summers, where they swam in the beaver pond every day, visited the Finnish farm family down the road whom we'd known for many years and who had an authentic sauna that they shared with us. He and the kids rented a horse for a week to ride while they were there. And I, at home in D.C.'s city heat, was working on the remainder of courses in graduate school to complete the requirements for my master's degree.

1971 Washington, DC

Those two years raced by, and upon completion of my course work, I received a MA in teaching from Trinity University. That summer, I was hired by the D.C. public schools to teach 10th and 11th grade English at my Ballou Senior High School. Oddly enough, the D.C. school system did not offer to our secondary level students an elective course in public speaking, even though that was a serious deficiency for many Southeast students because they lost out on front office jobs in businesses and certain government jobs after graduation due to their lack of standard English business speaking skills and consequently were often relegated to behind-the-scenes filing jobs after high school.

Our children, now 13, 11, and 8, had been spared the ugliness and potential scandal of Dan's sexual relationship with Julie, one of his confirmands who became pregnant by him during that period in New York before we left St. Paul's and were able to escape to the slums of Chicago. Sometimes, however, I wondered about Eric, our oldest child and a very intelligent and sensitive four-year-old during the period when Dan was having a relationship with our babysitter. Dan had frequently taken him to get ice cream and probably visit with Julie, our babysitter, who worked at the Carvel Ice Cream store in New York. I wondered sometimes what, if anything, might he have seen or intuited between his father and Julie!And now in 1971, eight years after I'd been through the heartbreak and trauma of Dan's affair with Julie, he still had never expressed any regret, sorrow, or even an apology to me for what he'd done to our relationship, to me, and to my sense of myself as a desirable woman.

After leaving St. Paul's, I never caught wind of any whispers or suspicions about his relationship with Julie from any former church members. It seemed as though to Dan, the whole tragic affair had never happened. But of course, it had— at least for me, it's possible emotional impact on our kids, and undoubtedly for Julie, as well. After that evening before I knew anything of her relationship with Dan when she'd come over to my house to talk to me about her possibly reclaiming her baby girl, I never again had the opportunity to talk with her about Dan.

Initially I'd attempted to mitigate the responsibility for Dan's involvement with Julie in my mind by partially blaming her for "seducing" him. She had often been seen hanging around the church office, at least according to Lyle when he initially assured me of the innocence of Dan's relationship with her. Eventually, however, I came to realize that Julie had been a victim, too, and possibly even more than I. Dan had been not just any thirty-five-year-old, married man and she a very young girl, but he'd been her pastor whom probably at some time, like so many other young girls in our church, she'd probably idolized him, had him on a pedestal just as I'd once believed. There could be no excuses for his betrayal of me and Julie!

As her pastor who had confirmed her, he was supposed to be her spiritual leader, someone she could trust and whom she probably loved. At 16, she'd had to leave home for six months to hide her pregnancy from her friends and the community and then had been coerced into giving up her baby for adoption. The loss of her first child, a daughter, to strangers was a loss she would never wholly forget, nor would I. Somewhere, probably here in the Washington area, my children, now grown, have a half-sister almost the same age as my youngest daughter about whom for years they knew nothing. I still wonder at times about the evening she'd come to see me soon after she'd had her baby, wanting advice from me about whether to take back her baby from the people who'd adopted her. There was a small window of time left when she could have changed her mind before the adoption became final.

Dan and I always had gotten along together, usually laughed at the same kind of things, and shared many of the same interests besides the lives of our children; his interest in me, however, both emotionally and sexually, seemed totally devoid of any real intimacy. So things remained just as they had been when we were living first in Pennsylvania, then New York, Chicago, and now in Washington, much to my disappointment.

We continued to avoid the whole "incident" of Dan's relationship with Julie. I never knew how he felt about it, whether he ever was in contact with her, nor how he felt about anything else, for that matter. Though we still shared a bed, we had sex only two or three times a year. I was sure I was probably the only woman on the planet who could honestly claim, though sadly and ruefully, that I'd never had need to use the "headache" excuse in order to avoid sex with my husband in all our years together as I'd heard other women joke about doing. And I certainly say that with no pride.

Though I tried to brush aside thoughts of possible current infidelities on Dan's part, sometimes I wondered about it. The implicit trust I'd once had in him seemed totally broken. Though I'd not given up hope that it could be restored since I still loved him and doubted that would ever change, there was always an empty place inside me regarding our relationship. I remember feeling envious when the wife of a clergy couple we knew quite well was showing me their newly decorated bedroom. I'd inquired quite innocently about the need for the several partially burned candles on tables in their bedroom, and Norma replied with a teasing smile and tone in her voice, "They're for atmosphere. We call this our 'sex room.'" I was surprised at her candor and I was also rather envious. How I wished that Dan and I had needed and desired candlelight for a romantic atmosphere in our bedroom.

During my sixteen-year marriage, I'd occasionally sensed other men's attraction to me, but no one had ever been directly outspoken about his feelings nor made a pass at me. From the time I was a teenager, I'd believed that I didn't know anything about flirting; I'd viewed flirting as a kind of art, a talent some girls seem to possess but that I didn't think I had. Besides, conscious flirting always seemed so contrived and even a dishonest game that some women played— at least in the movies. I'd never had the self-confidence nor the inclination to be straightforward with someone I was attracted to, probably for fear of being rejected. Though technically I'd initiated my relationship with Dan years ago by inviting him to a Sadie Hawkins Day sock hop, I'd used it only as a ploy to get back together with my ex-fiancé' Ken; I'd never anticipated falling in love with Dan. I had believed early on that it was always the man's place to make the first moves in any sort of romantic relationship.

Now, I was no longer just a somewhat invisible minister's wife and mother of three, but also an inner-city high school English teacher, a member of the Board of Southeast Neighbors, our local community organization, and a church member (though technically not an Episcopalian) at St. Mark's without the burden of playing the role of minister's wife. These were all places where I had identities in my own right beyond my home, three children, and my husband's career. Given the sad history of my marriage to a man so seemingly indifferent to me except as the mother of his children, it was not surprising that the inevitable would happen, and it did. I began working with a man on the Southeast Neighbors committee, whom I found increasingly attractive as I sensed he did toward me. Eventually he became unmistakably outspoken about his interest in me, and we had a brief affair. Men, I had learned early on, are somewhat reluctant to "hit on" the minister's wife, but they can be very attracted to the challenge. It was as though they thought we were some different breed of cat than most women.

Though some people call them flings and others call them affairs depending, perhaps, on how long they last and how serious they are, both are terms for describing breaches of fidelity— actually betrayals of one's partner if you are in a committed relationship together, though many might invent extenuating circumstances to justify them. Given the circumstances of Dan's betrayal of me and the seeming absence of any sense of guilt by him, it was fairly easy for me to justify my own fling outside our marriage as far as Dan was concerned. After all, I reasoned, I wasn't giving away any part of me that he seemed to want anyway, so I felt little guilt since he seemed to have no remorse over what he'd done to me early on. But an empty, short-term affair was not what I was looking for in a relationship, even with an attractive man. And I worried about how I could explain my having an affair to my children should they ever find out.

And there was guilt. What I couldn't reckon with was the guilt I felt toward the woman who the man was married to— his wife. What plagued me was how, given the extreme pain I'd gone through with Dan's betrayal of me, I could justify doing something, if not as egregious as his had been, at least similar to and been a party to the betrayal of another woman—and the great pain it would probably cause her if she found out. It was especially difficult because, though she wasn't a friend of mine, I'd met the man's wife at several community functions, which made me still feel like a first-class rat! I couldn't pretend she didn't exist.

Given my upbringing, my own spiritual beliefs, and my own heartbreaking experience of Dan's infidelity, I could not square my actions with my own beliefs about who I was or at least who I wanted to think I was. I was not cut out to be the other woman, even though it fulfilled a need in me to feel loved and desired sexually which I rarely felt in my marriage. I felt quite conflicted about it all. I knew I had to do something about this situation— either to learn to live with an emotionally empty relationship with Dan as things were or learn to live without him. I decided to go back into therapy.

I'd seen a therapist a few times since moving, but Dan was not interested in getting couple's counseling. Since he didn't want to discuss our relationship, the therapist's only concrete advice to me, besides possibly a divorce, was to take a lover. I was taken aback especially since the therapist had been serious. Though the mid-to-late sixties had brought with it not only the Civil Rights Movement and Vietnam, but also the beginning of the Women's Movement and the whole sexual revolution, I was neither a bra-burning feminist nor a supporter of three- or four-some sexual couplings. Consequently, I thought the therapist's suggestion surprising— something a woman would understandably do if her husband had been wounded in a war or something and was now incapable of sex. I'd always wanted a relationship with a man who not only loved and felt genuine passion toward me, but also real interest in me intellectually and emotionally— certainly not just someone who was there only for an occasional roll in the hay.

Since my insurance didn't cover routine therapy with an individual therapist, I chose to be part of a therapy group consisting of seven or eight other people led initially by a woman therapist who was a gifted practitioner of something called Gestalt Therapy, something I'd never heard of before then. Though I'd thought it a waste of time and money to have to listen to other people's problems (what they called "the hot seat" when the therapist homed in on a single individual's situation), I eventually realized that I learned quite a lot about myself from their interactions with her. Being on the hot seat was a daunting experience requiring that one not only share very personal things with the group regarding what was going on in one's life, but actually attempt to go back into the old emotions of that experience. What the therapist was after, I believe, was for an individual to shed the false persona people build up over a lifetime to meet the expectations of others— first our parents, then teachers, friends, lovers, the world— and we end up not really knowing who we are.

Entering any extended period of therapy with a skilled therapist is the beginning of a search for one's authentic self even though most people don't realize that initially. This is especially true about minister's wives about whom a congregation may have a whole system of expectations or possibly even think is such a sweet nothing bore that they don't even think much about her at all. And as a minister's wife, especially Dan's wife, I knew well what living inauthentically felt like. I'd had much practice pretending our relationship was fine to the outside world. And yes, I had lost track of who I really was, if indeed I'd ever actually known it.

That search was not fun, but eventually for me it was very worthwhile. And I discovered that the more I learned about myself emotionally, psychologically, and spiritually, the more inclined I was to tell the truth about what was so for me about almost everything (with the exception, at the time, of the secrets concerning Dan's past and our relationship, though I did share that with my therapy group). I stayed with the group twice a week and occasionally in individual counseling for several years.

CHAPTER 10

Here We Go Again

1971 – WASHINGTON, DC

D an came home one evening and told me that an opening as pastor of a Lutheran church in Georgetown had become available, and he was thinking of leaving his work with the Lutheran Planning Council and returning to the pulpit of that particular congregation if he got called there. Many church members had moved out to the suburbs, and now there were only about 50 active members in the congregation, a large number of them over 60. Dan believed that there were lots of possibilities for this seemingly dying congregation in Georgetown with a forward-looking minister there. Because of the uncertain state of our relationship and because I was happy attending church at St. Mark's, I was not eager to return to a parish situation where I would have to resume pretending despite the tenuousness of our marriage.

I knew that if I became active in any way, I would come to like the people there, as I always had in previous churches, and if we did separate, it would make going through the inevitable explanations about separating so much harder. I was willing to support him, however, when that congregation, which was eager to have a full-time pastor again, extended a call to Dan to be their pastor. The agreement was that I would not have to attend church there on a regular basis nor be involved as Dan's wife with the women's group, Sunday school, or choir. I knew that the congregation would probably view me as "odd" or a really unsupportive, almost "disloyal" minister's wife and would probably pity Dan his hardship being married to me. All of this made me uncomfortable, but that's the way it was. I was just tired of pretending, and I enjoyed having an identity at St. Mark's as something other than the minister's wife.

We still used our home phone number as Dan's number where he could be reached when he was not at church, and I was frequently answering that phone when the secretary was not at the church office and I wasn't at school teaching. At some point near the end of Dan's first year at Georgetown, he began getting what I thought were an inordinate number of calls at the house from a young woman named Jackie. When I asked Dan who she was and why she called so frequently, Dan explained that she was having serious marital problems and he'd been counseling with her and her husband. Though hints of alarm began going off in my mind, Dan assured me that there was nothing untoward about the frequency of her meetings or calls. Because of his natural talent as a preacher, Dan began to attract a wider and younger audience on Sunday mornings. In order to begin reaching this younger membership, he planned activities including a larger variety of music such as jazz, blue grass, and folk music on Sundays and for special concerts. There were also trips to current movie-discussion offerings featuring wine and cheese after viewing the film, which I attended and invited my friend Nikki to join me. The two of us drove to Georgetown in her car since Dan had taken our car needing to be there much earlier than I.

While standing in line with his group from church, waiting to get into the movie theatre, Dan introduced us to the rest of the group. With them was a young woman in her late twenties whom I didn't recognize. I found her staring at me frequently and then again during the rest of the evening, and my intuition told me that she was the "Jackie Bell" of the many home phone calls that Dan had been getting. Sure enough when we were introduced, it was that Ms. Bell, and her frequent staring at me continued after the film and back at church during the discussion of the film over wine and cheese.

When the evening was over shortly before eleven and we were all saying goodbye, Dan turned to her and asked, "Where are you parked, Jackie?"

"Two blocks away," she replied.

"That's too far for you to walk this late at night," Dan replied, "Since Joan's driving home with Nikki, I'll just drop you off at your car on my way home."

And so, it was settled though it felt very much like a kind of set up to me as Nikki and I were driving home. When Nikki dropped me off at the house about 11:15, I didn't invite her in. In anticipation of the guests we were expecting that evening from out-of-town, I quickly began picking up the messy living room that the kids had left behind earlier in the evening before going to bed. Our good friend, Lyle, our former youth director when we were at St. Paul's, had been ordained into the ministry while we were living in Chicago. He was now serving a church in Brooklyn and was bringing his fiancée, June, whom Dan and I had never met before, but they'd not yet arrived.

It was now 11:30, and I was expecting Dan any minute since he was only dropping Jackie Bell at her car and knew we were expecting Lyle and June. As the minutes ticked by and it was going on 12 Midnight, I wondered if he'd had car trouble or an accident, and then more and more as the time stretched out and still no word from Dan, I began to suspect that he was involved in some way with Ms. Bell. By the time Lyle and June showed up around 12:30 am. and I'd still not heard from Dan, I was sick inside with anxiety, eventually sadness, and the later it got, anger.

It seemed once again to me that I was facing the same emotional upheaval that I had endured eight years before in New York. Lyle knew me well enough to sense that I was upset by Dan's absence and the lateness of the hour. It was difficult to carry on a normal conversation with him and June with my mind totally elsewhere and not on our guests feeling as I did, and especially since June and I had never met before that evening.

Shortly after 1:00 am. I heard Dan's key in the front door lock, and as he came into the living room, he began greeting Lyle and June as though nothing was unusual. What came out of my mouth surprised me as much as it did everyone else.

"Dan, I want a divorce!" I blurted out, realizing I had lost total control over what I'd been thinking and what I was saying. No one said anything at first as the words sank into the silence. Talk about a pregnant pause!

Then Dan began to cover over my statement with demurrals. "Joan, you don't mean that…"

"Yes, I do!" I replied adamantly.

"We'll talk about it tomorrow." Dan answered cutting off the exchange. I'm sure even Lyle was taken by surprise, even though he knew the whole back-story about Julie and Dan eight years earlier.

As for poor June, who knew neither Dan nor me, shocked would have put it mildly. She must have thought she'd just entered some kind of ministerial nut house. This was neither the time nor place to begin a conversation about what had just transpired. Dan had to have known why I was so unhinged, but I have no recollection of what happened between us after my outburst. Probably Lyle and June went to bed as quickly as possible. The next morning, I made breakfast for all of us, including the kids, and nothing further was said about the previous evening.

After Lyle and June left, Dan and I talked briefly about his relationship with Jackie Bell, a woman in her late 20s. He told me only that she was having a tough time in her marriage, and that there was nothing going on between them. But then when I told him I didn't believe him, he finally acknowledged that they had lunch together "several times," but he made no real effort to dissuade me from thinking the worst. I've wondered occasionally since then if perhaps I'd been wrong, that possibly I'd misjudged him, but at that point I just didn't care. I'd had enough uncertainty about Dan and his lack of capacity for a committed, loving relationship with me. I felt sure that if our marriage wasn't on its last legs now, it certainly would only be a matter of time until he left me for another woman and undoubtedly a much younger one.

I also knew that at my age, my chances for starting a new life and marriage with someone else were almost negligible, especially here in Washington with many more single women than men and a city with the notorious reputation for men more interested in short term relationships. With this new dalliance of Dan's— if that's the right word— my love for him had finally seemed to breathe its last breath and quite simply died of malnutrition— the absence of the nurturing, emotional connection, care, and interest essential to any really loving relationship. I just didn't care anymore. Mostly I felt sadly numb.

My outburst in front of Lyle and June had been unexpected even to me— unplanned, and with no thought about how I would explain this to our children or how it would affect them. Throughout our marriage from the time I'd learned about Dan's relationship with Julie, the glue that had held our marriage together had been my love for him and the damage divorce would do to the kids. Divorce had never been a part of the plan for my life. I thought I would marry a man who loved me as deeply as I loved him and have a family.

When I met Dan, I thought I'd found a truly exceptional man, a bright, wonderful, gentle man, someone totally different from Ken, who'd always found so much to criticize about me. He was a man unlike anyone else I'd ever known or loved before. Those were my thoughts when I was twenty-one years-old, a relatively inexperienced virgin who'd thought on my wedding day as I stood holding the arm of my father and looking down the aisle at my beloved Dan that I was the luckiest girl alive to be getting a man who truly loved me and who I would never have doubts about when it came to his fidelity to me: this was a man I'd spent all of just eight or nine weeks getting to know face to face before he moved many hundreds of miles away to take charge of his first congregation.

At some point, shortly after Lyle and June had headed back to New York, Dan and I began to talk more freely. He finally indicated a willingness to get some marriage counseling. After the numerous times during the past 15 years that I'd wanted us to get counseling, his suggestion now, coming as it did after yet another possible affair— or whatever his relationship with this Jackie woman was or had been— it felt like closing the barn door after the horse had escaped. I should have felt exhilarated, hopeful, but somehow I felt nothing. Now he was even willing to at least start with the therapist I'd been seeing, which eventually we did. I did not want to turn my back on this offer of his, but my heart wasn't in it.

My therapist strongly suggested to me privately that for honesty's sake I should be upfront with Dan about the brief affair I'd had. Though I had my doubts about the advisability of this! I finally told him in the car on our way home from the therapy session. To my surprise he didn't believe me. I don't know if he thought I was too pure to have had an affair or if he thought I wasn't sexy enough for some man to even have propositioned me.

At any rate, I felt somewhat indignant that he doubted me, but not nearly as upset with him as I was when, on the way home from counseling the following week, he suggested that we not get a divorce but instead have an open marriage where we were both free to have sexual relationships outside of our marriage. I could hardly believe what he was saying, and I felt deeply hurt that he seemed to care so little about me that he was willing to do that. With our children still at home, I could also not imagine doing that and risk their finding out that I was having an affair with someone other than their father. And that this was an acceptable arrangement that we'd agreed on? What was he thinking? What sort of example of marriage and relationships would that set for them, and especially now that they were entering into adolescence? Was this what the so-called sexual revolution, that was upon us in this country, was all about?

Dan's suggestion about an open marriage became for me the death knell of our marriage. The emotional difficulty that I am having as I write this part of our story comes as a surprise to me these many years later. So much heaviness in my chest as I breathe. Many times I have wondered if somehow I missed some cue years ago— that I'd misunderstood Dan's intent— that all along he really did love me but could just not express his feelings— that my telling him of a rather meaningless fling that I had with someone I didn't really love— maybe that had been the kiss of death for him regarding our relationship. But then I realized that was just wishful thinking on my part.

I shared with my therapy group my response to Dan's coming home hours late after "dropping off" that woman at her car— the anger inside that I felt. Responding to my flat affect, the therapist, at that point, handed me one of those tightly stuffed, heavily padded devices called a "bataka," a flat bat that therapists sometimes use to help clients release the stored up negative energy in their bodies from the anger they may consciously or unconsciously have but are unable to express. The client pounds the bat, flailing it repeatedly on the floor to mentally whack the person or object they are angry with. Using that method to get in touch with and release long-buried negative feelings may seem bizarre, but it can be very effective and much safer than many other ways of either suppressing the anger, turning it against oneself, or expressing strong, negative feelings toward another person.

And so, using the harmless bataka, at first very dispiritedly, little by little I began to strike the floor more and more forcefully and began to give voice to the rising anger inside me. I began expressing some of the rage, hurt, and sorrow that had been buried inside me toward Dan for so long. I was exhausted when I was ready to stop— my anger spent.

That evening I shared with Dan what had occurred in my group that afternoon. I guess I hoped to get some response from him by way of understanding how extremely angry and upset I'd been the evening of the movie when he'd been almost two hours late coming home after dropping off the young woman who'd called so frequently. His response to my venting my anger at him using the harmless bataka bat and the floor (as a kind of surrogate for him) was to view it as kind of a joke. He laughed. And I came to realize that this had always been Dan's way of responding to someone else's strong emotions— fake it, especially if they were aimed at him.

The only personal incident he ever shared about himself vis-a-vis his family was in one of the counseling sessions we had with the therapist shortly before we separated. His reluctance (or perhaps it was an inability) to show any strong emotions had started when he was ten or eleven. His two older brothers used to tease him unmercifully when he was younger, and he would scream and cry in protest. Then they would make fun of him about his temper and his crying. He said it was then that he simply shut down and refused ever to show negative feelings.

Though our marriage counseling, as brief as it was, had seemingly not been successful from the standpoint of our marriage, at least it had helped convince Dan that he needed more therapy, and soon after, he joined a different counseling group conducted by the same therapist. Shortly thereafter we decided we needed to tell our children what was happening between us.

Telling our children must be a moment that sadness has almost wiped from my mind, for I'm having great difficulty remembering what the tearing apart of our family looked like, sounded like, felt like— sharing our decision to separate and how that took place. Perhaps I expected some big, uproar of protest, but I remember only deafening silence. Ann-Mari and Elizabeth just sat there silently on the couch as we gave them the news that we were separating. They just looked at us. They had few if any questions.

Eric would not be present until later that evening (though I cannot now understand why we didn't wait until Eric got home from visiting Dan's family and his cousins in Pennsylvania for a week before telling them all together.) We told him that evening on the way home from the airport of all places after picking him up. What a rotten homecoming surprise! What must we have been thinking to spring this on him so suddenly!

I do remember Dan's response in the situation. He, too, said little if anything, but below the surface I could hear from his sarcastic tone that he was angry; and in truth, though it wasn't always evident, the anger was often close to the surface thereafter. Divorce was not as prevalent then as it is now, so perhaps the girls' lack of reaction was due to not really understanding what lay ahead for them and our family. But then why should they? I certainly didn't. All I knew was that I could not go on forever with an empty, false relationship with Dan, putting up with affairs and waiting— expecting— that sooner or later he would leave me for someone else.

Prior to that time, there'd been no loud fights or arguments between Dan and me to give the kids clues that our marriage was in trouble. Dan's reluctance to ever honestly discuss his feelings about me and about his affair with our babysitter, or mine about my fear of his leaving me and our children, were probably a good part of the emotional distance between us. Perhaps if we'd ever had the normal arguments about all sorts of issues in our marriage— not just the devastating effects of his affair with Julie and his silence both before it began and afterwards— we might have had a chance to mend our relationship, but there was no real emotional honesty between us.

For years I had taken responsibility, somehow, for his disinterest in me sexually and emotionally. I believed for years that I just wasn't sexually attractive— that if I had been "different" in some way (though lord knows, I hadn't a clue what that different would have looked like) then maybe he would have loved me in a way that I recognized as loving me. Or if we'd ever had really intensive couple's therapy early on perhaps... perhaps... perhaps.

But we hadn't. And there was also the issue of money. We had none. Standard health insurance didn't cover that sort of relational therapy. One almost would have had to be on the verge of being institutionalized before insurance companies might cover the costs. And I'm not even sure they had such a thing as marital therapy back then, and even if they did, it was something Dan avoided like the plague, and I didn't entirely trust. The therapist who recommended that I "take a lover" suggested that Dan should go into intensive psychoanalysis. Not much chance of either happening!

I've wondered if the children ever sensed that anything was not as it should be between Dan and me. Whatever emotional fallout our children may eventually have incurred, Eric, being the oldest at the time and just four years old, was the most vulnerable. Dan frequently had taken him over to the Carvel Ice Cream place where Julie worked; I'll never know what, if anything, Eric had seen or heard between them. But kids can be pretty intuitive even at four, certainly ones as sensitive and intelligent as he was, especially when I would break into tears at least once every day for many months after learning of Dan's fathering of Julie's baby.

I had made the decision years earlier not to tell our children about what had happened in our marriage to cause us to leave St. Paul's— certainly not until they were adults and old enough to process that information more maturely. I did not want to prejudice them against their father whom they loved and needed very much. I also did not inform my in-laws, Dan's family, about the reasons for our divorce. They both were very old and sick, and I saw nothing to be gained at this stage of their lives.

But sometimes it wasn't easy to keep quiet. I remember a time after Dan and I had recently separated. Eric was in his early teens, and we were having an argument of some sort about the usual kinds of things parents and teenagers argue about. I must have been after Eric about not doing chores. He yelled back at me, "Nag! Nag!! That's all you ever do is nag. It's no wonder Dad left you!"

Even though logically I knew that in truth it had been I who instigated the separation, it still really hurt to hear Eric say that. Sometimes kids seem to unerringly sense where to stick the knife in for it to be most effective. Obviously despite what I'd learned in therapy, there was still a small voice inside that said "If you'd only been a 'better' wife, then Dan would have loved you more and all this wouldn't have happened!"

In the early 70s when divorces began to be quite common, the child rearing wisdom stated that it was better for parents to separate than for their children to experience dissension in the family between their parents. It wasn't until considerably later that the new experts stated that teenaged boys were especially vulnerable when families broke up. They especially needed their fathers at that stage of life. It certainly was true in our family as I would later learn.

It had been such a slow, silent, emotional death between Dan and me that I had scarcely been aware of it until his relationship with yet another woman from his church had become evident. So it's no surprise that the children were taken totally unawares when we announced that we were officially separating. Up to that point, I'd never given much, if any, thought about what separating from Dan would look like— who would live where? Who would pay for what? How we would support two households on two mediocre salaries, Dan's as a pastor and mine as a teacher. With three adolescent children, how would we now pay for private school since by this time we were paying partial tuition(with scholarships) at a small Episcopal integrated high school in Accokeek, Maryland.

Sending our children to middle and senior high school in Southeast, where there were far fewer, if any, white students was a different matter, however, than the elementary school experience in Southeast schools that had been so positive. Now that they were entering their teens, we felt that they should go to a school where they were not in such an extreme minority, and perhaps where they'd be challenged academically more.

We agreed that our separation would be easier on the children if they continued living at home with me. Dan would get an apartment closer to church, would continue to see the kids regularly and be with them on holidays, and they would go on Sundays to the Lutheran church where Dan now served as pastor. Since we didn't want to tear up their lives any more than necessary, we didn't even consider any alternative to legally sharing custody of them equally. Although it wasn't really equal sharing. Most of the parenting was done by me, as it always had been, because Dan's work schedule often extended into evening meetings and because now he would no longer be living at our house. Now I would be responsible for the children six days a week except, perhaps, on Sunday mornings and afternoons when they were with their father. It would not be easy, especially when I was also teaching full-time.

1973 Washington, DC

After Dan found an apartment and moved out with a modest amount of furniture, household utensils, and his books, we began to discuss drawing up a separation agreement. We knew we would eventually need a lawyer somewhere along the way, but since we were basically in agreement about the important issues including my continuing to live in the house with the kids, assuming the mortgage and utilities payments, and Dan paying child support and half of their school tuition until the children had grown up and left home, we agreed that having separate lawyers was not necessary. We would determine the value of the house at the time of our separation, and if I should remarry after the children were grown, I would pay Dan half of the value of the house at the time we separated. That it had been my parent's loan/gift of $3000 was never made part of our settlement discussions.

I made an appointment with a highly recommended lawyer, David Austern, who, after meeting with me and then with Dan, and seeing that there was very little in contention about the issues of the separation agreement between us, agreed to draw up the necessary documents and represent both of us for just $150, an incredibly small amount. He must have realized how little money we had.

Shortly before we separated, Dan joined a different therapy group, which was run by the same woman we'd been seeing together. Not long thereafter he began dating a young woman, Meara, from his group. Almost fifteen years younger than Dan, she was going through a divorce herself and had two small boys under three. Her financial situation, however, was considerably better than Dan's and mine. She lived in a comfortable-looking house in an upscale section of Northwest D.C. Her former husband (her boys' father) came from a wealthy family; her own parents were also people of considerable means, as well. Since Meara was so much younger than Dan and also of the Jewish faith, I naively thought that this would not be a serious or lasting relationship.

Needless to say, our kids were not happy about our family break-up. Not only did they see their father less frequently with the exception of Sunday mornings at church, but after he began seeing Meara, she frequently came along with her two little boys whenever our kids were scheduled to do something with their father. They did not see him often enough as it was, but it troubled them that those precious times with their Dad since we'd separated were now usually shared with his new girlfriend and her children.

CHAPTER 11

Muriel: Finding my Strength

1973 – WASHINGTON, DC

Life was considerably harder now that I was a single mom with three adolescent children, teaching five English classes a day in Southeast's inner-city, and then having to hurry home to begin thinking about what I could fix for dinner for my own kids that day.

I wasn't much good at planning ahead especially since I also had lesson plans and paper-grading to do for my 150 students at school each day, and helping with my own kids' homework if they asked— though usually they didn't ask me to proofread their writing because they knew I'd want them to make writing changes or corrections. But with only four more weeks until school was out for the summer, I could hang in there a little longer. And with school out, at least I would get the homework monkey off my back. Temperatures often reach into the upper 90s even in May. The hot afternoon sun baked down mercilessly even with the shades drawn and the windows open, and I breathed a deep sigh of relief as I gathered up the pile of student journals from the table in the teachers' lounge.

With three teenagers of my own, paper grading always got postponed till the last minute on Sundays, which was why I dreaded Sunday afternoons and evenings so much. It was time to get my stuff in the classroom and head into the afternoon traffic before the weekend pile-up became unbearable. There's something unnatural, almost eerie, about a silent, empty school building usually so filled with life and noise during the day. My heels echoed off the lockered walls as I approached my classroom, and I was surprised to see my door wide open.

"Muriel," I exclaimed as I entered my room and saw one of my students seated, her shoulders hunched over her desk. "What on earth are you still doing here? It's after four!"

Of all the students in my class, Muriel, a recent enrollee to Ballou, was the person I probably knew least well and was certainly the last one I'd expected to find there in my classroom on this late Friday afternoon. She'd recently transferred into my English class, having just come from St. Thomas in the Virgin Islands. That's all I knew about her since, as was often the case at Ballou, there were no accompanying school records from her former school.

She had a decidedly lilting, Caribbean accent especially difficult for northerners here to understand since she spoke softly and quite fast. Which may have been why she rarely spoke in class, probably getting frustrated at people asking her repeatedly, "What did you say?" as though she spoke some foreign language. Or maybe it was just because she was new...or shy. But she was also very different from the street-wise, local kids with their long Afro hairstyles, hooped earrings, bell bottoms, and often loud, outgoing ways. Quiet, diffident, dressed in simple cotton shorts and a top, Muriel's closely cropped black hair was pulled back straight and tight to her head with two short plaits fastened together with a plastic barrette at the back of her neck. Whether it was the absence of eye make-up or something in her bearing, she seemed so young, almost naive. She had to have been 15 or even 16 to be in my class, but she looked no older than 14.

Seated in her regular seat, her brown arms resting on the desktop, fingers splayed across her face, she didn't answer me when I came in and spoke to her. It was then that I noticed her shoulders shaking as though she were laughing or crying. "Muriel?" I asked again moving closer to her. When she finally looked up at me, her eyes were red, swollen, and wet with tears that covered her face innocent of all make-up. When she opened her lips struggling to speak, her face crumpled and her words were lost in deep, choking sobs that came forth from deep inside her.

Alarmed, I quickly pulled another chair-desk over to where she sat, leaned in closer and put my arm around her as she continued to sob. "What in the world is the matter, Muriel? Tell me, " I implored. She then began to pour out an unbelievable and sometimes difficult-to-understand tale between her broken sobs. Something about her father, the police, rum, and Miss Hughes, our school counselor— all of it in a jumble of words interspersed between more tears. She seemed terrified, and at one point bolted up from her seat over to the window, peering out anxiously and begging me to pull down the shades.

"Muriel," I reasoned, "we're three stories up from the street. No one could possibly see you in here." At that point she was so over-wrought, I was beginning to wonder if she'd taken leave of her senses.

Seemingly reassured that no one out there in the street could see up this high, she calmed down, and I pressed her to speak more slowly so I could better understand her story which became even more unbelievable. She told me that the evening before, her father had forcefully poured quantities of rum down her throat. He then raped her. This morning she'd told him she was going to the police and then back home to her mother in the Virgin Islands, but he told her there was no chance of that. When she left the house for school, she noticed that he began following her in his car, trying to head her off as she ran darting in and out of traffic on Alabama Avenue to avoid him. Eventually he pulled over and began chasing her on foot as she ran out into oncoming traffic to escape him. Two police officers in a cruiser witnessing this chase stopped their squad car and intervened.

Muriel told the officers what had happened at home the night before, while her enraged father shouted that she was a bad girl, a lying whore, and was trying to run away from home. The police took her with them in their car to the police station and had her father brought in another squad car for further questioning. At the station, the two were questioned by officers from what Muriel called the "sex squad." Her father continued to insist she was lying and had been nothing but trouble since he'd brought her here from St. Thomas several weeks before. Muriel had bathed after the attack so there was no evidence available in 1973 to substantiate her story but her word against his, as the police explained, and eventually they released them both. In 1973 in Washington, D.C., a predominantly white police force paid scant attention to violence within the black community, especially when perpetrated against black women. The police did drive Muriel to school where she sought the help of Miss Hughes, a school counselor who had come here from Trinidad. But Hughes told her that there really was nothing she, nor the school system, could do. (Nor, I surmised, did she relish tangling with the likes of her father, whom she'd met when he brought Muriel to Ballou to enroll her—especially not over so explosive an issue as allegations of rape and incest.)

As hard to believe as Muriel's story was, I tended to believe her, especially knowing what I knew of both the D.C. police and the D.C. public schools and their laissez faire about people of color in Southeast. But one needed only to see the real terror in her dark brown eyes to know she was telling the truth.

"I can't go home, Missus Pierotti, he'll kill me, I know he will," she cried as she got up again and, shielding herself from view, looked up and down the street from the window. "I know he's down there waiting, watching for me in his car!"

What to do now? I wondered. I couldn't leave Muriel here in my classroom, and I couldn't take her back to her father's. The only solution seemed to be to take her home with me at least for the weekend. Muriel seemed relieved at my suggestion, the first traces of hope playing at the edges of her frightened face. But she wouldn't walk out to my car in the parking lot. Instead she insisted that I drive around to another entrance where she needed only to take a few steps from the building door into my car. And she wanted to lie down hidden on the floor in the back seat, which she ended up doing. Frankly, I really thought she was over-dramatizing the extent of the danger. I had a bit of a chuckle inside my head at the seeming theatrical quality to this enterprise. Eventually, however, months later, I was to learn that she had not been exaggerating the peril at all.

My own kids, accustomed to strangers staying at our home from time to time, welcomed Muriel without the slightest indication that this was anything unusual. And Muriel, safe and away from the immediate danger of her father, relaxed into the usual nuttiness of a family with three teenagers and a dog, and added her own brand of fun, including her "invention" of a Coca Cola mixed with canned pears which my kids thought was wild. I had some misgivings about being charged with kidnapping or something, but given the circumstances of her being there, it was most unlikely that her father would press charges.

That weekend Muriel shared some more information about her father, whose name, I learned, was Junie. She barely knew him and had seen him only a few times in her life prior to moving to Washington. Born in St. Croix, he and her mother had never lived together as husband and wife. He'd moved to Washington some years before, finding work on occasional construction jobs, and had been down in St. Thomas visiting recently. He had insisted on bringing her back to Washington with him so she could finish high school and get a better job than was available in St. Thomas. Her mother had reluctantly allowed him to take her with him to Washington where he lived a mile or two from Ballou in Stanton Dwellings.

Stanton Dwellings, now mercifully torn down, was a housing project in Southeast Washington— notorious in D.C. as a hot bed of poverty, drugs, crime, and unsolved murders. It had been built by the federal government to house the many thousands of blacks who came up from the South in hopes of finding work after World War ll. The City of Washington, in its infinite planning wisdom had put almost all the public housing for those hundreds of thousands of migrants from the South in Southeast where there was cheap, available land. It was also a place where the newcomers would be out of the way and out of sight of the more fortunate white people in this Federal City. Here Junie lived with his common-law wife, their two-year-old son, and a 12-year-old half-sister of Muriel's from another partner of Junie's. Muriel later spoke of an angry row they'd recently had when Junie brought home a newborn infant belonging to him and another woman and demanded that his common-law wife look after it. The baby's mother was another of Junie's conquests. If Muriel's mother had any idea of where Junie was taking her daughter, she would never have let Muriel go with him.

On Monday, Muriel returned to school with me wearing a fresh change of clothes we'd purchased that weekend. We lived four miles from school and I assured her that there was no way her father could have traced her to my house. Still, leery of being seen by her father whom she was sure was scouring the neighborhoods around school for her, she insisted on traveling hidden on the backseat floor of my car again and of entering the building the same way she'd done on Friday.

And so it went for the next few weeks. I'd spoken with Mrs. Hughes about Muriel's situation, and she had no solutions to offer by way of assistance. Needless to say, I was thoroughly disgusted with the whole school system, including Mrs. Hughes, but not really surprised. That was how they dealt with the problems of the city's poor. Just ignore them and maybe they'll go away. Though Stanton Dwellings has finally been torn down to make room for more upscale, private townhouses in its place, the plight of many of the poor, displaced families has also become worse.)

As if Muriel's perilous circumstances were not enough, I was also in the middle of my separation from Dan. I was caught in a dilemma regarding Muriel. I believed that there were no real opportunities, nor much of a future for her back home, but here in Washington there was nothing either for a girl as vulnerable and unaccustomed to the city as she was. Returning to her father seemed out of the question, but my marital situation, with its attendant financial losses and many emotional adjustments for all of us, made my taking on another child to raise on my teacher's salary an impossibility. I'd needed to speak with Muriel's mother but she didn't have a telephone, so Muriel wrote to her with my telephone number asking her to return the call.

When school let out for the summer, the kids and I, along with Muriel, took a short trip up to Vermont where for a number of years, our family had spent many summer vacations renting an old farmhouse on lush, green, wooded farmland that was no longer being farmed. It was a magical place for all of us, but especially for Muriel who'd never been to a place like this (though her Virgin Islands— I later found out first hand— had their own inestimable beauty.) When we returned home to Washington, we were finally able to reach Muriel's mother. She called Muriel at our house, and Muriel had a chance to tell her some of what had happened to her at the hands of her father.

I, too, spoke to Muriel's mother and told her that I didn't think it was safe for Muriel to continue living in the Stanton Dwellings area of Southeast, not only because of her father, but because of the nature of the neighborhood where he lived. It was difficult enough for kids who were street savvy and had grown up in that area to safely negotiate the drugs and violence of that community, but for and inexperienced girl like Muriel it spelled disaster. When I described the area to her and told her I thought Muriel should return to St. Thomas, she agreed. I said I would do my best to find the money for a plane ticket for her as soon as possible.

Some days later when I was home alone with Muriel, our German short-haired pointer Nicky started raising an awful ruckus, barking for all she was worth and racing furiously back and forth from window to window. I went to the front door and opened it to see a stranger, a short, hefty, mahoga-ny-skinned man with a pock-marked face pacing back and forth on the lawn, about 20 feet from the front door. I knew immediately that this was the in-famous Junie.

"I'm here for Muriel," he shouted as he approached the porch. "I'm her father! I know she's here," he yelled with a distinct challenge in his heavily accented voice. Fear should have been my first instinctive reaction, but it wasn't. It was anger bordering on rage.

"And who told you she was here?" I asked equally challengingly. I couldn't believe that I had so little fear towards this man.

"I've found her. That's all that matters. I want her!" he answered.

I wondered if someone from Ballou, perhaps Mrs. Hughes, who I sensed had mixed feelings about my hi-jacking a student without parental permission. But it seemed Muriel's instincts about her father had been right. He had hung around Ballou, somehow learned that she was living with me, and eventually followed us home.

Muriel stood behind me at the front door, not knowing what to do. I knew her father would not dare to do anything to her in my presence, and I finally opened the door to him knowing that the dog was my back-up. I offered him a seat in my kitchen, and he proceeded to tell me the same cock-and-bull story he'd told to the police. When he finished, I told him Muriel's mother knew that she was here.

"Muriel's mother is dead!! She's been lying to you!"

"Oh, really?" I answered. "That's strange because I just spoke to Muriel's mother in St. Thomas the day before yesterday. I think that you're the liar, unless she spoke to us from the grave." He was flummoxed and speechless. I proceeded to tell him all that I knew about his rape of his daughter as did her mother, and that her mother and I agreed that Muriel should return home.

"And where will she get a ticket to go home?" he demanded.

"I'll buy the ticket as soon as I'm able," I replied

The belligerence in his face fell away. Clearly he was stunned and had little more to say.

"I am going to speak with Muriel," I continued. "It'll be up to her to decide what she wants to do—-stay here in Washington with you or return to her mother. But I promise you that you will end up in jail if you ever lay a hand on her again!" I knew that she would not want to stay with her father; however, seeing that he had been cowed in a way she had not thought possible gave her confidence that she would be safe at least for a short while. She decided to return to her father's house to be with her younger sister and to gather up her belongings.

It's interesting how the mind and our memory play tricks on us, causing a distortion our recollections, and sometimes the reality as we wished it or feared it gets replaced by very different memories. Many years later when Muriel and I were discussing this encounter I'd had with her father, she said, "Oh, I was so surprised. No one ever dared talk to my father the way you did. And was he ever surprised when you pulled out that gun and placed it on the table next to you!"

I was absolutely flabbergasted. "Why, Muriel. I had no gun. I've never owned a gun in my life!" I believe she'd seen my strength in standing up to her father's bullying as something one only dared do with the help of a gun.

Several weeks passed with only an occasional phone conversation from Muriel to let me know everything was quiet at her father's place. She'd had no trouble with her father since my encounter with him at my house. And then one afternoon in late July the phone rang. It was Muriel and she sounded upset. "Missus Pierotti, I have missed two periods now," she said, her voice quavering. "I brought a urine sample to the school nurse, but she never called back about it. I thought everything was O.K." She was clearly frightened and upset. "I don't know what I'll do if I'm pregnant. He'll kill me!" I thought Muriel was perhaps being overly dramatic but her words later proved to be prophetic!

I tried to reassure her that probably she wasn't pregnant. "There could be another reason you missed two periods— perhaps you counted wrong, or it could be something else…" My words trailed off, but I could hear the hollowness in my own voice. I told her we'd do everything we could to keep him from knowing and agreed to come pick her up and bring her home with me. I'd heard that there was a free clinic, which was housed in the basement of a Georgetown church. It was open to anyone who couldn't afford medical help.

After I hung up the phone, I found the number for the clinic and called to see if I could bring Muriel over there. Fortunately, an appointment wasn't necessary. Calling her back, I told her I'd pick her up in front of her house. Before the day was over, we'd brought a fresh, urine sample with us to the clinic, Muriel had been examined by the doctor, and the news was not good. She was, indeed, two months pregnant. My heart sank. The panic is Muriel's voice and eyes was unmistakable. "Missus Pierotti, what will I do if my father finds out? I don't want a baby by him!"

After learning of Muriel's precarious situation at home and that she was only 16, the doctor discussed performing a dilation and curettage— an abortion— with her, which she readily agreed to— anything to protect her from her father's control.

"But can my teacher be with me in the room when you do it please?" she begged of the doctor and to which he agreed. And so that's what I did, holding Muriel's hand throughout the procedure. We then went home to my house where she spent the weekend while she rested up.

Three weeks later, having purchased a plane ticket for her back to the Virgin Islands, I notified her father that she was going home to her mother.

He voiced no objections this time when I went to pick her up, and so with my girls and our dog as the farewell committee, we took her to the airport, and she was safely on her way back home to St. Thomas and to her mother. After saying goodbye to Muriel, I struggled with the question of whether she would have had more opportunities here in the U.S. if I'd been able to take her in as part of my family. But that was a moot question, however, for with my marriage ending, I barely had the financial wherewithal nor emotional energy to take on another teenager. Several months later, however, I received an answer to my inner questioning and the feelings of guilt I'd had regarding the advisability of sending Muriel home when I did.

I opened the morning Post five months later to the local news headline "Wife Killed and Plastered into Wall." As I read the gruesome story, I was shocked when I realized that the victim had been the common-law wife of Muriel's father! Junie had murdered the poor woman, plastered her into the kitchen wall, taken their two-year-old child, and fled the country. Months later he was captured in St. Croix, stood trial, and eventually died in prison in New York some years later.

Since most of what happened to her while she was in D.C. took place during late spring and early summer, no one in Ballou's administration ever learned what had happened either to Muriel or her father, nor my part in her returning to her mother in St. Thomas. Nor did anyone ever ask. But that shouldn't be surprising since during my 23 years at Ballou, we actually had twenty different principals and at least eight school superintendents! The D.C. school system changed principals at Ballou like most people change their underwear.

Even now Muriel and I are still in touch quite regularly. Over the years I have watched her as she finished high school, later married her high school sweetheart after returning to St. Thomas, and worked for many years as the desk clerk at a seaside resort in St. Thomas. She and her husband had three fine children, and my children and their families and I have visited them in St. Thomas a number of times over the years. I have never had any regrets about sending her back to her home when I did.

CHAPTER 12

Don't Cry, Kid, Swear!

1974 – WASHINGTON, DC

From my diary in July, 1974, one of my worst days as a new single parent.

Diary,

First thing this morning, the doorbell rang. It was a man from the gas company who'd come to disconnect our gas because I hadn't paid the bill for several months!! It never occurred to me that they'd actually do that. I had to give the man $150 immediately!! ($50 of which was a deposit that I'll lose if I'm late again within the next 18 months!) That pretty much cleans me out till payday.

Then Eric and I had an ugly argument over his doing so little to help around the house. We started yelling at each other and he ended up cussing me out (bitch, nag, etc.) all of which upset me so much that I began crying. I ran upstairs and into the bathroom sobbing so hard that while leaning on the sink for support, the whole sink broke completely off the wall. Water began gushing out everywhere and then into the hallway. I didn't know how or where to turn the water off, and everything got flooded including the hall carpeting and then through the floor and down on to the newly painted ceiling in the kitchen down stairs. I yelled for the kids to call Mr. Smith next door to ask him to see if he could figure out how to turn the water off. I went into near hysterics—was soaking wet myself—cried and cried and decided I just couldn't take any more.

I was due at the EST Center where I'd promised to do a few hours of volunteer work at 1:30 pm. I threw on some dry clothes, my hair dripping wet, eyes swollen from crying, and drove to Georgetown, still crying intermittently all the way. I finally calmed down enough to work at answering the phone. When I came home, the girls had cleaned up the wet carpeting and other mess really good, and I felt much better coming home to that. Eric had asked a friend of his to come over to look at the refrigerator which wouldn't stay cold, but the guy seems to have left it in even worse shape than it had been.

Right now, the refrigerator, the dryer, the dishwasher, my little TV, and my telephone upstairs are all on the blink. And even the dog is still not well from the diarrhea attacks she's been having. Everything at once! Tonight earlier I just wept again. I give up, God!! I can't handle much more, but I have to, I guess. Maybe God's telling me I should just sell the house and move to an apartment. I guess that would make a lot of sense all the way around— but I love this house. It's home, especially for the kids. I hate to give it up. I guess I shouldn't be so attached to things, to possessions, but I am. I called Carolyn in New York to see if I could come up there these weekends if at all possible. I need some very much time to myself. What a day!!

P.S. Thank you, God, for Mr. Smith, next door, who managed to get the water turned off and affixed the washbowl back onto the bathroom wall— a lot of work!

There were many days like this one, but few worse! Eric was now fifteen and working setting pins at the bowling alley near our house after school. I don't remember what I said or did that triggered his getting mad enough at me (or maybe at his dad), but one day not too long thereafter, my car wouldn't start so that I couldn't drive it. Once again I had to call on Mr. Smith next door, who came to the rescue. He diagnosed a missing distributor cap as the reason the car wouldn't start when I needed to use it. I suspected Eric had taken it though I had realized he was that knowledgeable about engines, and soon after he returned it. But I just didn't know what to do for us to be able to live in some semblance of harmony with the assurance it wouldn't happen again.

Maybe my son couldn't take living in the house with three females or just missed his dad so much after Dan moved out. At any rate, I ended up calling Dan and told him I thought it would be easier on Eric if he lived with his father and Dan agreed to that arrangement. Though he had to take additional public transportation from his father's apartment to get to the bus stop in Southeast D.C., he still seemed happier to be living alone with his dad.

What seemed like a good arrangement, however, lasted only a couple of months. Dan and Meara decided to live together at her home in Northwest D.C. Dan informed Eric that there would be room for him as well. From the start, however, Eric did not feel welcome living there. He always felt as though he was a constant intruder by Meara in her house, though being the extreme introvert that he is, he never told me that until many years later. And Eric probably was difficult for someone like Meara who was unaccustomed to living with a teenager, especially one who wasn't her own and who was struggling to adjust to a broken home.

David Austern, the attorney who was handling our divorce agreement, had sent Dan and me each a copy of our separation agreement so that we could look it over for any possible changes we might have. We agreed to meet at a restaurant so we could talk in private out of earshot from our kids. Toward the end of a rather brief discussion of the document, Dan said hesitantly, "Well I guess we're pretty much in agreement about most things." (Why, I wondered, did he suddenly feel like such a stranger now? Maybe he'd always been a stranger to me and I just didn't know it.) Up until this point in our meeting, I'd felt fairly relaxed even though there'd been a distinct distance between us, a kind of chill in our communications that didn't used to be there before Meara came into the picture. I tightened up almost instinctively as he spoke those phrases "pretty much in agreement about most things." Uh oh, I thought. What's coming next? And then Dan dropped the bomb.

"I've been talking to Meara and a couple of her lawyer friends," he began. "They're telling me I'd be crazy to let you have the house!"

There it was—the very heart of the separation agreement. "What?" I exclaimed incredulously and almost knocked over the restaurant table as I stood up suddenly.

"That we agree on most things, you say? Dan, the most important thing in all of this is that our children have a home— that our children have a place to live! You're not giving the house to me. Your share will go to the kids when they're grown, or if I ever marry, or when I die. Eventually it'll all go to them!"

What really set my hair on fire was that this new concern about the house was actually a message from Dan's girlfriend, Meara, and presumably from her damned lawyer friends, but had been delivered to me by way of Dan! What business was it of theirs? There were a few more words spoken, but I was too angry at the time to remember what was said. That, however, ended our conversation, not just for the evening but for some time to come. I walked out of the restaurant and left him sitting there. The next day I made an appointment with David Austern, our lawyer.

When I had first visited him regarding a separation agreement and shared with him the history of our marriage, he had said very little. Now, knowing that Dan, a minister, had not only moved in with some woman before we were divorced, but now suddenly also wanted me to pay him half the value of our house. Austern was visibly angered. "Fine!" he snapped, his lips tightening. "We'll just send Mister Pierotti a letter saying that we're suing him on the grounds of adultery!" I wasn't sure that was really ethical since, as far as I knew, Dan's relationship with Meara hadn't started until after we separated. But I didn't stop Austern from sending the letter. Our kids having their own home to live in was my prime concern. Dan eventually got another lawyer, but our divorce decree ended up containing the terms of our original separation agreement regarding the kids and my having the house until they were grown.

When our dear friend Jaye learned from me that Dan and I had separated, she and Emil were stunned. They had been totally in the dark about Dan's affair with Julie or that he had fathered her child while we were at St. Paul's. Jaye, a former kindergarten teacher who'd taught pre-school at St. Paul's, had Julie in class many years before, so she'd known her and her family well. God only knows what she thought about our separation, other than that she was dead-set against divorce especially between two people she'd loved and especially admired. Who knows— maybe she thought we or I had decided to separate as some kind of quirky New Age whim!! At any rate, she wrote me a harsh letter about our decision to divorce and told me how selfish I was being to our children and Dan. Finally, I decided that at least to these dear, loyal friends from our former church I would tell the truth. I'd never shared a word with them about the heartbreak and shame I'd been through with Dan those years before. Even with them, I'd attempted to hide my depression and despair. It was time to stop protecting other people's illusions about Dan all the time so as not to hurt or disillusion others. It was time to tell the truth at least to them.

And I did— the whole ugly tale. They were shocked, and Jaye later wrote a letter in which she apologized, saying she had learned an important lesson about withholding judgment of another's actions when one did not know the whole story!

That spring Dan called to ask if Eric could stay at our house over the Passover and Easter holidays while Meara's parents visited them from the Midwest. Of course, I assured him Eric was welcome. When spring break was over, however, and the kids returned to school, Eric called me from his school at the end of the school day.

"Mom," he said, his voice clearly upset, "I just called Dad and asked him to pick me and my stuff up from our house so I could get a ride with him back to Meara's house. Dad then told me that he and Meara had been talking it over and had decided that it was best for everyone if I didn't live with them anymore!! Mom, if Dad calls you asking if you will let me come back home to live with you again, I want you to tell him no! Just tell him no!" At this point Eric's voice broke. "I'm supposed to be Dad's responsibility now and it's up to him to figure something out about where I'll live!"

The hurt in his voice was audible. Of course, I would have let him come back home had Eric called, but then neither he nor Dan called me back. I assumed they had worked something out with Meara, and she had changed her mind. I later learned that the explanation given for that sudden and unexpected decision that Eric must leave had been Meara's decision. She said she couldn't tolerate hearing Eric, a teenager, bad-mouthing his father and felt it was "setting such a bad example" for her two small boys. Evidently she hadn't seemed concerned that this living arrangement they now had might be setting a bad example not only for them but for Eric, as well, who never ever felt welcome nor wanted in Meara's home for that brief stay, not then, not ever after that.

Later that week, I learned from Mr. McDuffie, the headmaster at his school, that Eric was not with his father. Somehow he'd gotten a key to the church, and that's where he'd been sleeping at night. Another friend of Eric's told McDuffie that while staying there those few nights, Eric removed all the lettering from the sign board in front of the church and replaced it with just the following cryptic message in large letters:

IF THY SON OFFEND THEE, CAST HIM OUT!

When I heard about this, I didn't know whether to laugh or cry at Eric's very witty but poignant paraphrasing of the Bible quote "If thine eye offend thee, cast it out!" I felt so sad for Eric and angry with his father and Meara about that whole situation. I am sure Dan removed Eric's "updated" words from the church signboard the minute he saw them.

Possibly Eric had hoped that he and his father might move back to the apartment when he was forced to leave Meara's house, but that's not what happened. Instead Dan found a seminary professor with a room to rent at his house in Northwest D.C., and Eric had a room there basically on his own until the following fall. I had no idea of how un-supervised he really had been either by his father or the family at whose house he lived during those months when he was just 15.

Essentially he'd felt abandoned by all of us! He'd always been a very introverted and sensitive person growing up, sharing very little of what he felt with people except possibly with his closest friend from elementary school, Bruce Jones. Bruce's father had died of a cerebral hemorrhage when they were in the 5th grade. Both boys' losses of their fathers served to forge a lifelong bond between the two.

Elizabeth and Ann-Mari were much more outgoing and seemed to have an easier time of it during those teenaged years, but they also had each other to lean on. Whatever pain or damage they may have experienced leading up to and after our divorce during those early teenaged years was less obvious. If I knew then what I know now, I would have waited until the kids were older before considering divorcing Dan.

Dan, on the other hand, seemed to be enjoying his expanding success in church membership increase and in his personal life with Meara, as well. Because I'd sensed in what direction our marriage was heading, I'd deliberately kept a certain distance from the activities at Dan's new church. Very little notice of our separation seemed to have registered within his congregation since I had only occasionally attended service there and now not at all. Also because

Meara and her children never attended services there, they were never evident around the congregation on Sunday morning to arouse questions.

Dan's novel approach and frequently entertaining preaching style and his innovative worship ideas were drawing many new, younger members. These were the 70's now and everything was much looser, especially in urban society. Dan's new worship-style was much more open and eclectic including such things as jazz and a departure from some of the older traditional Lutheran styles of liturgy and music.

Dan directed the musical *Celebration* that drew considerable attention and participation from the younger crowd in Georgetown. Even Elizabeth, who wanted to be a theatre major in college, had an acting/singing part in the show, and Eric worked on the lighting. Not everyone in the congregation, however, was happy about all the changes taking place at the church, especially a number of the more elderly original members who'd been there when Dan was first called to be their minister. Some of them wanted their old church service back the way it had been before Dan had become pastor.

Not surprisingly though, word eventually leaked out into the congregation that Dan was now living in what some people characterized as an adulterous relationship with someone besides his lawfully, wedded wife. Many of the older, tradition-bound members were outraged and demanded of the church council that they call a special meeting with the regional Bishop in attendance to investigate this situation, some of them demanding his resignation. For once I was almost glad that none of that mess involved me directly— at least that's what I thought!! My primary concern was for our children, and its impact on them emotionally as the pastor's kids at church, or if Dan should lose his job and have no income to help support them.

A congregational meeting with the Bishop was called and attended by almost 150 members with a number of members having their say about whether or not Dan was in an adulterous relationship with someone other than his legal wife. I chose not to be there for most of that discussion, but

I did slip in quite late and stayed in the back of the sanctuary until almost everyone present had spoken. For selfish reasons, I did not want to see Dan lose his job, his means of support, and consequently his ability to pay support money for our children.

I also believed that the core issue, now that we were separated, wasn't so much the adultery charge but rather that the older members resented the changes that had taken place in the worship service when Dan became minister and so many new, younger people began attending services. At this point I did not care anymore what he did, although when I earlier had learned that Dan had decided to move in with Meara, I'd thought it was a rather stupid thing to do on his part without expecting that his move, when it became common knowledge, wouldn't eventually effect his ministry. I was even more concerned about how Eric and the girls would fit into this new decision on their father's part.

Toward the end of the hearing, I came forward and spoke very briefly to the issue of adultery, briefly indicating that the essence of our marriage in truth had really ended long before. Dan's real adultery had taken place in our marriage ten years earlier, though I didn't mention that in what I said. My speaking up was not about defending Dan but rather, in truth, about my financial concerns regarding his ability to help support our children. Of course, I didn't mention that worry then.

Frequently Dan's actions and speech seemed to be done primarily for shock value especially coming from a minister and going as far back as his seminary days. Back then I'd considered him rather theologically avant-garde. Eventually I had come to believe he had a somewhat self-destructive streak in him. But if I thought the worst was over, I was mistaken.

When I came to school early one April morning a week after the congregational meeting, a good friend and colleague in the English department, came up to me, newspaper clutched in her hand and said excitedly, "Joan, I presume you saw this morning's *Washington Post*?"

"No, I haven't" I answered, sensing there was something I'd missed that I should know about.

"That's your Dan, isn't it?" she said obviously knowing that it probably was he. She thrust the paper under my nose where a 5" x 6" picture of Dan smiling broadly, replete with a newly grown beard and mustache, looked up at me from the front page of the Metro section of that morning's *Post*. He was standing in front of the same outdoor church sign that Eric had changed some months before. This time the phrase "Actually, Jesus UNSAVES us" (a supposedly clever take off on the familiar "Jesus Saves" phrase) was clearly visible on the signboard directly behind him. What Dan had meant by that I did not know, other than it was there presumably for clever shock value. Beneath the picture was the headline "Pastor Resigns in Dispute Over His 'Sinful' Lifestyle" and a six-column spread of a rather sensational story.

"What is this?" I thought as I grabbed the paper and read on, hardly believing that he'd actually given this quote to the Post reporter. In it, I was supposedly indirectly quoted along with him as saying, "We discovered that we had been married for all the wrong reasons!" I was shocked by what I was purported to have said, but absolutely dumbfounded when he added, "I understand the Ten Commandments… and that they say to be faithful in relationships. They also basically mean that you should not use or abuse one another to satisfy your sexual needs, which is precisely what my wife and I were doing." I was incredulous! He then went on to characterize his relationship with Meara by telling the reporter "It is the most moral, upright, delightful relationship I've ever had! We're not married. We may never be. One of the problems in the church today is that the clergy have not been honest about their sexuality."

His comment about his new relationship and how "moral and delightful" it was stung me, of course, especially given the pathetic emptiness that our almost non-existent, physical relationship had been for me. And initially it certainly made me sound like some kind of chopped liver as a wife. But his saying that he and I had used and abused each other for precisely that reason— to satisfy our sexual needs' came as a shocker to me and was so far from the truth regarding my actions, that it was hard to believe that he would actually say what he had said in reference to me. It sounded positively kinky, which it certainly never was, sad to say! If anything, I'd always felt sexually "un-used" and emotionally abused!

Since at that time we were probably the only Pierottis listed in the whole D.C. phone book, it was fairly obvious to my colleagues at school that the article was about Dan and me. No hiding there! But I never had a question about that article from any student or colleague except my friend, a regular Post reader, who'd discovered it. Though I'd experienced what most people might call "emotional abuse" from Dan through his indifference towards me over the years, I'd also received the benefit of a lot of healing psychological therapy and life- saving answers to prayer. Already I'd begun to develop a freeing, personal openness about my life that I'd never had before. It no longer mattered quite so much what other people thought. Consequently, his intimate references to our marriage and Dan's latest affair spread out there on the front page of the Post didn't devastate me quite as much as they might have earlier in our marriage.

I don't remember if I ever confronted Dan about what he'd said in that *Post* interview. To this day, I have no idea of why he would have concocted such a twisted and disparaging take on our relationship, the problems in our marriage, or why he seemed to be aiming such undeserved vindictiveness towards me. Perhaps it was intended as a back story to help justify his current life style to Meara, her friends, and Dan's church members, and colleagues by inventing a marriage "reality" which purportedly had transpired during our years together. By this time, however, his actions no longer had the power to hurt me as deeply as they once did.

Throughout all of this time and thereafter, I never received even a phone call or a note asking how I was doing or ever inviting me to any social functions from any of Dan's and my clergy colleagues or their wives whom we'd known throughout Dan's ministry. Perhaps they'd read what he'd said in the *Post* and felt I might feel too humiliated by the whole matter to even appreciate a call.

It was as though I'd disappeared from the planet. Friends, especially those who'd been through a divorce themselves, have conjectured that perhaps I was seen as a threat to our ministerial friends and their marriages in some way—-a situation that was so bizarre, something that just wasn't supposed to happen in a minister's family, so they shut their eyes so as not to see this betrayal that went against their sense of the proper order of things especially in ministers' families. I've been told that this seems to happen to many people who divorce. We become the persona non grata that married couples don't know how to communicate with. That seems also to happen to couples who aren't even clergy related. Their friends also frequently disappear.

Shortly after the congregational meeting, Dan was asked to resign from his pastorate by the congregation. Despite his resignation, however, he was still eligible to serve other parishes in Lutheran churches elsewhere. Ultimately, however, he chose to resign from the Christian ministry entirely. Possibly this decision was made because of his relationship with Meara. However, it could also have been due to his leaving behind him a trail of betrayals that only he, Julie, Lyle, our youth director in New York, and I had known about. Eventually not only were our marriage vows hopelessly shattered, but his sexual relationship with Julie, whom he had confirmed at St. Paul's when she was just fourteen and which resulted in her pregnancy, the loss of the baby girl she'd given birth to and then was forced to give up for adoption— all these betrayed the most fundamental vows he'd taken both when we married and when he was ordained into the ministry.

Possibly he carried inside himself a sense of shame and regret especially toward his betrayed relationship with me, his children, and with Julie. But if he did, he never spoke of it to me. And if he'd ever believed in any of Christ's teachings about forgiveness, where better a place to find healing than in service to others? He still possessed excellent writing and speaking abilities and still had much to contribute, especially in the spheres of opening the consciousness of churches and synagogues to the fundamental racism, civil, and voting rights issues and abuses endemic in our society. When Dan left the traditional parish ministry he could still have served in a less restrictive position as a chaplain at VA hospitals (where he'd served when we lived in Erie,) regular hospitals, or even prisons.

I would guess that Dan's relationship with Meara played a major role in his decision to leave the ministry entirely, though he would probably have denied that at the time. I doubt she'd have taken on the role of a minister's wife under any circumstances. Explaining to our children his decision to leave the ministry and eventually the Christian faith entirely could not have been easy, if he ever did.

Leaving his original chosen calling without seeking any other form of ministry left Dan without any immediate means of making a living, and as I had feared, he very soon began many months where he could not pay child support nor his share of the school tuition for our children, which left me to pay what I could and to negotiate with our private school for the tuition deficit.

Fortunately, dear Mr. McDuffey, the headmaster, and the school administration were helpful with financial aid and very patient with my paying off our indebtedness. As Meara and her children became the primary focus of Dan's life almost to the exclusion of our three children, the harder it became for them to accept Meara. Their feeling as though they were increasingly becoming outsiders in their father's new life with Meara and her children epitomized for them when he and Meara decided to get married a year after Dan resigned from his Georgetown parish and left the ministry entirely. Their wedding was a non-denominational ceremony performed by a judge at a former mansion and reception facility. Ann-Mari was then 13,

Elizabeth 15, and Eric, 17. He had come home for the weekend from college for his father's wedding, having just started his freshman year at a college in Minnesota.

When the kids came home after attending their father's and Meara's wedding, they had very little to say to me except that there had been a part of the ceremony when Meara's two small boys were brought up to stand with their mother when she and Dan exchanged wedding vows. They had inserted into the ceremony vows by Dan to love, support, and care for Meara's two boys as his own. No similar promise about Dan's children, however, was made by Meara. As far as they were concerned, they were just part of the audience remaining anonymous, silent observers to this event along with all the other guests.

This exclusion of Dan's kids from his and Meara's wedding could not have been just an oversight. These two people were educated, presumably sentient beings. What could they have been thinking not to have included Dan's children in the same or a similar family-embracing way?

Sad to say, the occurrence of their seeming invisibility at their father's wedding, as well as numerous other occasions over time, probably sealed in concrete the paradigm of their relationship with their father and his new wife in their minds for years to come. Confirmation of this came some months later when Dan announced to our children that since Meara's divorce had recently become final and she intended to sell her house in NW. Washington, they had decided to move to Madison, Wisconsin, because, as Dan told them, "it was a comfortable university town with good schools and not far from Meara's parents, who lived in Evanston just outside of Chicago." They'd found an English Tudor house in Madison large enough for their growing family— Meara's boys and the daughter and son that would be born several years later. Unfortunately, the move just happened to be almost a thousand miles away from Dan's other three children in Washington— just part of the collateral damage of divorce.

Over time, my kids usually received birthday cards, an occasional phone call or now and then a weekend visit from their father. He usually sent them modest Christmas presents, though he no longer celebrated Christmas himself. He, Meara, and their children celebrated Hanukkah and other Jewish holidays. The two children Dan had with Meara, along with her two boys from her first marriage, all made their bar and bat mitzvahs. Dan, however, did not convert to Judaism himself.

The whole experience of their father's moving away did not come without emotional scars for my children and especially for Eric. Though the kids and I still celebrated Easter and Christmas with friends, neighbors, and Jaye and Emil always visiting us from New York, they just stopped attending church completely after Dan resigned from his church in Georgetown, even as they grew from their teens into adulthood. The kids missed seeing their dad conducting Sunday services, just another painful reminder of his absence from their lives.

It seemed strange to me that Dan would cut himself off from any relationship with the church anywhere, after it had been the focus of his life for over thirty years. His reasons for moving to Madison seemed entirely secular, and a little cold. But what he didn't tell us, of course, was that Madison was also a good place for him to take on a whole new identity in a new community, actually a new life, without the unpleasant memories from the past in Washington, just as Chicago had been an escape from the potential scandal at St. Paul's in New York ten years earlier.

That second-best treatment of our children by their father and Meara, over and over again as the years passed, probably led to my becoming the favored parent by default, but I didn't see that as a particularly good thing. It broke my heart to have to stand by helplessly and watch them be hurt and displaced by the father they had loved and revered all their young lives. It meant that I had to try so much harder to be both mother and father to them over the coming years.

I certainly did my best, but nothing and no one else could have taken Dan's place as father in their lives. And it continued through the years as their father's new family grew to a total of four children counting Meara's two boys and the birth of an additional son and daughter. Because both Meara's and her ex-husband's families were financially very well off, there was never any question about sufficient funds for family travel, a vacation home on a lake in the woods of Wisconsin, summer camps, ballet, gymnastics, sports, and music lessons. All of these were extras that my children could have benefited from, but were too expensive on my single parent's salary.

Nonetheless, Dan's unsteady income after leaving the ministry was not sufficient to regularly pay me what was due in child support and his half of school tuition. There certainly was nothing there to help pay his share for their college tuition— separation agreement or no separation agreement. Back then taking him to court was quite fruitless. It also became obvious to me that he and Meara probably had a pre-nuptial agreement before they married to protect her family's considerable wealth. How else to explain the disparity in life style between our two families regarding our children? Many are the times I had to remind them over the years that Meara's money was Meara's money and not their Dad's. I suppose my blaming the huge difference between what was Meara's and what was Dan's income was my feeble way of trying to protect my kids from being disappointed again and again by Dan's lack of ability or interest in providing for his first born children what was routine for his second family. That ploy didn't work forever, however, not as they grew older and compared their life style to that of their father's second family.

All three of my children worked through high school and also in college— Eric in a bowling alley and ice cream store and the girls both clerking in our local drug and department stores. Shortly before Dan and Meara's marriage, Eric matriculated to a small state college in Minnesota because it had been recommended by one of his teachers and also had a relatively modest tuition that he paid primarily using federal college loans. Because

I always considered him to be the quite intellectually gifted, I was especially distressed when he left school after two years, staying in Minnesota and working for a tire company near his friends from college. I always felt this decision was related to his father's absence.

The one positive side to our impoverished circumstances was that my status as a single parent supporting three kids on a beginning teacher's salary and living in the District made both the girls eligible for financial aid at George Washington University from which they both eventually graduated. Liz worked in a department store and saved money all through school as did Ann-Mari as a bank cashier and later a kitchen designer. With a full tuition scholarship, Liz earned a B.A. degree in Theatre Arts. Eventually Ann-Mari earned a master's degree in speech language pathology.

When it came time for the children in Dan's new family to go to college, the disparity between our two families was striking. All of his and Meara's children were able to attend prestigious and expensive schools. When Ann-Mari needed a $1000 to help pay tuition for graduate school at the University of the District of Columbia (a relatively paltry sum compared to the tuition at the Ivy League-caliber schools of Dan's and Meara's kids), however, Dan had no funds that he could spare to give her.

For years, Elizabeth would sometimes refer to Dan sardonically as "my dead father," not only for financial reasons, but rather because of his essential absence from her life after our separation. The fact is that they all felt abandoned by their father, and in actuality they had been.

There were times when I regretted sheltering my kids from the truth about their father's past and the original reasons for the breakup of our marriage. Perhaps the pedestal I protected with our secret would not have seemed so high and ideal to them when he stepped off and moved far away to start a new family when they needed him most.

I had done my best to tell the truth about everything to them when my children asked questions over the years, except, of course, the more shameful aspects of some of their father's behavior about which they'd never asked. Eventually the time for truth telling made itself clear, however. I was driving Ann-Mari back to Wagner College on Staten Island shortly before she was to finish her sophomore year there. As we sped along Maryland's Route 95 and after a long pause of many minutes, Ann-Mari turned to me and then seemingly clear out of the blue she asked, "Mom, when you and Daddy were married, was Daddy ever unfaithful to you?"

I felt totally blindsided. I stopped breathing for a few moments. As I finally released my breath but before I could speak, she jumped in with "I KNEW it!! I just knew he must have!" she replied to her own question without my saying a word. "I didn't say he had," I replied lamely. "If he hadn't, you'd have answered right away," was her immediate intuitive retort. And she was right. I would have eventually told them when they were a little older and after rehearsing some less abrupt way to tell her or her two siblings. Thus began a conversation in answer to the question I'd been half expecting for almost twenty years.

But a simple "yes or no" answer would never have sufficed for Ann-Mari, always the curious one. The resultant conversation should really have been called a Q and A, for it lasted all the way to Staten Island, with all my answers triggering more questions— who? what? where? when? What she didn't ask was "why?" Why had her father been so morally and spiritually reckless— perhaps a better word would have been "corrupted"— to seduce and profoundly betray Julie, an innocent, really vulnerable young girl, one of his own confirmands at St. Paul's? Why had he also betrayed not only me but his own children in such a hurtful way? Why over all these years had he never once told me that he was sorry for how profoundly he had deceived me. That why question was one I could never really find a satisfactory answer to, for in truth I did not know the why myself. I could have understood if he'd had a love affair with an adult woman in our congregation, for I'm sure there'd have been a number of them who had crushes on him, perhaps imagining that he was the epitome of a "perfect husband" in their imaginations. This is quite common among clergymen. And after all these years, I'm still not sure why, though the answer may lie within the glimpse of what he revealed about himself in that mysterious letter at the end of this narrative, written by Dan in February of 1957, several months before we married. I refer to it as "mysterious" because I had no recollection of having ever received it until after his death in 2014 when it appeared in the pile of old letters from him to me written shortly before our wedding.

What surprised me most was the seeming equanimity with which Ann-Mari received my answers to her many questions about her father, his affair with our babysitter Julie and the other daughter that he'd fathered, who would have been her half-sister born just six months after Ann-Mari. What also surprised me somewhat was that my other two children, Eric and Elizabeth, did not come to me for confirmation of that information about their dad that I know Ann-Mari shared with them soon after. Perhaps at the time, my confirming it would have made it so in their minds, and they just weren't ready to hear it from my lips. And actually, my referring to it as an "affair" was probably my way of not facing the real enormity of that transgression against a girl as young as Julie at 15 or 16 had been, by her own minister— a sexual relationship that I later learned lasted at least two years, a tragedy which would undoubtedly have landed him in jail had it been revealed today.

PART 2

CHAPTER 13

The Dating Game

1976 – WASHINGTON,DC

As an almost 40-year-old woman, no longer married, I was totally unprepared for the dating scene in the latter part of the 1970s. The women's liberation movement and the sexual revolution were in full sway. So much had changed, especially for women like me who'd been indoctrinated with the belief that one should be a virgin before marriage or at least sexually faithful if one were in a loving physical relationship with someone even if not married. The sexual revolution turned that notion on its head. It seemed as though being sexual was just the entry fee to exploring the possibility of a relationship rather than getting to know a man first, perhaps fall in love with them before being so intimate.

At my age, it was very difficult to meet men in the Washington area, where the ratio of women to men was said to be five to one. Add to that, the paucity of men who were not married, were straight, or actually interested in a committed relationship with a woman with three adolescent children. Married to a minister for 16 years, I'd never attended the kind of social meeting places for singles such as bars, nightclubs, and dances. Ann Landers always recommended church as a good place for the availability of single men. Obviously, she hadn't spent much time looking there herself! I've personally never known any people who'd met their future partners at church, but I could be wrong. I just found that most men at the church I attended were already married or never intended to be.

Actually, at the time, I doubted there was a man on the entire planet looking for a divorced, 40-year-old woman with three kids!! My social life, at least with eligible, interesting men, was almost nil. And so, to find personal friendships and activities outside my teaching, running a household as a single parent, and being a mother, I took printmaking and calligraphy classes. I also returned to the comfort of watercolor painting, as I'd done when Dan, the children, and I lived for that difficult and uncertain year above the TV repair shop in a Chicago slum.

Now, as a single woman hoping to meet some nice man, the only problem with courses like that was that very few men took what they called those "artsy" classes, so I met very few men in them. I even took sailing lessons with my friend Nikki, as well as a class in canoing.

Someone had told me about an organization called PWP (Parents Without Partners), which had been formed to help single or divorced parents with children meet others in the same situation. I had been told that PWP was just another meat market where most men came primarily to find sexual partners rather than to establish lasting relationships— a rather dismal introduction, but I thought I'd at least check it out for myself. I went to their next planning meeting, which turned out to be a small group of eight or nine people at the apartment of a divorced woman (Jolen but nick-named Josie), who though born in China, had grown up in the States. She was a single, divorced mother, raising her two-year-old son.

She was the first Chinese person I'd ever met socially, and we became good friends. Besides both being single mothers attempting to raise emotionally stable children on very little money, our mutual search for potential husbands or partners and our pathetic track records with the two men we'd married helped us bond quickly. Eventually we began attending an occasional PWP dance together so that if there were no interesting men at the dance, we could always go out for coffee or a glass of wine together and the evening wouldn't be a total loss. What follows is an account from my diary entry in July 1976, describing one of my first "social" experiences at PWP and later at a bar with Josie:

July 1976

This evening I went to a Parents Without Partners dance event with Josie at Bunny Robinson's house. What a drag!! 55 women and 25 men, and you wouldn't believe those men!! The most interesting male there was Bunny Robinson's springer spaniel, Mike! I had really gone with a positive frame of mind to just have a good time dancing (and not be looking for anyone special), but I didn't even want to dance with any of them. I think I've just about had it with PWP (which Josie says stands for "Pussy Without Participation" since she feels that's all the men are there for— to get laid!)

At 10:30 pm. Josie and I decided to leave and go to some bar she knew of, the Royal Warrant on Connecticut Avenue, where she said they had a regular piano player, people dance, and she felt like dancing. I'd never done anything like that before. Actually, I'd never really been in a bar before in my life. Josie didn't believe me when I told her that, but it was true. It was really an interesting experience. I sat there through the whole evening like I was at a movie— really an observer. Some guy named Charlie, slightly drunk, came over to our table, sat down with us, and started talking, primarily with Josie. Before too long he and Josie were sitting there, kissing passionately. It was really kind of both funny and bizarre, sitting there at the same table watching this whole scene going on feeling like I was some kind of voyeur or maybe even invisible!

Some guy came over and asked me to dance, and that was O.K. because he was polite and didn't attempt to put the moves on me or mess with me in any unwanted way. I guess Charlie, Josie's new found friend, didn't know what to do with me either, sitting there at the same table with them while they necked not two feet away. Finally, he told me to pick out a guy, any guy at the bar that appealed to me; puzzled, I picked out the best looking one I saw, thinking he was joking. Shocked, I watched as Charlie got up, went over to the bar, and brought the guy over to our table! I really didn't care one way or the other whether he came but then there he was!! He was actually quite a nice guy. Ed was his name— some kind of executive with Pepco. We talked for a long time, and I gathered from what he said that he thought I was a pretty nifty woman. He wanted to call me and see me again, but he was married and, from negative past experience, I told him I didn't mess with married men— not anymore. There was no future, I'd learned, in that kind of relationship. And at least he was honest about being married, which was a rare occurrence.

Some months later at a PWP affair, I did meet an attractive man, Ray, a single parent who worked as an economist with NIH. He had custody and was raising his two children, eleven and nine. I didn't see many men raising their children by themselves, and I really admired him for doing that, especially since Dan hadn't seemed to have struggled much over his decision to move so far away from our children

We saw each other for five or six months, our families once having Thanksgiving dinner together, and when Ray's father died and he had to go to the West Coast for the funeral, I kept his children for two weeks. Early on he'd begun pushing me for a commitment to get married; he was, however, an excessively rigid person and a strict disciplinarian with his kids, a parenting style very different from mine, which I knew would surely cause problems in a blended family. Also, his habit of several martinis every evening, which often left him "a sheet or two to the wind," was a part of his life style that I, who'd never really developed a taste for most alcohol just couldn't share with him.

When I couldn't commit myself to marriage so early in our relationship and so soon after my separation and divorce, he began to distance himself emotionally from me, and eventually the relationship ended. I sometimes wondered if what he primarily wanted was someone to help him raise his children. Though I cared for Ray— even believed I loved him— and initially had hoped things might work out for us, I knew well from my own experience how lonely having a relationship can sometimes be, even when one is married, if there is no basic emotional honesty and connection. I realized that Ray and I just didn't share the kind of emotional or sexual connection that I wanted in the person I wanted to marry eventually. Add to that equation five adolescent children between us from two different families, and one had a recipe fraught with potential problems.

CHAPTER 14

Nobody But Yourself

1977 TO 1982 – WASHINGTON, DC

As a Speech and English major in college, I'd taken both acting and theatre courses, so for two summers, I took classes in improvisational acting led by director Bob Alexander and the well-known actor Bob Prosky at Arena Stage theatre with my daughter Liz, who was now in her teens, and hoped to major in theatre when she went to college. I was still teaching English at Ballou and eventually was able to convince the principal, Bob Royster, a fellow former member in the Urban Teacher Corps, into letting me teach an elective acting class as part of my 11th grade English teaching load.

Due to the overcrowding and shortage of space at Ballou, there really were no suitable places such as an empty classroom or even the stage in the school auditorium large enough and available to use for a drama class. We finally ended up using my English classroom up on the third floor both for the 11th grade English class and for the theatre class, which involved the daily time consuming moving of all thirty-five or forty desks over to the room's perimeter in order to make space once a day for the movement and action in the class.

To help loosen up and encourage the kids to relax (and also to cut down on the noise for the class next door), I required that they work in their stocking feet on their improvisations and theatre exercises, which meant that they had to remove their shoes in class. This created quite a stir 'til they got accustomed to being shoeless. Something so simple turned out to be a big deal for those kids and there was some opposition— embarrassment— possibly socks with holes in them— I never did find out— but eventually when all the shoes started being taken off by the more "daring" kids, the rest of the class eventually went along with the program and removed their shoes as well.

Many of those students turned out to be real naturals when it came to acting. Most of them had never even seen a live stage play in their lives before, but how they loved doing it! Despite the inconvenience of insufficient space in my classroom, they still seemed to have a great deal of fun learning how to improvise. So did I!

Their lack of exposure to the arts should not have been surprising to me, however. Far more shocking was realizing when I first began teaching at Ballou that though most of the public schools in Southeast, D.C. were just a few short miles from the Mall, an area rich in extraordinary museums and theatres, seldom were those children from southeast taken on school field trips to any of those places. Too many of them have never set foot inside the doors of most of those museums. It's almost as though segregation were still in place as it once had been until after the Brown vs. the Board of Education Supreme Court decree in 1954. Some public places were still considered "white" places by blacks, now not by law but unfortunately by custom and consequently not frequented by many blacks. Why risk a confrontation going to a new place where once you'd been told you weren't allowed to go?

Just making trip arrangements with museum personnel for group guided tours; reserving school buses months ahead of time because they were always in such short supply; wrangling permission from the principal, from other teachers, and the parents to take those kids out of their other classes; or even just recruiting parent chaperones, most of whom worked, and finally getting the kids onto those buses and into a museum or theatre— it was— and probably still is always such a big, difficult deal for most DCPS teachers.

And it's especially so when field trips are regarded by others as a kind of holiday off from school rather than an important part of the curriculum. Few teachers undertake to go through all the red tape required in order to take their students on field trips.

Unfortunately, these many years later, not much has really changed in that regard in the District, and the missed educational opportunities for those children still continue to be an unacknowledged form of segregation on the part of the school system and the U.S. Department of Education. It's a kind of criminal negligence in my opinion— a form of what Senator Patrick Moynihan once referred to as "benign neglect." Finding the money for sufficient numbers of buses and making field trips a curriculum priority, especially for kids whose world view already is often so limited. Whatever else it takes to get those children to some of the many educational opportunities on the Mall, so close to home, shouldn't be rocket science. Any D.C. resident can tell you how crowded our city is during the spring, summer, and fall, filled with thousands of busloads of school children brought here from all over the rest of the U.S. to see the wonders of the seat of our Federal Government. Those tour buses unfortunately are rarely filled with our own District children!

Very few visitors to our city are aware that we, who live here in D.C., have no representation in Congress— no senators or representatives— because our almost one million D.C. residents are not considered a state. But we still pay some of the highest income taxes in the country to our federal government. "Taxation Without Representation" has been emblazoned on our auto license plates courtesy of our D.C. City Council to inform the many people from other states, many of whom have no idea that we have no representation in Congress.

Because of my previous associations with the improvisation classes that my daughter Liz and I took at Arena Stage, a group of my students from Ballou were invited by Bob Alexander, to be one of the few classes in the

213

city working with their new company of young talented actors at the Living Stage, a special program begun that year especially for school-age kids. I remember vividly the day my students went to their first student workshop there. Since Alexander felt that the presence of teachers tended to inhibit free, emotional expression on the part of participating students, teachers were not invited to even observe the workshops. Actually, we were specifically dis-invited from attending.

My students were picked up at Ballou by a van from Arena Stage but had to get home by public transportation on their own. I'd instructed them to take the bus directly home rather than having to waste an extra bus fare to get back to school for just the last half hour of classes that day. To my amazement and delight, however, instead of their going home early after their workshop, the students returned to school on the city bus. They came bursting into my seventh period English class completely turned on, not by pot or PCP, but by excitement and enthusiasm bordering on joy. They explained that they just had to come back to tell me about their day. This had been their first exposure to this type of improvisational participation where they actually developed or improvised the plot with the actors.

They were filled with talk of "transformations" and "living statues," theatre exercises used in improvisation to stimulate creativity and involve students in scenarios taken from their own actual lives and geared to addressing the real-life problems and experiences that teenagers often encounter. The kids excitedly wanted to know when they could go to Arena again. They seemed, indeed, to be transformed by an experience that used an almost magical alchemy of improvisation, music, poetry and Living Stage's professional company of young, dedicated actors inspired by the actual life story plots shared by my students and their actual improvisation assistance in the unfolding of their stories. Alexander and his company were really impressed with the energy and cooperation my class had displayed and invited them to come again monthly until the school year ended.

Some weeks afterwards, a group of those kids came to me with the idea of putting on an inter-school improvisation demonstration that involved the audience as well. I was somewhat reluctant, not knowing what kind of pandemonium might ensue, but they were so excited by the possibility that I agreed to go along with them providing they did at least the basic planning. Their performance was held in the school library, and to my surprised delight it went very well.

Soon after, they announced that they were ready to do a "real" play for the school. Thus theatre came to Ballou with our producing of Douglas Turner Ward's *Day of Absence*, a satirical play about a typical southern town depicting the aftermath among the white people when all the black people mysteriously disappear one day, and there's mayhem in town when no one is left to do the work.

The next semester two of my students won Best Actor awards at a city-wide high school play competition for scenes they performed from *The Miracle Worker* and *Day of Absence*, and we later celebrated with a spaghetti dinner at my house.

There was one student in the acting class that I still remember especially well because he'd been unusually unpleasant. His name was Mack, and he carried with him a nasty swagger and the unmistakable look of trouble. He was a tough, cynical, young man who was new to Ballou and was recently enrolled in both my English and Acting classes in mid-year by one of the counselors. Rumor had it that he'd been involved in some sort of shooting involving a member of his family. Never have I seen anyone alienate others so rapidly with threats, sarcasm, and insults as he did. Within two weeks, everyone in both classes hated him. Even I referred to him privately as "Mack the Knife."

Initially Mack refused to volunteer or participate in either the English or the acting class. And only reluctantly would he join the Living Stage group on their Arena workshop outings. Little by little, however, his hard shell began to crack, and the mask began dropping off to reveal a lonely, struggling kid who was living pretty much on his own in one of the projects, Stanton

Dwellings, one of the public housing projects in Southeast. He began participating and eventually actually began volunteering. When he discovered that there were places where it was safe to be "for real," which was the coin of the realm with the other kids, he gained acceptance from the others and actually became the self-appointed "sergeant-at-arms" to keep the drama class students "on task" during class.

Mack ended up passing both my courses at the end of the year, graduated the following year, and eventually became productively employed. He came to see me from time to time after that. Gone was the surly, defensive expression on his face that he'd carried when he first joined my two classes. In its place was a look of seeming confidence and self-respect that had developed as a result of what I call "therapeutic" theatre: learning, which along with skills and course content, hopefully heals something important in the soul of a student, as well. The early Greeks referred to it as *therapeia*, (literally meaning the healing power of fresh air and sun!) Given the opportunity to trust others and to share honestly what is going on inside one's self is indeed like the healing that comes from fresh air and sun being allowed to express or cleanse one's soul or psyche.

Mack was a kind of miracle to me when I saw the changes that took place in him over the remainder of the year, which I can only attribute to the support and love he received from the people at Living Stage, his classmates, and I hope from me, as well. We are all mind, body, and spirit. I concluded that only when our educational systems eventually begin to address all of those three essential parts of what it is to be fully human, will those systems begin to be fully functional. When Mack later visited me after graduation, he still spoke of the plays and improvisations we'd produced in the acting class, his English class journal writing, (which he said he still continued on his own), and his work with Living Stage.

One of the most memorable teaching experiences I've ever had— it still makes me laugh when I think of it— took place during that acting class. Trust is an essential part of improvisation and does not come easily to inner-city kids, given the challenges involving trust that they face daily in Southeast D.C. Developing it in acting classes centers around what Viola Spolin in her authoritative book *Improvisation for the Theatre* calls "trust exercises" and is used in acting classes to develop a sense of trust between acting students and their fellow actors.

In one of those exercises, class members take turns lying down on the floor and with their eyes closed, allow seven or eight other class members to surround the student and then, placing their hands under him or her, carefully lift the student off the floor to the group's waist level where they slowly and gently rock the student for 15 or 20 seconds. The group then slowly lifts him or her to their shoulders and carries them, whose eyes are to remain closed, around the room for perhaps a minute. The student is then gently lowered to the floor, hopefully having enjoyed being gently carried while giving their trust over to the group of carriers. It usually has a very positive experience of allowing one's self to trust others as well as the feeling of being lifted, held, gently rocked, and carried.

I used that exercise with the twenty or so students in the improvisation class after much coaxing from others in the group. One at a time, they all had a turn allowing the others to lift, rock, and carry them. Ultimately, they all had participated in that experience of totally trusting and also being trustworthy. When they noticed that I was the only one in the class who had not been carried, they began to coax me into letting them carry me. "It's not fair if you don't do it, too, Missus P," they intoned. Though in theory I believe that teachers should not expect class members to do something they wouldn't do themselves, I didn't believe I'd be so sorely tested on my so-called teaching theories!

Reluctantly I finally agreed to be lifted and rocked on the condition that I could choose the eight kids to do the carrying. Of course, I chose those who I figured were the strongest ones to carry me since I was no flyweight!

I then gingerly lay down on the floor, crossed my arms, shut my eyes and began to just breathe deeply, trying my best to relax. Eight of my stalwart students then carefully lifted me up to their waist height, gently began rocking me, lifted me up onto their shoulders and proceeded to carry me around the classroom like I was an Egyptian mummy or something.

I was able to relax, keep my eyes closed, and eventually, actually began to enjoyed the experience— a little! They then finally lowered me carefully down and laid me gently on the floor. A few moments later, my eyes still closed, I heard what sounded like stockinged feet quietly scampering off into the distance. I opened my eyes and to my astonishment discovered that I was looking up, not at the ceiling of my classroom but rather at the ceiling of the hallway, a considerable distance from the classroom door! Still prone, I turned my head and heard the light laughter of the class, all of whom were looking at me from the classroom door at the other end of the hall! Somehow they had silently managed to carry me quite a distance without me even realizing we had left the classroom.

Before I had time to pick myself up off the floor, the doors to the stairwell from the second floor swung open, and onto the 3rd floor, where I still lay prone, and in walked the school psychologist, Dr. Sigamoni, who happened to be from India. Without batting an eye, he glanced down at me as he passed, nodding and smiling slightly, and in his charming Indian accent greeted me politely and continued on his way down the hall. No questions, no comments, and just as though he was accustomed to finding me there on the floor every day at that time— perhaps he'd thought I was meditating or something! I have never forgotten that wonderfully funny experience nor those students as well. For me, it was a great lesson in allowing myself to trust, not only in my students but in myself as a teacher, as well.

Another trust- exercise the acting students did was to divide into couples and go out on "blind walks" mostly around the school outdoor premises. Students were blindfolded and then led each by another student, trusting him or her to safely lead the other both inside and around outside after which they switched sides. Perhaps word had gotten out around school about some of our more unusual class activities, (or by then I'd gotten the reputation as a kind of kooky English teacher at the very least by Dr. Sigamoni!) At any rate, no one on the staff ever inquired of me what on earth we were up to, and rarely did any of the administrators come around checking on my classes or any of the other third floor classes except to observe our teaching for our yearly evaluations. For all the administration knew, we English teachers could all have been fornicating on the desks up there all those months for all the oversight or support we received from them.

Rarely was I assigned the senior college bound English classes such as the advanced placement, honors or Humanities courses— those students were headed for college and thus were usually more academically compliant since their transcript grades were at stake. Those senior classes always seemed to be assigned only to certain teachers. I never learned what the main criterion was for the selection of those teachers who got to teach those classes, but I assumed they were set aside for those who the assistant principal thought were the "good" teachers or were friends of hers. I don't know this for a fact, but it certainly seemed to work out that way. Perhaps I was assigned the classes I got because I rarely complained about getting them. I usually was assigned the average or below average students. I'd like to think perhaps that I'd been chosen by the Universe for other reasons. Perhaps God-Spirit-All-That-Is had somehow hand-picked those students that I'd fit in well with— the ones who maybe needed an extra dollop of patience, creativity, or extra tutoring. Or maybe I was just pegged by the administrators as some dummy who wouldn't put up a fuss if I didn't get the "good" students. At any rate, I loved— or tried to love— the students assigned to me and made an effort to know them as individuals, as much as possible.

This I often achieved through the use of the required regular journal writing I had them write, which was graded solely by the number of pages each student had written. It was due every three weeks. My main goal was to keep them writing, writing, writing! This was part of their English grade they had total control over. It could be on any subject or aspect of their lives or interests that they chose. If it was too personal, they could write DO NOT READ on the top of the page. The deal was that if they didn't want me to read it, I wouldn't read it except for one line on each page— my way of checking to make sure their writing was not copied from another source. Over my many years as a teacher reading student writing, I could spot plagiarized writing a mile away, usually by the flawless spelling or grammar that a student may have copied from professionally published writing.

Only once was I wrongfully over-confident in my "fraud" detecting when Aaron, a new student, wrote a composition that seemed so technically perfect that I was virtually certain he'd copied it from somewhere. I confronted him about it, and he was righteously indignant at being accused of cheating, so I asked him to write another piece, this time in class. It, too, was excellent, and I was embarrassed about misjudging him. I apologized to him and talked to him about his transferring to a college prep class or a Humanities class, but he would have none of that. I was somewhat sick at heart when he wrote a letter to me explaining that his church affiliation actually discouraged college attendance, believing it lessened their young people's desire to do the regular evangelizing door to door after leaving high school. This young man could have easily gotten a scholarship to almost any college he wanted. I hope that eventually someone convinced him to do that.

I still had my own diaries I'd kept all through my own high school years and fortunately had saved them all. They'd been valuable to me as a mother to my three teens and served as a realistic reminder of who I'd been in my own teens when years later my own children would sometimes rage at me for some reason or other. I remembered the struggles, arguments, and tears with my parents, my sister, and even some boyfriends during those tough adolescent years. Eventually when I was introducing the journal form to my students, I decided to bring some of my own old diaries from high school days into class and passed them around for the kids to read if and when they chose. They seemed excited about getting to read them, probably thinking that they might get glimpses of my hot teenage sexual experiences or something. They didn't realize that I, too, had a mother who was not above reading my diaries, so there certainly was nothing looking like "hot sex" in them. How disappointed they must have been! But those old journals served as one kind of model for ideas of what a personal diary could be about. I'd treasured them and was gratified that the kids never defaced them in any way.

I did not correct their journal writing with a mess of red remarks (actually I never marked anything in red pencil!) except occasionally for misspellings or word misuse. There sometimes was something kind of "sacred" to me about the nature of what some students occasionally shared with me regarding their lives. Also, they could guarantee themselves B's or A's on a journal if they managed to churn out those 8 to 12 pages of free journal writing required and due every three weeks. That may not seem like much writing to some people, but for most of the inner-city students I taught, who'd rarely been assigned sufficient writing all through school, it was a lot!

Frequently they'd even write "READ THIS!" at the top of the pages, especially if they wanted to ask for advice or for me to just comment on what they'd written. Hoping someday to write about them, I asked and got permission from several of my students to keep some of their journals. I still have them and haven't given up using them someday to share perhaps in a book more fully as I'd promised those students I would.

In addition to journal and composition writing there was also what constituted the standard DCPS English curriculum, which was always dependent on what textbooks were available. Rarely did we have enough books, and we'd have to duplicate short literature pieces and composition assignments that some of us teachers copiously and illegally copied from published literature so that each kid had a copy. I sang the praises of whoever invented the Xerox machine! I had no qualms about duplicating copyrighted material in the name of seeing that my students had some of the necessary assignments found in books we didn't have enough of. I felt that those students had been cheated out of so much in their lives in the D.C. schools, that to enable my students to at least have access to necessary school material, then my thievery was in the cause of justice.

Literature textbooks were often in short supply and particularly ones that gave sufficient representation to African American literature, poetry, and essays especially of the many outstanding writers from the Harlem Renaissance. These writers were often unknown or unavailable to many English teachers since their work was often not included in typical high school literature texts, which consisted mostly of the works of white writers and poets. Because of the Urban Teacher Corps' program that I'd been part of at Ballou in 1970, the English department for a time had a more forward looking collection of literature books which included appropriate and inclusive literature by noted African American writers especially for a school with a significant-sized African American student body.

The year I served as chairman of the English Department, the school population was so large that when I went to retrieve literature books from the book clerk, there simply weren't any more. The book clerk suggested I go down personally to the D.C. public school book warehouse and see what they had there. This I did, hopeful I'd find an unexpected treasure trove of lit books they didn't know they had. I'd never been there before, but my hopes were dashed as soon as I saw what a wreck the building was. All I could find in the high school English book section was a single class set of American literature books published in 1950. Though those books were still intact (i.e. managing to stay together) and the contents still legible, they'd actually been in a fire so that they reeked of smoke, the book covers all wrinkled and in dreadful shape from the heat of the fire.

When I was a kid, part of the anticipation of the start of school each fall was getting a fresh, new, unused, un-scribbled-on textbook. It gave the unconscious message to me, as the recipient, that I was worth something. What message would these pitiful, smoke contaminated texts give to one of my students about whom their school system thought they were? Though I brought those books back to Ballou, I simply could not bring myself to pass them out to my students. Instead I eventually gave them out piecemeal to the occasional guest who was interested in education as a souvenir of how the school system regarded its clients, Washington, D.C.'s children.

CHAPTER 15

The Possible Human

1978 – WASHINGTON, DC

My early interest in things psychological and spiritual, (and even certain aspects of spiritualism) dovetailed with the recent spiritual exposure I was getting through the predominately Christian teachings of Unity where I'd begun to attend church. Though I missed the traditional hymns and liturgical practices that I'd found as a child and young adult in the Lutheran and Episcopal Churches , Unity's basically Christian teaching emphasizing the part of God which is immanent in all of us and everywhere in the Universe, along with the use of meditation and prayer as a way of going within made far more sense to me than the kind of piety I'd found in churches that required a definite conversion experience and that one be able to give the time, date, and location when one first accepted Jesus "as their personal savior." Finally, the notion of God, Spirit, and the teachings of Jesus took on a greater reality for me in the here and the now than I'd ever had before, both as a Christian and certainly later as a result of my painful experience as minister's wife.

Toward the end of 1978, I took a two-weekend workshop with the unlikely title of the EST Seminar Training, named for Werner Ehrhart, who'd created the program. There were those who considered Ehrhart to be a kind of kooky charlatan, but I found the content quite interesting and for the first time I began to learn the kind of deep breathing similar to meditation. It was intended to introduce people to greater self-awareness and psychological growth. One goal or "breakthrough" was enhancing the ability of seeing something in a new way, which enables a person to see new opportunities and new openings for action that one couldn't see before. The EST Training, as one person cleverly described it, was a way to help people to discover how much more they knew that they didn't know they knew!! It was not a religion by any means, but some of its material touched on aspects of Buddhism, and it certainly helped me to at least begin to learn to pay attention to what I was thinking and to take the first steps toward learning the value of meditation and greater consciousness.

Soon thereafter in December of 1979, *The Washington Post* featured a fascinating article about someone named Dr. Jean Houston, who with her husband Dr. Robert Masters was the founder and director of the Foundation for Mind Research. Here was a woman with two Ph.D.'s, one in psychology, the other in the history of religion. She was and still is a prolific writer, author of numerous books, some focusing on whole-brain learning, areas that became of special interest me. As a researcher, historian, and scholar, and who at the time was the president of the Association for Humanistic Psychology, Jean Houston is considered one of the primary founders of the Human Potential movement. According to the Post article I'd read, she was to be the primary presenter of an upcoming two-week-long workshop/seminar, *The Possible Human: Enhancing Your Physical, Mental, and Creative Abilities.*

Though I was not familiar with her research, I was quite excited after reading the *Post's* article about her. Here was someone who was actually doing serious research into areas that most people were totally unfamiliar with— the brain and learning, human development, LSD research, a leader in the whole field of human consciousness research, and spirituality,— areas encompassing both science and religion, and all of considerable interest to me. I was pressed for money but determined to attend if at least for the first weekend. To my good fortune, I was able to receive a scholarship so that I could attend not just the weekend but also the whole weeklong event.

Dr. Houston (or Jean as we came to call her) turned out to be the most extraordinarily gifted speaker, teacher, and communicator that I'd ever heard in my life before or for that matter, since that time. I'd never seen nor heard anyone speaking so authoritatively about the human potential— physically, intellectually, spiritually— of every human brain, mind, and body. Unfortunately, we treat these incredible gifts (if we even have an inkling of how laden with them we really are) with such careless ignorance.

That knowing opened up a much further appreciation for me of the wondrousness of the brains of every one of my students, not just in caring about them as people with incredible latent potential but realizing that inside of everyone one of them was this incredible "God stuff." If I had told them that they were all "God in hiding," which is what I believe, well, that would for sure have guaranteed that I was some kind of nutcase and belonged over at St. Elizabeth's Psychiatric Hospital down the street from Ballou. And I never, even to this day, cease to be sickened whenever I read in the local newspaper of the many thousands of these young incredible brains that are being blown away by the mindless use of guns. And now those statistics no longer are just true in the impoverished streets of Southeast D.C., but all over the U.S. and other parts of the world.

The waste of talent, potential, and possible undeveloped genius (or as Jean described them "evolutionary wonders, each a trillion cells singing together in a vast chorale" simply boggles my mind especially because those students themselves are unaware of their own intrinsic value. And the whole system that purports to educate them is also usually unaware of who those children, teenagers, young adults really are, largely because they come perhaps disguised as poverty and a certain color, and therefore are adjudged to be worth less by far too many ignorant people.

In 1982, I enrolled in a three-year graduate-level study program on human potential in the Human Capacities Training Program, designed by Jean Houston. The program met for three years, each year comprised of one intensive summer month for 8 to 10 hours a day, meeting on the campus of Ramapo College in Mahwah, New Jersey, and also for two weeks each of those winters in California. During those summers, we spent a number of the weeks not just studying but experiencing aspects of a variety of the teachings, history, and cultures of Judaism, Christianity, Islam, Sufism, Buddhism, and Greco-Roman religions through the use of lecture and personal processing primarily using meditation, dancing, music, art, dress, etc. Each afternoon our group of about 100 students worked with Bob Masters on what he called the Psychophysical Method using physical exercises, hypnosis, and disciplines stressing mindfulness and awareness – from Egyptian, Buddhist, and Taoist traditions on to contemporary teachers such as Gurdjieff, Alexander, Erickson, and Feldenkrais.

During those three years, we also focused on the psycho-neurology of learning— the brain/mind connections and special focus on the Triune Brain theory of Dr. Paul MacLean, head of the Department of Brain Evolution and Behavior at the National Institutes of Health. In the 1980s and before, neuroscience was still in its early stages of discovery, research and development. Much of what MacLean had been brilliantly researching and writing about was the striking similarities between the structures in the modern human brain and the evolutionary brains found in the reptilian, old mammalian, and neo-mammalian brain structures— all of those early structures accounting for our neural capacity for thinking, feeling, emotion, and action. Learning about the brain became an incredibly fascinating area of special interest to me for the remainder of my life.

One of my colleagues in the training had the opportunity to meet with Dr. MacLean, and knowing of my extreme interest in the brain, she invited me to join her when she met with him. I was surprised by MacLean's willingness to share his work with us two women, total neophytes to neuro-anatomy, and of his interest in what we were doing, both of us teachers. We had a lengthy and delightful conversation, and I felt so fortunate to have met him, especially when he told us, at some point, that he felt that teaching was the single most important profession there was!

Through this study of the brain and other aspects of neuroscience, I came to appreciate the importance, when teaching, of engaging students' whole brain/mind/body system, wherever possible, in any activity involving learning— whether through story, music, emotion, dance, movement, artwork, rhythm, etc., and also of sharing some of this brain information with them.

I finally figured out why Jean Houston's trainings and lectures always were so rich, varied, entertaining and totally engaging— they truly employed the epitome of whole brain learning.

I worked for many years with Houston's circle, expanding my own whole-brain learning throughout my life. The summer of 1995, I took what turned out to be the trip of a lifetime for me to the island of Bali in Indonesia along with ten other women friends, all of whom I was well acquainted with from Jean Houston's Human Capacities Program. Robin Van Doren, one of Jean's guest lecturers who'd been to Bali many times, knew many of its people, was fluent in the Indonesian language, and led our group for this unbelievably wondrous three-week trip.

Virtually all of the Balinese people are artists of one kind or another— dancers, musicians, painters, sculptors, architects— and all of them are deeply spiritual people whose art forms, whatever they are, are always an outpouring of their faith. Robin knew many of them and was able to connect each of us to whatever artist-type we chose, who agreed to take us on as students of theirs. Each of us met with and were taught each morning for two or three weeks. I had brought my watercolors with me on the trip and chose to work with two artists, Wayan Sukra, and Ketut Alit who taught me much about the Balinese style of watercolor painting and especially a painting I did of Saraswati, the Hindu representation of the divine feminine.

I was so enraptured with Bali, its beauty, and its wonderful people that I was determined to return someday and went so far as to take a semester course in Indonesian. That was many years ago and I have yet to return. Unfortunately, I've forgotten most of what I learned of their language, but I have not forgotten *terima kasih*, Indonesian for "Thank you" which I still surprise Indonesian people with when I use it appropriately to them.

My trip to Bali enhanced my appetite for further travel even when it meant going alone. In addition to returning to Sweden to visit my six cousins and their families several times more, I traveled also to Rome, Venice, Florence, and two trips to England especially to see their artwork. Those trips were instrumental in strengthening my self-confidence as a single woman.

Whole brain learning brings us closer to ourselves, and should be part of all education initiatives. I came to understand why our public educational systems are frequently failing— far too much emphasis is being placed primarily on test scores! The current focus on STEM courses does not necessarily make their content any more interesting to average students and average teachers unless that content is presented in a more holistic and interesting way. Our schools are competing with so many other vehicles of entertainment and communication which are much more absorbing to students. Classroom learning must also be engaging. Except for a small percentage of students, too many kids are frequently totally bored stiff once they get past second or third grade. One thing neuroscientists have determined— our human brains LOVE variety and usually perform optimally when learning activities introduce variety!

One of the later presentations in our program dealt in part with the brain and the negative impact of stress, not only on the early development of the brain when babies are still in utero, but also on all new learning regardless of age when the brain is confronted with learning a new task but is frequently enveloped in tension and stress. I came to realize that there were physiological, intellectual, and psychological benefits to the release of tension and its concomitants (such as cortisol) when my students had the opportunity to express their emotions either verbally or through their journal writing. More recent research in neuroscience began to indicate that sustained negative emotions (often as ordinary as every day stress) can have a harmful impact on humans at any age, even on the most minute cellular level— what we now call the mind/body effect, found in much if not all adult illness.

Gun violence killed twelve of Ballou's students during the years I taught in the District schools. (Eventually shootings became so frequent that the administration at Ballou stopped announcing each of those killings of our students over the school P.A. system when they occurred!) Because of the many emotional struggles due to homelessness, racism, street drugs, gun violence, and problems at home that my students experienced, I 'd become convinced of how valuable their journal writing was for them not just academically but to their physical and emotional health. I consequently decided to try holding a kind of weekly classroom "tribal council" similar to the one I'd experienced in one of the Human Capacities Trainings I'd taken in that program.

Based loosely on Native American and African tribal decision-making traditions, it was primarily designed to encourage group members to communicate whatever was on their minds, to express their feelings, and to respectfully listen to others when it was not their turn to talk. Initially I'd expected that my classes would think it was a stupid idea, but something impelled me to give it a try anyway. Chairs were arranged in a circle for what we simply called "Council." Students could talk when they had the object designated as a "talking stick" in their hands, and no one commented or gave advice, as often happens in group therapy.

When everyone was seated in the circle, a class volunteer lit the Council candle I'd placed on a chair in the middle of the circle, and that same person dedicated that day's Council to some special situation or intention he or she had that week. The intention might possibly be for a friend or family member or for a difficult situation they themselves were facing. Lighting of the candle signaled the opening of Council, and a suitable object we'd designated as the talking stick was then passed around to each person in the circle. (Eventually an African craftsman I knew, carved a real "Talking Stick" for us.)

Council was held once a week usually on Fridays for one period and had only a few ground rules:

- No one was to talk or interrupt unless he or she had the Talking Stick.
- Council was to be a kind "sacred time and space" for sharing.
- Whatever was shared in Council was not to be a source of later gossip with outsiders.

Our first Council attempts were initially a bit messy (some kids making inappropriate comments, interrupting, etc.), but no one set the room on fire with the Council candle or anything like that!! Just getting the kids to respect one another when someone else had the talking stick and was speaking was the hardest part, but they did begin to do that just almost automatically as kids got used to sharing, very soon after our first gatherings.

My 11th grade English class in particular had been assembled after the semester had started. It was comprised of students that several other English teachers had sent to me to reduce their class sizes. Needless to say, they definitely didn't send me their easiest-to-manage students. (Initially I had doubted that one could even hold Council with them because of the huge, 30-person circle of chairs required). But by the third Council meeting, students were beginning to relax and trust one another more. They were also beginning to learn to be respectful when another class member was talking.

Things really began to move, though, when one boy broke down as he shared with the group about being with his two cousins when they found the body of a third cousin who'd been missing for several days. He'd been shot to death and left lying near his car in a secluded park area in Arlington. He was the catalyst that sparked a flood of pain, fear, and even anger in the ensuing weeks of Council.

Tina, a student who rarely ever spoke in class, told the group of three deaths in her family in the past three months, the sadness and disbelief of seeing her most beloved grandmother disintegrating with Alzheimer's disease, and somewhere in this barrage of woe the casual mentioning of her own rape five years before by an older cousin.

James confided to the group that he was despondent over the impending break-up of his four-year relationship with his girlfriend, and his loneliness at home because he had no real communication with his father even though they lived in the same house and played in a band together frequently. He described a recent fight in which they came to blows with each other. Also, he missed his mother, who now lived in Georgia, and said, "I know you guys will think I'm a real wuss, (his word!), but last night I just laid on my bed and cried!"

When he'd finished, Neisha, one of the more difficult girls in the class, asked for the talking stick and in an attempt to give comfort to James (and after warning her classmates that they'd be sorry if they told anybody what she was about to say) she began to tell James about life with her mother! She described how out-of-control she'd been for a long time, how she'd become engaged in fights with her mother that necessitated the neighbors calling the police to come and restrain her. Her relationship with her mother had been difficult, and she confided that her mother had been in reform school, herself, when she was a teenager. She turned to me and told me that her bad attitude and behavior toward me was not my fault— that she'd had a lot going on— but that things were better now.

Just as the bell was ready to ring, Neisha stood up and said, as she walked toward him, "James, I just want to give you a hug to let you know things aren't as bad as you think they are." And she hugged him in a gesture of affection and support. There were some wet eyes in class that day! Incidentally, her relationship with me improved markedly. She even smiled at me sometimes in the halls when she saw me! That third period class surprised and deeply touched me by the tenderness students began to show toward one another eventually, especially when someone was clearly hurting. And their openness opened up the space for others to also become more open.

I will never forget when Trise at another Friday session broke into tears when she shared that her mother had taken her dog out and had abandoned it on a busy roadway after Trise had neglected to walk the dog one winter day. She revealed that her mother also had lied to her about who her real father was— clearly a taboo subject among the kids that I had never encountered in their journal writings nor heard mentioned before in any of the Council groups I'd witnessed.

Even more surprising and heartening, when Trise had finished, the next three boys in that same circle shared one after the other the absence and pain they felt over issues related to similar questions about unknown, jailed, or missing fathers! I was struck by what a sensitive and almost generous response from those boys, who usually would never have admitted to those truths which were usually kept hidden. I was surprised and deeply touched by the tenderness students eventually began showing.

Using the Council format to empower students to communicate not only with me, but more importantly with each other, probably turned out to be one of the single most successful activities I ever used as a classroom teacher. I became convinced of that by an unusual "Council" incident that occurred in another of my classes some time later when I was teaching at Duke Ellington. Tim, a quiet, somewhat introverted class member, whose turn it was to have the talking stick, shocked the group when he began by saying, "This will be the last time I will be speaking in Council," to which the rest of the group turned to one another in surprised wonderment.

He then continued, "Wasn't what we said in this council supposed to be 'sacred time and space,' not to be repeated outside the group?" Most of the class nodded in agreement, as did I. Tim then looked over at me and nodding politely said, "You, Ms. P, you broke that rule!" I looked at him questioningly, thinking he must have been mistaken or joking. He then proceeded to remind the class of how he'd spoken in our Council recently of the very upsetting suicide of a good friend of his.

Assuming he'd told his mother about his friend's suicide, I'd related this event to his mother several weeks earlier by way of a possible cause when she had a parent conference with me about his seeming depression and poor grades. To my chagrin, she had known nothing of his friend's suicide. Tim was right. I had blabbed to his mother what he'd said about the suicide in council. I'd assumed he had told her, but she knew nothing about it until I mentioned it to her. I'd totally forgotten the Council's confidentiality rules.

I apologized to Tim and to the class for revealing his sharing outside of the group, readily acknowledging my unwitting "big mouth" problem and expressing a hope that he'd reconsider his reluctance about contributing during Council. I also told Tim how pleased I was that he'd been so forthright in calling me out on my thoughtlessness about such an important matter and even more important, his having the courage to confront me respectfully in the presence of others during class.

So much good, so much important sharing took place when a space was created, a situation where kids— people— could put down the masks they too often wore. I, too, shared from time to time my struggles as a single parent.

My life at Ballou was not totally without its untoward incidents. Twice during those years, I had my purse taken, although never by one of my students. Once, a student I did not know popped into my empty classroom a half hour after school let out as I sat at my desk grading papers, grabbed my bag from off the top of my desk, and ran out the door and down the steps with it. I jumped up and chased him down the three flights of empty hallway stairs, yelling loudly after him. At some point, he turned to see me still following him, dropped the bag, and kept on running. I didn't catch him, but I did get my bag back.

One other time my purse disappeared from my bottom desk drawer. I mentioned losing it during my homeroom period. The next morning during first period class, a young man came into class with a large, brown grocery bag in hand and asked if I was "Missus Perello." Figuring I was the "who" he'd meant, I said, "Yes?" He plopped the bag down on my desk and disappeared out the door before I could blink. Inside the bag was my purse with everything in it— everything including money and credit cards. I then realized with a flush of warmth inside that someone in my homeroom or maybe in one of my classes had been looking out for me (or as kids say today, "he or she had my back"). They'd found out who had made off with my purse and put the screws on them or their friends to make sure I got it back.

Usually I did not have problems with students that could not be handled in or just outside of my classroom door. I learned early on how to avoid, if at all possible, throwing down the gauntlet by confronting problems with difficult students in front of their classmates— to avoid a showdown with them in front of their peers, which, of course, they would then have felt obliged to try to "win" in order to save face in front of their friends. Students were usually more than ready to settle things outside of the classroom door alone— just the two of us.

Over the years, when people I met learned that I taught at Ballou, which had the reputation of being one of the worst high schools in the District, they'd often say something like "Oh, wow! You should get hazard duty pay or a medal for teaching there!" They just couldn't wrap their minds around how much I enjoyed working with those teenagers— the joy of watching another person unfold and especially if you have had a part in that unfolding. What basically good, decent, and cooperative people most of them actually were, especially if they sensed that you were really honest with them about everything (no pretense, for kids are powerful "crap detectors"), that you did not look down on them, and hopefully that you genuinely liked them. It also helped enormously for a teacher to have a good sense of humor.

A number of people's fantasies regarding my working with students from Southeast D.C. were that I often needed to fear for my life in school, surrounded as they thought I must have been by rough, noisy, cursing, angry, knife wielding, dangerous black kids just like Hollywood and other media invariably depict them in film or TV— especially young black men, who in general are depicted like the ones whose sullen arrest photos are featured along with the daily headlines in newspapers. They are the stereotypical ones many white people think should be followed around in stores to make sure they don't steal everything not tied down— the ones you'd better click the lock on your car door against if you catch sight of them nearby, or you cross the street if they're coming toward you on the sidewalk. Add to them the ones who are stereotyped as driving around in likely "stolen" Cadillacs or BMWs and perhaps buying steaks with their welfare checks. These grossly racist views are not exaggerations. I have heard them numerous times over the years from white people who have themselves rarely ever had the privilege of or opportunity to have an African American as a personal friend or close neighbor. Didn't they have co-workers of color?!— yes, frequently, but usually only at work. I think that's too bad. They don't know what a rich experience they are missing.

Too many white people I've met, sad to say, still think in those stereotypical ways that have rarely, if ever, been my experience. I simply do not recognize them at all in those descriptions, especially when depicting the young, mostly black men and women I ended up teaching for almost thirty years. Perhaps I see them through different eyes because my family and I have lived in fairly close proximity with them for over fifty years.

I have had the good fortune to get to know much more about who they were inside by what they wrote in their journals, what immense financial struggles, homelessness, and family issues they sometimes were dealing with at home and in the very dangerous streets of certain sections in Southeast D.C. where easy access to guns and drugs are an everyday potential threat.

Generally, several days before Ballou's fall semester was to begin, a faculty meeting and get-together was always planned. It was customary for any new faculty members to be introduced to the faculty, followed by a luncheon and get-acquainted game where every new faculty member had get the signature of every other teacher along with his or her teaching specialty. When the physical education department's new teachers were introduced, one of them, a handsome, young man with a dazzling smile, who was well over 6 feet tall, stood up to introduce himself. He was here at Ballou to do a teaching internship under Ron Smith, head of the physical education department. He'd graduated from Montana State University several years before with a degree in physical education and music, and was here to complete an internship required for him to get a secondary teaching certification in the District.

As we were all sitting around after lunch casually finishing dessert, the newcomers were circulating, getting the signatures and teaching specialties of the other faculty members. I sat chatting with a good teacher friend, Andre Martin, one of the few openly gay faculty members back then, when I saw that tall young man heading toward us.

As he approached to introduce himself and have us sign his get-acquainted paper, I turned to Andre and said jokingly but sufficiently loud enough for the new intern to hear me, "Ah, here he comes now, Andre. Isn't he the prettiest man you've ever seen?" That comment just popped out of my mouth spontaneously. Nowadays a comment like that from a woman in her forties might jokingly brand her as a "cougar," a woman who prefers younger men, but I was at least 40 and felt safe saying it because though I did mean the comment as a statement of fact, I'd never have said it in his presence if I'd actually had any designs on him. I presumed it was obvious I was teasing with both of them.

Andre, of course, jokingly agreed with me, and the young man laughed warmly as he reached out to shake my hand and said, "Hi, my name is Jules" laughing a bit embarrassedly but obviously enjoying the compliment he'd just overheard, nevertheless.

A couple weeks later after fall classes had begun, Jules showed up at my classroom door armed with a notebook pad and pen just before my 6th period acting class. Since this was his free period from the P.E. department, he asked if he might observe my class. Though rather surprised, I welcomed him, of course, introduced him to the class, and found him a seat in the back. To my surprise he then began attending that drama class fairly frequently during his free 6th period, and I found him to be quite relaxed and engaging, especially in interactions with my students.

One afternoon not long afterwards as school was just letting out at 3:00, I ran into him as we were both leaving the building. "Any chance of catching a ride with you to somewhere nearer my apartment on your way home? I have some questions to ask about handling one of my P.E classes?" he asked as we approached my car.

We chatted easily about a minor discipline matter he was having, and when we stopped near his apartment, he said rather ruefully, "Well, I guess I'll see how I do with cooking that steak I got yesterday. How long should I cook it to make it medium rare?" Coincidentally, I, too, was making steak for the girls and myself for dinner, and since I assumed he'd be eating alone I thought perhaps he might like to join us. Eric was away at college in Minnesota, but I was sure Liz and Ann-Mari would like him. "Get your steak, Jules, and come have dinner with my girls and me." He brightened visibly, hopped out of the car and returned just a few minutes later, steak in hand.

After dinner, he stayed on until almost ten before he made a move to leave and catch the bus home. It had been a warm and laughter-filled evening with an easy interchange between Jules and my daughters as later in the living room they showed him some of the latest dance steps the kids were doing those days, and he good naturedly got up to try doing them himself to their delighted applause.

After he said goodbye to the girls, I led him to the front door, and was totally surprised when before stepping out from the screen door, Jules turned back toward me, leaned down and gave me a quick kiss goodbye and said, "A big thank you, Mrs. P. It's been great." I was struck by at the unexpected kiss and especially from a man much taller and years younger than I. And I finally knew what it was like to feel like that "fragile flower" I'd always wished I'd been long ago when standing next to some man.

"He really likes you, Mom," Liz called out matter-of-factly moments later as she headed up the stairs to her bedroom. "Yah, you bet!" chimed in Ann-Mari shaking her head knowingly as she followed behind her sister.

"Oh, come on!" I protested emphatically. "He's at least fourteen or fifteen years younger than I am. Don't be ridiculous!"

But to my total surprise, that's how my relationship with Jules began. We'd been accustomed as a family to having friends of the kids and our neighbors in and out of our house routinely, so Jules' coming around more frequently felt quite normal. At first, though I found him to be enormously attractive and engaging, I could not even entertain a "real" relationship with him. Though I sensed that he was attracted to me, as I was to him, I couldn't imagine anything coming of this attraction let alone lasting more than a few weeks. But that attraction grew to a month, and then it became months, and then eventually years!

Customarily women my age coming of age during the 50s, 60s, and before, routinely sought relationships with men their age and usually older— men older and almost invariably taller seemed to be the standard, and more often better educated, also, because women themselves were shut out of the good paying jobs. If it was a real career, they had to be satisfied with the usual career choices— nursing, secretarial work, maybe teaching, or as an airline stewardess if they were slender, attractive, and 5'6 or under etc. Men were said to be less "comfortable" with women they thought were smarter than they. So, women often avoided challenging men intellectually or even academically, and might even pretended to be less smart—dumber, actually— than their partners— at least until they'd married them and could be more truthful. Coming, as I did, from my Swedish background where one did not presume to act as though he or she thought they were "better than" anyone else, I also didn't want people to think I was showing off by wearing my Phi Beta Kappa key, as Dan's friends in seminary had thought about their buddy Irv, who'd worn his Phi Beta Kappa key on his necktie. That was the primary reason I never wore the key I'd earned in college— which Dan had suggested I could always just hang from the toilet handle!

No woman that I'd ever known personally had ever had a relationship with a man any younger than they were. I'd even been a bit surprised when I learned that Dan's sister-in-law was a year or two older than Dan's brother! Both Dan and my former fiancé Ken had been six years older than I.

Unlike the way it was for women, it was actually almost routine for men to marry women 10, 15 or even 20 years younger than they. But for a man to date, let alone marry a woman 15 years older than he? Almost unheard of!! Not even in Hollywood did women take the risk that a younger man would eventually throw them over for a younger woman, or they assumed that most men would never even seek a woman older than they. Some of those unwritten rules began to disappear when the feminist revolution in the 70s and beyond began to take effect, and women's self-esteem began to grow. But those rules are not totally gone, yet.

But there was also one other stumbling block to a relationship with Jules. He happened to be a young, black man, and in the '70s and early '80s there were even stronger racial barriers than there are now, especially regarding dating and inter-marriage. Actually, there were still a number of states where inter-racial marriage was still illegal. That has changed by and large, thanks to a more recent Supreme Court decision. Mixed marriages are fairly common now, especially in the Washington, D.C. area and other large cities, but they weren't then. Even though most of my neighbors were African American, themselves, initially I was a bit uncomfortable wondering what they were thinking about their white neighbor with this tall, younger looking black man in tow. But they never said anything untoward and continued always to be cordial.

When Jules and I went someplace together, heads frequently turned, and especially since he was also tall and attractive. If anything ever was said, it invariably came from a white man in places like bars and restaurants, people whom neither of us knew. Occasionally a younger, unknown, black woman might grouse a bit under her breath about my leaving the eligible black men in D.C. alone!! Given what I knew about the dreadful treatment of black women historically in our culture, that was understandable.

As for the months while Jules was interning at Ballou, we were both very circumspect about being seen together there, and at least I never heard any gossip. I had begun attending a Unity church in D.C., which by then was quite integrated compared to other white congregations, and when Jules attended church with me, there were no discernible stares, and we seemed to blend in.

He was a warm, friendly, loving man interested expanding in many things and whom I expected would be an excellent teacher. One would have assumed that with his considerable height (6'6"), he would have played basketball in college, but he actually didn't care all that much for the game other than to watch it (and later teach it). His years going to college in Montana, an overwhelming white state, equipped him well for being comfortable with white people, who as a consequence, usually seemed quite comfortable in his presence. We often went out with my friend Nikki, who was French, and her fiancé Dick, a former Catholic seminarian from my therapy group to whom I'd introduced Nikki. When they married, Jules and I served as witnesses at their wedding.

Jules spent more and more time at our house and eventually ended up living with us and our dog Nicky. When I let myself think about it, I imagined that at some point whatever emotional connection Jules and I had would fade, that he would want to be with younger women, perhaps want to marry, have children, and our relationship would come to an end. I tried to prepare myself for that eventuality, but that was easier said than done.

The longer we were together, the deeper my love for him grew, and the harder it was to cut myself off from those feelings. I didn't even try. We shared the kind of emotional intimacy that I wished I'd had with my husband but that he'd seemed incapable of having. When I speak of emotional intimacy, I'm speaking here not just about a sexual relationship. I'm speaking of the whole range of the sharing of one's real feelings— the places where we are all so vulnerable— where we can open up our heart and our hurts to the other.

Finally, I knew what it felt like to feel really loved by a man. And Jules and I laughed together, often just about stupid things. Private jokes. An image that stays in my mind still, after all these years, is how often when he came home from work, he'd sometimes come running through the house toward the kitchen, his necktie flying behind his neck, yelling "Where is she? Where is she? I haven't had a hug all day!" as he'd come bounding into the kitchen, wrapping his arms around me, and kiss me roundly.

When Jules completed his teaching internship, he took a job at the

Scan Company, a Scandinavian design furniture store in Georgetown and was quite successful at salesmanship, so it was several years before he decided, with our family's persistent encouragement, to apply for a teaching position at several of the school systems in the D.C. area. During that time, Jules and I were attending a Unity Church in D.C., and at one point they held a fund-raising lottery. The First prize was a two-week trip for two to Paris. We each took ten tickets to sell— twenty tickets between us. Then we both promptly forgot we'd taken them. It wasn't until the Sunday of the lottery drawing on our way to church that we realized that this was the morning and we both had neglected to sell our tickets.

Since we'd forgotten to sell any of our tickets, we each bought ten tickets and agreed that we'd split the prize if any of our tickets won. Ours were among the last tickets in the barrel before they turned the barrel upside down to draw the winning ticket. My heart sank when I realized our tickets were now on the bottom. Hopeless, I knew, so I paid no further attention to the drawing until a friend's voice yelled out to us, "It's yours! It's yours!" and we realized that one of those tickets we'd bought was the winning ticket. Neither of us had ever been to France, nor had we ever won anything in a lottery. People seemed very happy for us that we'd won. People from Unity Church might have called that "divine order." I called it incredible good luck!

So, there we were two months later on an Air France plane headed for Paris. My friend Nikki was there for the summer visiting her mother in Paris where she'd been born and grew up, and she was there to meet us at Orly Airport. She'd found us an inexpensive small hotel, one with those small, open, metal lifts in the lobby to take guests upstairs; it was just blocks from where Nikki's mother had a tiny apartment. Dick arrived a few days later from the States, and he and Nikki spent the whole week showing us almost all the fantastic sites of Paris before Jules and I took a train to spend the next week in the French and Swiss Alps.

At one point we were the only ones in that closed French train compartment, and somehow we were able to make love and not get caught by the conductor making his rounds! It was lovely— very much like one sees in a romantic movie. It was a risk I never regretted taking, and so unlike anything I could have imagined taking ever before in my life!

It was interesting to see how much more accepting Europeans were of inter-racial couples than in the U.S. No one in France seemed to look twice at Jules and me. That absence of extreme race consciousness compared to the U.S. also explains why so many black artists, writers, and musicians early on gravitated to France to establish themselves artistically. They became ex-patriots there because the French took their talent far more seriously than it was ever taken in the U.S. The French were freer of prejudice at least of the racial variety than Americans were.

At the end of that wonderful trip together to France and Switzerland, Jules was due back to work at Scan, and I took advantage of being in Europe to visit my six cousins in Sweden before heading home. By now, we'd been together almost four years. There were times when my old fears of being betrayed, as I had in the past by some of the men I had loved, reared its ugly head. I would occasionally see an especially lovely, much younger woman than I, and torment myself imagining that if Jules could have a relationship with her and a family of his own, he would no longer want me.

Whether separating from him was inevitable given the disparity in our ages, his lack of sufficient experience in the area of relationships, or that my very fear in that happening somehow created it to happen, I can't say. But the evening he told me casually that he'd been thinking of getting a place of his own, my heart plunged to my toes. I didn't throw a tantrum or call him out for what he was suggesting, but I knew that comment, out of the blue that it seemed to come was probably the beginning of the end. I didn't want him to stay because he felt guilty. We were not married. I had no claim on him nor he on me. I'd had almost five years of as happy a relationship as I'd ever had with any man, receiving more love, tenderness, passion, and happiness, than I'd ever had before. That was far more than I'd ever expected.

My head told me what I'd learned years before— that people can't own one another much as I might like to, and that some people must have room to grow. My heart, on the other hand, silently felt devastated. It stamped its feet and yelled "No! No! No!" It cried and cried. And that's what I did that first night after Jules told me that he wanted to get a place of his own. I slipped out of the house to my car in front of the house where I actually did cry until I had no tears left. I knew if I carried on like that in the house giving vent to my hurt in front of him, perhaps Jules might have changed his mind about leaving, but eventually that need to fulfill whatever he needed to find out about himself would have come back. Some weeks later, he found a room somewhere in Arlington in a house-sharing situation with three other people.

We continued to see one another after he moved out but less and less frequently. A year or so later when we had a conversation, he told me something I found really hard to understand— that he'd left because he felt out-classed by me— that was the word he'd used. Is it possible that we separated because he felt intimidated, and I felt "too old and no longer pretty enough or slender enough?" Perhaps we both had self-esteem issues! But that's probably true for the majority of people on the planet or at least in our American culture.

Since then I've come to consider the possibility that there are those people who pass through our lives for just a brief period of time, and they're there for some reason— a purpose for which neither of us are aware and which we may not understand at the time. Much later we may realize that another person or experience was perhaps foreordained to be there to enable us to experience something about ourselves we needed to learn or to serve as the conduit to lead us to another step in our own unfolding spiritually or psychologically.

CHAPTER 16

The Rescuer

I was quite young, five or six perhaps, watching my Mother's almost reflexive response to another person's need for food, when I became a kind of occasional "rescuer" of all things in need. During the Depression and the beginning of WW II. Hungry, homeless men would occasionally come to our back door in Chicago asking for something to eat. If my mother had extra food, she would share it, if not she would at least make them a sandwich.

I remember once on the way to Lambert's delicatessen to get bread for my mother, I noticed a small, rubber DyDee Doll on a shelf in the shoemaker's shop. The doll was naked, covered with dirt and grime, and actually quite pitiful looking. It was still there when some time later, I was sent to the shoemakers to pick up a pair of shoes.

"Whose doll is that?" I asked the shoemaker.

"Oh, I have no idea," he said. "Someone left it in here weeks ago."

"Could I have it?" I asked timidly.

"What do you want that dirty, old doll for?" the shoemaker said disbelievingly, and then continued, "Yes, of course, take it! Take it home and give it a bath!"

Delighted, I reached up and took the doll down from its perch on the shelf above the counter, thanked the shoemaker and hurried home to do just that— give it a bath, find something at home to dress it in, make a bed for it, and adopt it as my own. Frequently over the years I felt compelled to rescue all manner of things— lost, homeless, or abused dogs, cats, rabbits, toys, and sometimes even people as I grew up.

When I was about ten, a cocker spaniel stray that we'd taken in and I named "Pepper," later bit a neighbor and was required to stay caged for rabies observation at the city dog pound for a month. When I went to visit our "Pepper dog," as we called him, I'd been so sickened by the filthy conditions and crowded animal cages there that I decided I wanted to own a proper animal shelter someday. I even drew up plans for it. I'd have liked to become a veterinarian, but girls didn't become veterinarians, or human doctors, either, for that matter. Career choices for women were very circumscribed.

Perhaps that penchant for helping people and other living creatures led eventually to my becoming a teacher and perhaps fulfilling my belief that as a Christian, it was consistent with my faith to be of service in this world and to leave it in a better place. But it may also explain an unexpected event in my life that took place many years later— an event about which I rarely speak because it's so difficult to share so that others could understand, and because it's always created a sense of shame or embarrasses much like the one I once felt about my husband's infidelity somehow being my fault.

In 1984, two years following the end of my relationship with Jules, I put a personals ad in the Washingtonian magazine. One of the people who answered my ad was an attractive-sounding man, Christopher Griffin, who like me, was from Chicago, where he worked as a stock trader. He began to write and eventually to talk with me regularly by phone. Eventually, I learned that he was calling me from the Federal Correctional Institution in Petersburg, Virginia, but had been afraid to admit that fact to me for fear I would cut off all communication with him.

Remembering the admonishment by Jesus in the book of Matthew about visiting those in prison, I eventually agreed to drive to Petersburg just one time to visit Christopher at the Correctional Center in Virginia. Having never been inside or outside of either a jail or prison. I was appalled the first time I saw this huge building and the forbidding exterior of that place, the harsh razor-blade coils above the barbed wire fencing, the fingerprinting and searching of visitors, the clanging of gates and doors. When the reality of imprisonment struck me, I was prepared to feel sympathy for anyone detained there! It would be the first of many visits.

I remember bundling up against the cold, checking to make sure I had all I needed, driver's license, money, bubblegum, snapshots, or whatever I would try to sneak into him (like oranges and freshly baked coffee bread I brought on Christmas Eve that he wouldn't eat because he said his grandmother warned him I might try to poison him!) Then I would walk the long walk from the parking lot (it really wasn't that far, but it seemed interminable) and I would be stopped by the guard in the tower who would question me about any possible contraband I might have and I would repeat, "No. No. No. No..." in answer to each of the guards questions about guns, knives, weapons, drugs, food, etc.

Then the walk to that building, dreading the wait at the window as the prison guard checked my license, checked the visitors list, slipped the questionnaire through the bars for me to fill out... I could never remember my license plate number so I always made one up and wondered if they ever checked. Then he would finally signal the guard behind the control window and the heavy barred door would slowly roll open and I would step through and wait while he searched my small bag. For some reason, he never unzipped the top zipper compartment where the bubble gum, notepaper, pen, and snapshots were stashed.

I could have smuggled lots of dope in there if I'd been a dope smuggler! I guess he figured that I didn't look the type. He then took out his electronic metal detector, ran it up and down my body as it clicked wildly away and

I would hold my breath wondering illogically if by some chance it might discover the oranges or apples I had in my coat pocket or whether the bulge from them would give me away. Then it was time for what I referred to as the Invisible Stamp Routine and I felt like an internee at Auschwitz as one of the guards stamped the soft underside of my wrist with some invisible magic word which became my passport to leaving the prison at the end of the visit when it was viewed under the ultraviolet light. (I suppose that was so that Christopher wouldn't don my high heels, coat, and scarf and leave posing as me while I took his place in prison!)

Finally, another guard would signal the man behind the glass control booth and another set of barred doors would open admitting me to the visitors' room where I then made my way to the guards at the front desk who would ask whom I was there to see. And I would wait, and wait. And I would pace the floor, try to find a table as far from their view as possible, deposit my coat, pace the floor some more, get a hot chocolate, smoke cigarette after cigarette. I hardly smoked at all until I began those trips to visit Chris.

I ended up being swindled by Christopher Griffin. He was able to convince me over six months that his imprisonment was due to a wrongful, unjust court decision by a racist judge in Chicago at a time when the Gray Lords scandal among judges and lawyers in Cook County, Illinois, took place. Griffin, along with the assistance of a lawyer, was able to talk me into temporarily posting the bail bond by mortgaging my house, for a total of $64,000. The lawyer was then to take the money, which I had transferred (through Griffin's lawyer) to the Cook County court to post a bail bond for Christopher Griffin's conviction in Cook County-Chicago. The bond was supposedly to have been a loan to be returned to me by the courts but was, in truth, a total swindle!

Perhaps some might take me for a lonely, desperate woman willing to throw away $64,000 after swallowing hook, line, and sinker the romantic blandishments of a young, good-looking convict. It wasn't true, but it's difficult to describe adequately the extent and enormity of Griffin's deceit, an incredibly clever and calculating strategy by a person totally devoid of conscience, tricking me and at least a few other women into helping him financially and in many other ways. Initially Griffin had managed to conceal not only his true age and background but also after three months of phone calls placed to me by having a girlfriend place three way calls, the fact that he was incarcerated.

He also managed to enlist the assistance of a Richmond attorney to serve as the go between for funds and to corroborate his lies that my money was to be used for legal fees and in my case to post a $50,000 appeal bond with the Cook County Courts as well. Along with other "talents," Mr. Griffin is a consummate actor and on several occasions literally cried in my presence over his fear that he would be killed when he was to be returned to Joliet Prison to complete his sentence if I did not help him to make a bond. I believed him, and in his innocence.

To me, given my meager teacher's salary, this was a fortune in 1984. I turned for assistance and wisdom to David Austern, the lawyer who once had helped with my divorce, the U.S. Attorney's Office and eventually the F.B.I. By then I had learned that Griffin never had been a stock trader though he certainly talked like one. I also learned that he had a long history of swindling women. A total of ten women, altogether at that time, many of whom had been visiting him at the Petersburg, Virginia prison during the same period that I was visiting. They'd only been found by the F.B.I. through my initial complaint and Griffin's visitors list at the prison in Virginia.

It took almost three years for a grand jury to bring an indictment against Griffin through testimony from these ten other women. Yet none of these other women reported Griffin's crime, probably out of a sense of shame for having been completely duped, betrayed by someone purporting to love them. I had been the only one who went to the authorities to report his activities after losing the mortgage money loan.

I never got my money back, though. From prison, Griffin was able to move my money from bank to bank using the girlfriend's 3rd party phone service to hinder the FBI from freezing his accounts. By law they needed to get a new subpoena from a judge each time they caught up with the money at another new bank. But by time the money could be subpoenaed, the money would already have been moved to yet another bank. Eventually his brother in Chicago withdrew my $64,000 from Griffin's account, while Griffin was still in prison. After almost three years, Griffin was charged with the theft of my money, pled guilty and received a five-year prison sentence, which was eventually reduced for good behavior to three years.

There are no words to tell you of the physical pain, disillusionment and financial loss I experienced during those 2 1/2 years. I had seen such potential for good in Christopher Griffin, and I tried to help him begin to realize that potential. He knew full well where my finances stood after mortgaging my house. He knew that I would have only $500 a month to live on after paying the monthly payment on the house. He knew it was only a matter of time until I would be forced to sell my home. I had visited him almost every week for almost six months in Petersburg because after seeing what conditions were like in prison. He knew there was no way that I could turn my back on him. I cared what happened to him. He seemed like a human being truly worth trying to save. That was my big mistake— trying to play God. And for my efforts on his behalf, he totally used, manipulated and cheated me and betrayed my friendship.

I realize that the courts view fraud as a lesser offense—not nearly equivalent to crimes committed with a gun. These are not considered crimes of violence. Fraud is white collar crime. But I tell you there was nothing white collar about this crime. I could not have felt any more violated had I been beaten or held up at gun point. I would much rather that Griffin came as a stranger out of the dark and put a gun to my back to steal my money. At least he would have only gotten my money. This way he not only stole my money and almost three years of my life, but he also stole my faith and trust not only in myself and my fellow man but also, for a while anyway, my faith in God. At times, I felt like I just wanted to fade away. Fortunately, I did not attempt to hide this mess from my family, friends and co-workers, and consequently their love and support and God's grace have helped me survive, that man may have taken my money away from me, but he wasn't able to take away the me from me!

Even during his sentence for swindling me, in a new prison in Danbury, Connecticut, Griffin again swindled three other women through the mails, by phone, and then through their prison visitations. Between those three women, one of whom was the vice-president of a well-known women's clothing store in New York City, he was able to steal over a million dollars!

Christopher Griffin is a coward who would never stand up to a man. Instead, he preys on women and their vulnerability in order to manipulate them for his own purposes. He is an extremely clever man, and he is also the most consciously evil person I've ever known. He was gifted with an articulate mouth, a cunning mind, healthy good looks, and warm, honest eyes. That is why he is so dangerous. I have taught in a public high school in one of the poorest neighborhoods in Southeast Washington for over 18 years. I have taught virtually thousands of poor, African American young-sters, some from the most appalling environments. Some of them you might consider to be hoodlums. But I have never been cheated or abused in any way by any of them. Without a doubt Griffin is the lowest human being I have ever encountered. He loves no one, and his own self-loathing must be enormous. And he doesn't seem to have learned anything from his impris-onment except new ways of victimizing people. His activities even after his more recent indictment bear witness to that.

I have learned since this happened that using the personals ads to bilk women of their money by playing on their loneliness and their sympathies is a con game rampant in prisons these days. Very few women ever acknowl-edge that they've been swindled because they are too humiliated by having been gullible and naïve. I found solace in the fact that I was not the only one tricked by Griffin. I hope the other women's shame was lessened by that as well. This was a club I never thought I would find myself a member of, but I am proud that I fought back through my shame and embarrassment to hopefully slow if not stop the abuses Christopher Griffin inflicted upon so many of us.

Griffin has now seemingly disappeared and as of 2019 is still on the loose for having broken his parole that he'd been serving for the theft of my money. I never did get the mortgage money back. I write this in brief as a matter of record but especially now when online dating is so prevalent and has become a fertile harvest ground for potential "lonely hearts" thieves and other swindlers.

What is it we do, or allow to happen in the raising of our daughters that makes them so vulnerable in their search for love and acceptance in a male-dominated world? What happens to us so unconsciously as we're growing up that we allow ourselves to be subordinated and abused and then shamed so that we don't even recognize that we're not to blame— that we've been "had," so to speak, and consequently are reluctant to report that physical, emotional, or even financial abuse to the authorities? And if we do report it, cannot even count on being listened to?

I have chosen primarily to write about it now, not because I really want to go back in memory to that event, but because it is a far more common occurrence now with social media connections and networks than it was when I was swindled out of a large sum of money by a prospective partner by way of a personals ad in a magazine. And it is still rare for any woman to share it with her family, friends, or the police.

CHAPTER 17

Innovation Can be a Lonely Place

One of the hardest parts of teaching was dealing with some of the decision-making insanities of the D.C. Schools' central administration, which was responsible for such decisions as the changing of principals at Ballou twenty times just during the twenty years that I taught there.

When test scores continued to consistently bottom out at Ballou, the school superintendent and central school administration decided that the fault was poor teachers—after all, who but a poor teacher would stay in a school with so many problems! Whatever their "logic" was, they gave involuntary school transfers to 70 percent of Ballou's 120 teachers. The other remaining teachers were either fired outright or required to re-apply "from scratch" to be considered for teaching jobs at Ballou again.

During that period before the mass transfers and firings, I had applied for and received a two-year educational leave of absence to complete the course work toward a doctorate in new brain research and its impact on educational psychology. During that period, I managed to support myself as a communications trainer with the U.S. Office of Personnel Management (OPM) from 1988 to 1990. Only when my educational leave was over and I was about to return to teaching at Ballou was I informed that I, too, had been "involuntarily" transferred to another high school.

When all of those teacher transfers and the hiring of new teachers didn't solve the problem of test scores, the system then transferred the entire Ballou administration including the current principal at the time, four or five assistant principals, all the counselors, and eventually even the cooks and janitorial crews. After that, Ballou was left with no internal memory, the stabilizing force that we experienced people had once provided. Things for the students went from bad to worse. Eventually after several years, the DCPS central administration decided to solve their problems by closing the school, tearing down the whole building and eventually erecting a new school next door!! Now there's a way to solve a problem! Just tear it down!! As for me, I stayed in the system six more years, but some of the happiest and most productive years of my teaching had been at Ballou.

I mentioned earlier that Ballou had a negative reputation in the school system because of its low test scores and its location in Southeast. Its serving one of the poorest sections of the city with a population of people (most of whom were lower income African Americans and were not accustomed to having any real voice in the city's decision-making) meant that Ballou was often used as the dumping ground either for teachers and principals who had in some way run afoul with the D.C. School Administration or where they often sent new, inexperienced teachers to teach. Because Ballou and other middle and elementary schools in Southeast serviced mostly low income families, the D.C. system got away with cheating the students in every conceivable way— insufficient books, supplies, art materials, musical instruments, teachers, substitutes, and even personnel or systems in place to effectively track down chronically absent students or at least make sure parents were notified whenever a student was absent. Having one's daughter or son truant and not being apprised of it for weeks would not have been tolerated by the more affluent and predominantly white parents in more prosperous

District neighborhoods. It made me sick to see our students consistently short-changed.

Being involuntarily transferred to another school in the system was viewed by many principals as a sign that a prospective teacher must be deficient in some way, transferred for some reason, especially if it was from a school with the problems Ballou had. Nothing changed, however, even after giving involuntary transfers or firings to the vast majority of Ballou's teachers and filling our positions with new teachers. After the change in staffing, there were no significant increases in student achievement averages such as reading tests or other performance criteria. And so it went from bad to worse, but predictably with no test score increases! And to add to the problem, every few years, the District of Columbia was also changing the system wide school superintendents.

When I received notice that I, too, had been given an involuntary transfer, I was at first indignant to have been involuntarily de-selected and then just very disappointed that I would not be coming back to Ballou again. As problematic as it had been, there had been a whole cadre of loyal teachers who cared about the school and its students and had hung in there year after year. I really loved that school and its students!! Even now in 2019 when former Ballou teachers happened to accidentally run into one another years later, we invariably greet each other like long, lost, Vietnam vets even if one teacher had not been particularly close to another years before. It was a unique experience both for the teachers and the kids.

I initially thought the news was good when I learned that I was being transferred to a high school called the School Without Walls, which was intended to be a kind of specialty public school founded for the purpose of encouraging students, who could not perform well amid the conformist strictures of a traditional classroom but could perhaps flourish where they could do semester-long internships in areas of special interest to them. Located in Northwest D.C. next door to the campus of George Washington University, it was originally an old elementary public school (circa late 1800s,) now it had less than 400 students, but it definitely had walls! I was excited about this new, different teaching challenge.

The bad news was that I was not wanted there... actively and obviously not wanted by the woman who was the principal and who made that very clear to me the first day I reported for duty. I'd never felt so unwanted in my life. She wanted a particular part-time chemistry teacher not some cast-off Ballou English teacher (my words not hers!) She'd been locked in a battle of wills with the Assistant Superintendent over this missing part-time teacher (probably because she had threatened the assistant superintendent with the same talk about her influential connections "downtown" with one of the City Council members, who'd evidently been responsible for her being moved from an elementary school position to being a high school principal. His strings she thought she could pull just as she'd threatened me. I had gotten caught in the middle of their battle. The Asst. Superintendent wanted me at School Without Walls and the principal didn't— clearly a personal clash of wills strengthened by my having been involuntarily transferred from Ballou and now not feeling so accommodating about being pushed around some more.

For the following six months, the principal assigned me no classes and with the exception of an occasional stony-faced nod in the hallway, literally ignored me for that entire semester. One of the English teachers allowed me to use her coat rack and a small table for my belongings in her tiny office that once had been the janitor's closet.

I finally had to ask the office secretary for a mailbox in the office but was never listed with the faculty on their bulletin board or on any other places listing the faculty. I attempted to keep busy substitute teaching for other teachers, teaching a voluntary lunchtime English refresher class to tutor any students needing extra help, assisting with other teachers' field trips, and helping with anything teachers might ask of me. I coached a new student, Eric, in a dramatic reading he'd chosen from Shakespeare's *Richard*

III for the English Speaking Union's City-wide Shakespeare Competition in which he won First Place. Eric was new to Walls after being sent to D.C. by his father from the South to live with his aunt because of some trouble he'd been in at his old school. I joined him and his aunt in New York City for the ESU national competition where he won Second Place nationwide. I called a Washington Post reporter, Courtland Milloy, who came out to the school, interviewed Eric on his *Richard III* win and then wrote a long Sunday feature article about him. I also worked with another student, the senior class valedictorian, coaching him in preparation for his graduation speech.

These were just some of the attempts I made to convince the principal that I would be a useful addition to her school. I finally became quite depressed by that inimical environment that I could not even use my spare time at Walls to work on my dissertation. Eventually I realized that there was nothing I felt I could do considering my financial responsibilities at home and graduate school tuition due so I finally withdrew from the doctoral program.

I'd never encountered anyone in the school system as vindictive as this principal. She regarded Walls as her school, as her property. I later learned that I'd not been the only person she had treated badly. Though Walls had originally been set up for kids who didn't "fit" in traditional schools, this principal selected only the "good" readers and excellent students, and actually pretty much ran it like her own private school.

By summer, I decided I'd put up with her abuse long enough. When she called me at home late in the summer just before the opening of another school year, she again told me there was "no place for me" at School Without Walls. I knew that she would have to keep me as long as the assistant superintendent wanted me there.

I believe she finally decided to bribe me into leaving by offering to find a placement at the Duke Ellington School of the Arts. Though Ellington was a much farther commute from home than School Without Walls, I agreed to the transfer hoping it would ultimately lead to a regular teaching position. It was time to bid adieu to the principal from hell as I referred to her ever thereafter.

That "placement" that the Duke Ellington principal had in mind when he agreed to take me on sight unseen was for what he referred to as a public relations position. I was given the task of proofreading and Xeroxing school brochures and advertisements for the arts programs at Ellington and helping get out the mailing lists. I also became the unofficial substitute for any absent teachers.

A year later, I finally was assigned a half time position at Ellington teaching 11th grade English plus the half time Public Relations paper pusher position and shared a classroom with another English teacher. As an English/Communications teacher with over twenty-three years with the District school system at what 1 felt was very successful teaching experience, a Master's degree, and all the course work toward a Ph.D. level in academic credits, I felt demeaned professionally when I was reduced to a kind of high paid Xerox machine operator and a part time English teacher. But I had made this deal to get away from the principal from hell so I just kept quiet!

I'd taken a considerable number of psychology, brain, mind, and healing related courses in addition to those dealing with consciousness and human potential that I had taken with Jean Houston. At one point, I took a weeklong training course in the MBTI (Myers Briggs Type Indicator), the personal-profile type instrument. I received certification to administer and score it and gave it to my 11th graders. Not knowing how they would respond to it but hoping it would expand their knowledge about their own personality characteristics, academic strengths, and interests, I also hoped it would give them an appreciation and understanding of others quite different from themselves. Surprisingly, they really seemed to enjoy what they learned about themselves their preferences, how they learned optimally, and how they interacted with other classmates different from them. In a two-week unit we completed, they learned not just about themselves but also about other students' preferences and temperaments through class discussions, comparing those differences, and then writing about the validity of what they'd learned about themselves.

I had also taken several Loving Relationship Trainings with Dr. John Gray. I began to use Gray's "Love letters" exercise in school. I would have each of my 11th graders write a letter to someone they had strong feelings of animosity against, starting with whatever negative feelings they had toward the other person and writing sentence after sentence working up toward more positive ones. The point was not to actually send those letters, but rather to work on releasing the anger, resentment, or negativity they felt so that it didn't continue to poison them and their relationships. Finding this helpful, my students began to use that technique in the context of their journals.

On several occasions, after the Christmas break at Ballou, I passed out to each student two fresh envelopes. They were to fill the first with a letter of good wishes which they would give to me to insure of its being mailed to whomever it was addressed. The second envelope was to contain a letter listing any of their negative feelings. They would seal that envelope and pass it to the front of the class. I placed those envelopes in the trashcan and then I lit them on fire calling on the students to see this as a symbol of the release of the negative forces in their lives. That caused quite a stir, believe me, and it worked quite well. When you were up on the third floor of Ballou High School you could do almost anything.

Having the opportunity to teach at an arts related public high school like Duke Ellington, whose students had chosen to attend and had auditioned to get accepted to it, was an inspiring way to finish my years in the

D.C. Public School System. Students' school days were long, running from 8:00 am until almost 6:00 pm., but because so much more of their brain was engaged in things like dancing, music, theatre, art, etc., things they really loved doing besides their academic curriculum, they didn't mind the long hours. I loved the environment at the school, the general climate of respect and affection that the arts program teachers (all of them professionals in one field of the arts or another) had for the students. And by and large, the kids seemed to love and appreciate their teachers, as well. Most of the teachers teaching the traditional academic courses came from the collection of D.C. Public School teachers, and on the whole we seemed to be a pretty good group of teachers. Over 90% of Ellington's student body ultimately ended up attending college or arts oriented professional schools beyond high school.

Still at Ellington early in March 1996, I learned that Vice-President Al Gore's wife, Tipper Gore, and Dr. Donna Shalala, Secretary of Health and Human Services, were to address the D.C. Press Corps and other guests in Ellington's theater and deliver remarks to launch a Children's National Mental Health Initiative. I was delighted to learn that these efforts to provide a much needed service were being considered by the Federal Government. I knew that Gore had an advanced degree in psychology and I wrote to her regarding non-medical remediation that could be used by teachers in schools to help their students and I told her a little about my efforts to that end in my own classroom. I was disappointed, however, that I was not going to be able to attend the press conference myself because I had a class to teach that morning when it was scheduled.

The morning of the conference, however, someone from the school office came up to my 3rd floor classroom to tell me I was wanted in the office. When I arrived, there was Tipper Gore, Vice-President Al Gore's wife. I was introduced to her and then taken up to be seated along side her and the other speakers. Both Dr. Donna Shalala and Ms. Gore gave brief presentations. What I wasn't prepared for and really surprised by was that

Tipper Gore read parts of the letter I'd written to her. The following is an excerpt from the speech Tipper Gore gave at Duke Ellington School on March 6th, 1996.

It is an honor for me to be here to underscore my wholehearted support for this important mental health initiative. Let me tell you about a letter I received from Joan Pierotti, a teacher at the Duke Ellington School. In her letter, she told me about the personal struggle she has experienced as a teacher, a struggle that stems directly from the pain, hardship and trauma many of her students have gone through.

Joan wrote about the culture in which many young people today are forced to live and learn. For some of her students, their safety has been jeopardized by neighborhood violence. Many are homeless, their friends and loved ones have been lost to drug addiction and their self-worth has been demolished by sexual abuse and racism.

But, as Joan wrote in her letter, there is hope. I would like to read the message of hope that Joan communicated to me.

"In my many years of teaching, much of it in the most economically deprived, crime-ridden area of this city, I can count on one hand the times I needed to call in a parent because of behavior problems that couldn't be handled in the classroom. I truly believe this was the result of her ongoing commitment to attempting to honor the totality of a student's identity as not only an intellectual being, but as an emotional and spiritual one as well. Somehow, having their emotional and spiritual natures acknowledged and addressed perhaps enables them to get beyond much of the turmoil in their lives and attend to the business of learning."

That's why we are here today, to promote total health and effective learning among our children. Today, we inaugurate a new era of awareness that mental health problems among the Nation's children are real, painful, and can be severe.

We also know, as Joan Pierotti pointed out so eloquently in her let-
ter, that environment can contribute to mental health problems.
Regardless of the balance of causal factors, effective treatments are
available even for the most serious emotional problems, whether it's
anxiety disorder, or severe depression, or schizophrenia, there is hope.
We want to send this message to every parent, caregiver, and teacher,
and to every individual who possesses the capacity to help a child with
a mental health problem.

Rarely was I acknowledged by administrators for any of my efforts in the D.C. School System except a monthly paycheck. This was true for most other teachers as well. The system seemed not to be aware of the importance of acknowledgment other than a paycheck for teachers, especially those in the inner city. The most important acknowledgments that I received during those years were from my students, which is what mattered to me especially when they contacted me through their journal writing or after they'd graduated. But Tipper Gore's acknowledgment of my letter meant a great deal to me. Within three months I was fired from the DC Public School system.

I taught at Duke Ellington from 1991 to 1996. The Ellington principal who'd hired me, was no longer there. In his place was the former assistant principal, who informed me several weeks after Tipper Gore's presentation that I was among the six teachers from Ellington who were selected to be part of their system-wide Reduction in Force RIF.

In the mid-nineties, the City of Washington, D.C., was on the verge of financial bankruptcy. The Congressional committee overseeing the District of Columbia rescinded the regulation on teachers' tenure being based on their number of years of service and required that the District of Columbia School System institute a minimum Reduction in Force (RIF) of 500 teachers either by firing them or forcing them (if minimally eligible) into retirement.

Those selected for the RIF were 500 of the more senior (and consequently the higher paid teachers). That included me. Like so many others teachers, I sought help from the D.C. Teacher's Union and had a hearing before a so-called judge (not one in a traditional court) who for the most part ruled against all those who'd lost their jobs. Teachers who hadn't enough years to take retirement, received several months of severance pay. Those like me, with enough years and age to take early retirement, received no severance pay and were forced to take early retirement at a considerably reduced rate in June of 1996.

The D.C. Teachers Union claimed it no longer had funds to hire its own lawyers to defend us. And technically that was true because, as it turns out, our teachers union president and a few members of her cabal had stolen many millions of dollars of our union dues from the union treasury, and consequently all the union funds were gone. Though eventually she and her crew ended up in jail, the money for legal help was still gone and never replaced.

June 30, 1996 was my last day in the D.C. Public School System. I was sixty years old.

September 1, 1996 was the first day of the new school year for students. I happened to be in Georgetown just as the kids were pouring into Duke Ellington to begin their first day of classes for the year. I pulled over across from school and sat there in my car on that bright sunny September morning, watching the streams of kids entering the building.

My eyes began to flood with tears as I looked up to the third floor classroom where I had taught 11th grade English and imagined those new kids entering my former classroom. I would miss them, but despite the tears, I realized how lucky I'd been to be a teacher to them these past years. And actually, lucky to have spent those past 29 years, with those and many other D.C.

students doing something with my life that I'd always enjoyed immensely.

As for Ballou, located in one of the poorest sections of the District where the vast majority of students could not read at grade level, it had not been an easy place at which to teach or even to administer, especially when principals were changed like underwear every year or so by the D.C. School system.

To begin to seriously meet the needs of those kids, the school system should have placed the most skilled and dedicated teachers and principals available, and not the newest, least experienced teachers or administrators. Nor should they have used Ballou, among the most impoverished locations, to be the unofficial "punishment" assignment for so-called recalcitrant teachers and administrators as sometimes was rumored to be the case. If that meant an increased financial incentive to tempt experienced teachers, who not only knew their subject but also actually liked inner-city kids, or where an additional team teacher was always available when needed to support new teachers then so be it.

Without question, along with smaller classes, there should always have been sufficient books and supplies. Expensive? Yes, probably, but well worth the savings to a society where we now spend between $32,000 to $60,000 thousand dollars per prisoner per year in our prisons, along with the huge cost of lost human potential, lost human lives, and broken homes. But that's not what the DCPS did, nor what it still does not do, based on city budget constraints. And to most people it sounds like wishful thinking— having a school system geared not only to the academic and intellectual needs of its students, but also their emotional, psychological, and spiritual needs regardless of where they live. But that is what was/is needed to help heal some of the multiple of problems in our society today.

It seemed much easier for the school system to construct a new building than to encourage students in the classroom. "Frank W. Ballou Senior

High School" was again re-named after Frank W. Ballou, who from 1920 to 1943 was the Superintendent of Schools, an era when schools were still segregated in the District of Columbia.

What the system didn't take the trouble to research was that Frank W. Ballou, along with being a school superintendent, had also come from a family of wealthy Southern slave owners. Frank Ballou's name will be remembered unfortunately, not because a high school was named after him, but rather that he'd had the distinction of being one of the two city officials who refused permission for one of the most celebrated contraltos of the 20th century, Marian Anderson, to hold a concert in a D.C. high school after she'd already been refused permission to sing at Constitution Hall because she was black.

That concert was finally held outdoors to an enormous crowd at the Lincoln Memorial on April 9, 1939, thanks to the intervention of Eleanor Roosevelt and Harold Ickes, F.D.R.'s Secretary of the Interior, who made one of Washington's most famous monuments available for the site of Marian Anderson's concert.

Knowing I would have to supplement my retirement pay, I called the Graduate School, USDA and the US Office of Personnel Management to tell them I was again available to teach the Communications courses that I had taught there for both agencies when I was in graduate school. For twelve more years I taught the following courses for the Graduate School until 2012: Basic Communications, Voice and Diction, Interpersonal Communications, Speech Improvement, Essentials of English, Proof Reading, Fundamentals of Writing, Effective Listening and Memory, and Learning How to Learn.

I was grateful that I had acquired the education and teaching competencies in a variety of courses over the years. Discipline or attendance problems were rare since all my students were adults working for the Federal Government. But for all those advantages, I knew they would never be... could never be... as enjoyable or as challenging as those students of mine in the public schools of Washington, DC had been.

CHAPTER 18

The Gifts

MARCH 2014

Dan Pierotti died in Madison, Wisconsin, just a few weeks before this was written. I was sitting on the couch in my living room in Washington, D.C., the box of old letters on my lap —letters he wrote to me over sixty years before. This was just a few months before my graduation from college and our marriage in Chicago, five days later.

Now I was re-reading those letters for the first time since I'd received them. There was one letter from him, however, that I especially puzzled over because I was certain I'd never read it before. Its contents were so uncharacteristically personal, so seemingly self-revealing, and consequently so unlike the Dan thought I knew. When I read it recently, sixty years after it was written, it came as a total surprise.

2/24/1957

Dearest Joan,

I have been lying here thinking about you and became so terribly lonely and wanted so much to talk to you. I am not sure how I can say what I want to say— it probably won't be intelligible to you, but I'll try anyway. You may not realize it, but you are engaged to a person who is terribly weak and immature. I've been thinking back over my life— what a miserable mess it is! It is no use to go into details – but I have never actually done anything of which I am honestly proud. Anything I have done that might be considered an accomplishment in other people's eyes has always been marked with my own weakness and deceit. I have never learned to trust my real talents. Not trusting my own abilities, I have gotten where I am by relying on falseness and deviousness. I've built myself up in my own and other people's eyes mostly through talk and proud action for so long that I cannot seem to do anything in truth and honesty.

The only two things I have done in my life that I am honestly proud of are my decision to enter the ministry and falling in love with you. I certainly am not worthy of the task I have now—and I'm not doing a good job because I refuse to work with my real talents, and instead fall back on my old device of merely talking a good game. I still tend to do this, however, and I suppose I understand Paul when he says, "The spirit is willing, but the flesh is weak." I want so much to be a successful pastor.

I think I more clearly understand myself now than ever before. I have a terrific battle ahead of me, and I am not sure I can win, but I am going to give it a try. I must substitute my wild day dreaming with honest work. I honestly believe God has called me and has also given me the ability to answer his call. Now it remains for me to get myself out of the way so I truly can answer that call.

There are so many things that have mixed up my life. You are not getting any prize package- that's for sure— and, I need your help. Since I cannot always believe in myself, I ask you to believe in me – enough for both of us. Since I cannot honestly be proud of myself, I ask you to be proud of me. I need your love, darling Joan, more than anything else. I think I can straighten out my messy life, but I need your help, your love, and faith in me, which I do not have in myself.

*I suppose this letter will just leave you confused, dear one. I am sorry.
I don't know that I can tell you any better. There are a lot of things I
should tell you and perhaps I will from time to time— or maybe never.
I am sorry to have to write this. Please understand.*

I love you very much – this much I know, Dan

It appeared among those old letters, a kind of gift to me almost an explanation for what had transpired between us in our marriage— the pain and heartache long before Dan died— a letter, the tone and content of which were far more forthright, introspective, and self-revealing than any further experience of the man I was soon to marry and whom I once thought I knew. In truth, that letter makes much more sense to me now after his death than it did many years before when in truth, I never knew him at all.

Perhaps, I thought, including it might help our children toward understanding the seemingly stark contradictions in the man who'd once been a beloved father to them, but who then abandoned them, moving a thousand miles away.

In 2018, I received a very surprising phone call from Julie Preston, who was the babysitter to our three children more than fifty years ago. After the passage of so many years, Julie was calling to ask my forgiveness for the relationship she had with my husband, the pastor of her church when she was just fifteen or sixteen. From that relationship, she had a baby girl whom she gave up for adoption. I had neither seen nor spoken with her since I learned of that affair in 1963.

I learned that in the ensuing 53 years Julie had revealed to no one, not her family or even her best friend, the identity of the father of her child— a secret that still burdens her now.

Quite early on, I'd given up the notion that my husband had been "seduced" by her. It probably had been my way of absolving him of some of the blame. I came to realize that as a thirty-five-year-old minister, and especially this young girl's pastor, he had been wholly responsible for her pregnancy in a relationship that lasted almost two years largely at his urging. He would be in jail had this happened now and was known to the authorities. As for Julie, fortunately for me I had been able to forgive her years ago, and especially after learning what major heartache she'd carried over the years. Julie still carries the shame of this secret, still fearful of what her now grown children would think of her affair if they knew of it.

The psychotherapy I received during those early years following the heartbreaking discovery of my husband's betrayals not only of me and our children but of the eventual end to our marriage and our family breakup eight years later was not without its gifts, much good that came out of that tragic period in my life. At the time, however, I could not see much that was good, and no one could have convinced me it existed. The God I thought I knew seemed silent.

It wasn't until I heard a lecture "*Betrayal: The Search for the Beloved*" that Jean Houston gave to our Human Capacities group in which she stated:

Betrayal, of all the woundings that may be suffered by the soul, can ultimately be the greatest agent of the sacred... and of healing. The only way to forgive truly is through love. In giving much more than one thought one could, one discovers that one has much more still to give. This is the mystery and miracle of love, and it changes the very fabric of reality, the very structure of our lives.

Eventually I began to experience some of those gifts of self-understanding and consequently a greater capacity for understanding the struggles, motives, and the hidden places which open up the place for much greater love and tolerance for others— friends, family, and my students.

Ugo Betti, the Italian playwright, put it so beautifully and so succinctly when he wrote:

Everyone has inside himself...what shall I call it...A piece of Good News! Everyone is a very great, very important character. Yes, that's what we have to tell them up there!! They need great, great hope, and they need it especially if they're young!! Spoil them! Yes, make them grow proud.

That's what's needed, don't you see that? Nothing else matters half so much. To reassure one another... to answer each other. Perhaps only you can listen to me and not laugh. Everyone must be persuaded, even if they're in rags, that they're immensely, immensely important and how much they are loved.